PRAISE FOR *BRUINS 365*

Bruins 365 is a must for you or any Bruins fan in your life! As a Bruins fan myself, I learned things I didn't even know. This book is a fantastic way to embrace the history and nostalgia of your favourite team.

— CAYLEE ALLARD, social media manager, NESN

As a kid growing up a Bruins fan then getting the chance to wear the spoked-B myself and now calling games from the booth, I thought I knew it all — but *Bruins 365* still surprised me. It's packed with stories — some legendary, some unexpected — that remind you just how rich this franchise's history really is. A must-read for any Bruins fan.

— ANDY BRICKLEY, Boston Bruins colour analyst, NESN

Bruins 365 stirred memories from my childhood and rekindled lost facts on this rich NHL franchise.

— JOHN BUCCIGROSS, ESPN

The Big Bad Bruins have been around for more than a century. From the early Art Ross days to the Lunch Pail A.C. era, Mike has curated a full calendar of moments that every Bruins fan will love.

— JAMES DUTHIE, broadcaster, TSN, and author of *Certified Beauties: More of Hockey's Greatest Untold Stories*

Mike Commito has blended the tenacity of an avid researcher with an appealing writing style and a deep appreciation of hockey history. We in the ice business are fortunate that his unbound energy has produced yet another 365 gem — this one about the Boston Bruins. Having had the pleasure of watching the Beantowners in action since my first visit to Boston Garden in 1952, I have a deep appreciation of Bruins' history. And there's a ton there, from Eddie Shore to Dit Clapper and on to Bobby Orr and his Big Bad Bruins. Yes, and even up to that whippersnapper Brad Marchand. Hey, you don't have to be a Bruins fan to love this book. But if you're a hockey fan, this volume is for you!

— STAN FISCHLER, author and historian

There is no one better at documenting hockey history than Mike, and as a life-long Bruins fan, *Bruins 365* is the gift that keeps on giving. It will be mandatory reading for my kids.

— MIKE GRINNELL, executive producer, *Spittin' Chiclets*, and host, *Chiclets University*

Bruins 365 is a must-have for every fan of the storied franchise! Awesome stories and information that have helped shape the amazing 100 years that is Boston Bruins hockey.

— BILLY JAFFE, Boston Bruins studio analyst, NESN

Just when you thought you knew everything about the Boston Bruins, along comes this book. From the well-known to the obscure, Mike's thorough research is going to teach you something about the Bruins every day of the year.

— MATT KALMAN, author of *100 Things Bruins Fans Should Know & Do Before They Die*

Bruins 365 is filled with a year's worth of tales and triumphs from the illustrious history of the Boston Bruins. A must-read for any Bruins fan, young or old.

— MARINA MAHER, Barstool Sports

Nobody does books like this better than Mike Commito. If you've read anything from the 365 series you know the quality of research that goes into this. The latest is a treat not just for Bruins fans but for all fans of hockey who want to learn more about one of hockey's most interesting teams.

— JEFF MAREK, *The Sheet* podcast on Daily Faceoff

Bruins 365 is a must-read for any fan of the Bruins and the NHL. Readers will continually refer back to this breezy and informative read.

— JIM MCBRIDE, Bruins/NHL beat reporter and writer, *The Boston Globe*

The Bruins have had no shortage of memorable tales over their 100-year history, and Mike does a superb job of chronicling the Original Six franchise.

— CONOR RYAN, Bruins beat writer, Boston.com

BRUINS 365

The Hockey 365 Series

Bruins 365
Habs 365
Leafs 365
Hockey 365, The Second Period
Hockey 365

MIKE COMMITO

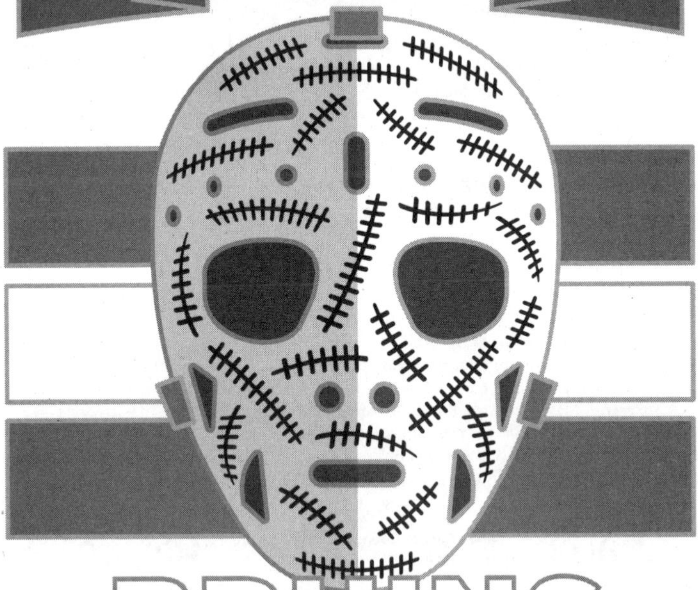

BRUINS 365

DAILY STORIES FROM THE ICE

Publisher: Meghan Macdonald | Acquiring editor: Kathryn Lane | Editor: Patricia MacDonald

Library and Archives Canada Cataloguing in Publication

Title: Bruins 365 : daily stories from the ice / Mike Commito.
Other titles: Bruins three sixty-five | Bruins three hundred and sixty-five
Names: Commito, Mike, author
Description: Series statement: Hockey 365 ; 5
Identifiers: Canadiana (print) 20250220393 | Canadiana (ebook) 20250220407 | ISBN 9781459755192 (hardcover) | ISBN 9781459755208 (PDF) | ISBN 9781459755215 (EPUB)
Subjects: LCSH: Boston Bruins (Hockey team)—Anecdotes. | LCSH: Boston Bruins (Hockey team)—Miscellanea. | LCSH: Hockey players—Massachusetts—Boston—Anecdotes. | LCSH: Hockey players—Massachusetts—Boston—Miscellanea. | LCSH: Hockey—Massachusetts—Boston—Anecdotes. | LCSH: Hockey—Massachusetts—Boston—Miscellanea. | LCGFT: Anecdotes. | LCGFT: Trivia and miscellanea.
Classification: LCC GV848.B68 C66 2025 | DDC 796.962/640974461—dc23

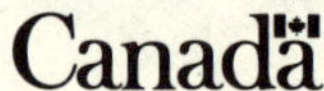

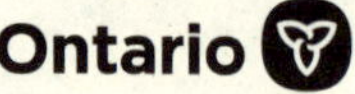

We acknowledge the support of the Canada Council for the Arts and the Ontario Arts Council for our publishing program. We also acknowledge the financial support of the Government of Ontario, through the Ontario Book Publishing Tax Credit and Ontario Creates, and the Government of Canada.

Printed and bound in Canada.

Dundurn Press
1382 Queen Street East
Toronto, Ontario, Canada M4L 1C9
dundurn.com, @dundurnpress

For my dad, Tony

AUTHOR'S NOTE

This book is called *Bruins 365*, but there are more than 365 facts. Way more. Some stories have more than a dozen micro-facts. These can include everything from where a player is from, what his childhood nickname was, when he was drafted, and all sorts of other nuggets that I pack into every story. And when a story is about a game or a particular scoring play, I need to include things like the time of the play, who set it up, and who was in the opposing net — and then verify it all happened the way I described it. All that to say, I am juggling a lot of information. I did extensive research and double-checked my facts to the best of my abilities, but humans make mistakes. Hey, look at the Bruins' draft in 2015. They had three picks in a row in the first round. They could've taken Mat Barzal, Kyle Connor, and Thomas Chabot, but instead they went with Jakub Zbořil, Jake DeBrusk, and Zachary Senyshyn. Nobody's perfect. And at least I didn't torment you further by putting that story in the book. So it's possible that you may find a mistake in *Bruins 365*. If that happens, all I ask is that you resist the urge to let me know. While I appreciate how carefully you have read the book, truly I do, after it's gone to print, there's really nothing I can do about errors. Finding me on social media or tracking down my work email address (yes, that has actually happened) is not going to change anything. It's not going to make you sleep any better at night, and it's most certainly going to cause me pangs of anxiety. I'll tell you what … if you happen to stumble upon an error, write it down. You know, with a pen and a piece of paper. Once a year has gone by, if you still feel you need to share it with me, you can mail it to me in a letter. I'll give you my address and even pay for the postage.

PRE-GAME SKATE

If you're familiar with some of my other books, then you already know I am not a Bruins fan. If you somehow thought I was, well, this is the third team-specific book in the Hockey 365 series — I would be a pretty lousy Bruins fan if I wrote books about the Leafs and Habs before I finally got to the black and gold. And while it may surprise you that I am not a Bs fan after spending the better part of a year writing a Bruins book, the truth is that, in an alternate timeline, I am probably a member of the Boston faithful. Even before I wrote this book, which includes 365 stories about the Bruins, one for every day of the year, there are a number of things I could point to that would have made me a prime candidate to cheer for the Boston Bruins.

My mom, Patti, grew up in Sault Ste. Marie, Ontario, as a Leafs fan because her *baba* cheered for Toronto. The simple reason for that allegiance was that Joe Klukay, a good Ukrainian boy, grew up down the street from them in the Bayview neighbourhood, a stone's throw from the steel plant. Back in those days, having a hometown kid in the lineup was as good a reason as any to root for a team, and since nobody wants to disappoint their *baba* — trust me, I know from experience — my mom went with the Leafs.

While she cheered for Toronto, her father, my papa, was a Bruins fan. He passed away when I was just a baby, but I learned much later he was an exceptional hockey player. He certainly didn't pass down those skills to me, but, hey, I'm doing my best. My papa had been invited to Detroit Red Wings camps and even spent a year playing hockey in Italy to help try to grow the game in the country where his family hailed from. He might have initially been a Red Wings fan because of his connection to the team, but I understand he was a Bruins fan because of Phil Esposito, who was also from the Soo.

The family legend goes that when Phil was growing up, he idolized my papa. I have it on good authority that he talked about wanting to play like Donny Lato when he got older. Even if my papa wasn't initially a Bruins fan, after Phil went to Boston, he cheered for the black and gold. So you could argue that, by rights, my mom should have been a Bruins fan, but it didn't quite turn out that way.

And on the other side of my family, my father, Tony, was actually a Bruins fan, at least in his younger days. Growing up in Onaping, a small northern Ontario mining town, all his classmates followed *Hockey Night in Canada* and always talked about how their favourite teams did at school on Monday morning. But my dad felt left out. He didn't necessarily have a squad to root for because they didn't watch too much hockey in his house. His parents, my nonno and nonna, were Italian immigrants. As much as my grandfather knew that old hockey sticks made for perfect stakes in a tomato garden, he didn't know much about the sport. So, when my dad told him about his predicament, my nonno's advice was simple: find an Italian player on a team to cheer for. It wasn't too hard. My dad learned about Phil Esposito and instantly became a Bruins fan. I don't know how long he stuck with the black and gold, but evidently not long enough for me to inherit his childhood allegiance.

By the time I was old enough to start watching hockey, my mom was the more diehard hockey fan between the two of them, so I followed in her footsteps. As I got older and continued cheering for the Leafs, enduring heartache after heartache, there were still some signs that suggested I had been a Bruins fan in a past life.

Growing up in Sudbury, I spent many a bleary-eyed Friday night at the Beef 'n Bird tavern, founded by hard-nosed Bruin Jerry Toppazzini after he hung up his skates and returned to the area following his NHL career. The Beef was once a veritable black and gold shrine, a nod to his time in Boston. Staring up at pictures of Bobby Orr and Gerry Cheevers after a few too many beers, you couldn't blame a guy for falling in love with the Bruins.

But despite all the time I spent at the Beef on Fridays or on Saturday afternoons for porketta bingo, a delicious version of bingo in which you gamble to win a pound of Italian pork roast — arguably the best thing you have ever put to your lips when you start drinking before lunch and haven't eaten anything all day — I resisted the pull from the dark side.

Even when I left Sudbury, the Bruins could have followed me. While at McMaster University, I did my Ph.D. on the history of black bear hunting and management. Seriously, that's the topic I chose to dedicate my life to for five years. It wasn't too long before I was colloquially known as "the bear guy" because of my doctoral work. This led to practically everyone in my orbit buying me kitschy bear stuff at every opportunity. I had bear ties, bear placemats, and more bear shirts than I could count. My eventual wife, Chantal, finally drew the line when someone, probably my parents, gave me a bear-themed toilet seat. Needless to say, that did not make it into our first house. But with so much bear memorabilia, I could have easily just said to hell with the Leafs and made an easy transition to a team with a bear as its identity.

Even as I'm writing these words, I am looking down at my left arm, which is adorned with a bear tattoo, commemorating the work and years I spent studying the history of black bear hunting and management, but if I squint hard enough it could easily be a Bruins tattoo. And this isn't even old ink. I actually got it a few days before I officially launched *Leafs 365* a couple of years ago.

And when it came time to pick which team we were going to do after *Habs 365*, I was the one who picked the Bruins. The publisher was actually pushing for *Wings 365* (sorry, Wings fans; you'll have to wait a little longer), but I said I wanted to do *Bruins 365*, pretty much for all the reasons I just described.

Wait, am I actually a Bruins fan? No, I am not, but this book brought me as close to rooting for Boston as I possibly could. Over the last year, I definitely spent more time with the Bruins than I did with my own team. I'm lucky to catch a couple of Leafs games a week, but I spent nearly every weeknight with the Bruins in some way.

If I wasn't writing, I was researching, and if I wasn't researching, I was watching old clips or reading stories about the Bruins. And as much as it was painful at times to write a Bruins book as a Leafs fan (please see 2013, 2018, 2019, and 2024 for more context), I came away with a begrudging respect for the franchise I hadn't had before. It confirmed that I would want Brad Marchand on my team in a heartbeat, and it made me a lifelong booster of the Lunch Pail A.C., a group that had such skillful hands they could both score on you and pummel you.

I think that if I, a lifelong Leafs fan, can come away with these feelings — although, I should stress, conflicted — about the Bruins, then I think you just might, too. You may not become a full-fledged Bruins fan by reading this, but if I have done my job as a historian and author, hopefully you will have a better appreciation for the team. And, of course, if you already are a Bruins fan, hopefully this book will remind you why you fell in love with the black and gold in the first place.

JANUARY

JANUARY 1

FENWAY HOSTS WINTER CLASSIC, 2010

For nearly a century, Fenway Park had been the home of the Red Sox, but for one crisp afternoon in January, baseball's oldest stadium had a new tenant: the Bruins. On the first day of 2010, the Bruins hosted the Flyers at Fenway for the Winter Classic, the NHL's annual outdoor game, which had become a New Year's tradition. There was no scoring in the first period, but there were fisticuffs. Boston's Shawn Thornton dropped the gloves with Philadelphia's Dan Carcillo for the first fight in Winter Classic history.

Regulation ended in a 1–1 tie, so they went to overtime on Yawkey Way. Less than two minutes into the extra session, Marco Sturm tipped in a Patrice Bergeron pass to win the game. Almost exactly 13 years later, the Winter Classic returned to Fenway. But with New Year's Day falling on a Sunday, the NHL pushed the game to January 2 to avoid competing with a full slate of NFL games. Jake DeBrusk scored two third-period goals to give the Bruins another victory at the cathedral of baseball.

JANUARY 2

CAM NEELY RECORDS 10TH CAREER HATTY, 1994

Cam Neely told reporters that he considered himself day-to-day for the rest of his career. A two-time 50-goal scorer for the Bruins, Neely, who was known as "Bam-Bam Cam" for his physical game and penchant for finding the back of the net, missed significant time with a knee injury after being hit by Ulf Samuelsson, one of the game's dirtiest players, in the 1991 playoffs. After missing much of the next two seasons, Neely returned for the 1993–94 campaign. Although his knee was never the same, it was the best he had felt in years.

And although he had missed 17 games, he was still filling the net. On January 2, 1994, Neely recorded his 10th career hat trick, giving him 26 goals in 22 games. Despite the wonky left knee, his torrid pace continued. He eventually reached the 50-goal mark in just his 44th game of the season, but because he didn't accomplish the feat in Boston's first 50 games of the year, some people don't feel it is an official 50 in 50. Those people, however, are wrong.

JANUARY 3

EDDIE SHORE MAKES IT TO MONTREAL, 1929

Nothing was going to stop Eddie Shore from getting to Montreal. After narrowly missing the team's train out of Boston, Shore, arguably the game's toughest and most skilled defenceman, was determined to join his teammates for a road game against the Maroons on January 3, 1929, especially if he hoped to convince coach Art Ross not to dock him $500 for arriving late to the station. But if Shore was going to make it, he would need to drive through a blizzard.

Many people would have turned back, but Shore urged his driver to continue and even took over for stints behind the wheel. After driving all through the night, they were nearing Montreal when the chauffeur went off the road. Shore later recounted to the great Stan Fischler that he had to conscript a team of horses to pull the car out of a ditch. Shore eventually made it to his destination, and lucky for the Bruins he did. The sleep-deprived blueliner notched the only goal in a 1–0 victory. He was not fined by Ross.

JANUARY 4

BOBBY ORR SETS GOAL-SCORING RECORD FOR DEFENCEMEN, 1973

Bobby Orr changed hockey. His dizzying end-to-end rushes and offensive brilliance redefined how defencemen could play the game. Although there were plenty of smooth-skating blueliners who came before him, such as his predecessor Eddie Shore in Boston and Doug Harvey in Montreal, Orr revolutionized the position, so it's no wonder that he rewrote the record books for defencemen. He held the benchmark for the most goals, assists, points, and nearly every other offensive category you could think of for a blueliner. Heading into a game against the Blues on January 4, 1973, he was about to topple another one.

With 162 career goals to his name, Orr was tied with Red Kelly for the most ever by a defenceman. Kelly had patrolled Detroit's blue line for more than a decade, before he shifted up front to centre during his tenure in Toronto. Late in the second period in St. Louis, Orr found the twine to set the goal-scoring record. But what's incredible is that while Kelly accomplished the feat in 841 games, Orr did it in just 428.

JANUARY 5

JIMMY HERBERT NOTCHES FIRST BRUINS HAT TRICK, 1926

Some newspapers referred to him as Jimmy Herberts, but his last name was actually Herbert. The fact that he never bothered correcting reporters is still evident today — nearly a century after his playing days were over, the NHL's official website still records his surname as Herberts. While his last name may have been up for debate, most of his teammates knew him as "Sailor" because he worked on the Great Lakes in the off-season. An original Bruin, Herbert made his big-league debut in 1924, along with the Bruins, leading the team in both points and penalty minutes.

In his second campaign with the Bs, Herbert continued making a name for himself, notching the first-ever hat trick in franchise history on January 5, 1926, when he scored the club's only goals in a 3–0 win against Pittsburgh. Herbert was later traded to the Leafs for cash and Jack Arbour, a move that reportedly started a feud between Boston's Art Ross and Toronto's Conn Smythe, who felt he had been swindled into taking a player he believed to be washed up.

JANUARY 6

RAY BOURQUE STAYS HOT, 1994

Ray Bourque was on fire. After collecting five assists in an 8–2 rout of Washington in Boston's first game of 1994, four days later, on January 6, he racked up four more points against the Jets, to start the new year with nine points in two games. Bourque was only a few seasons removed from a 94-point campaign with the Bruins, but he had turned 33 years old just over a week earlier, and some felt that his production would decline as he got long in the tooth.

But Bourque wasn't like other defencemen. After making his Boston debut in 1979, it wasn't long before he established himself as one of the best blueliners in the NHL. Like Bobby Orr who came before him, Bourque was a swift skater who was able to effortlessly get the puck out of the defensive zone and contribute offensively. While Bourque couldn't continue his red-hot pace to close the 1993–94 season, he finished with 91 points to take home his fifth, and final, Norris Trophy as the league's top defenceman.

JANUARY 7

JOHNNY BUCYK HITS 300, 1970

Johnny Bucyk knew exactly what he was going to do with the puck. After finding the back of the net with just over a minute remaining in a game against the California Golden Seals on January 7, 1970, to record his 300th career goal, becoming the 14th player in NHL history to accomplish the feat, Bucyk already had plans for how he would commemorate the moment. One of his friends had made him a gold leaf–trimmed plaque on which he proudly showcased some of his milestone pucks. He was pleased with how the display was taking shape, and noted it would look even better now with the 300th on there.

I'm not sure how big that plaque was, but Bucyk would need more room. He finished the season with 31 goals, a career high since joining the big leagues 15 years earlier, only to top that the following year with 51 tallies. When he finally hung up his skates nearly a decade later, he had 545 goals with the Bruins, a franchise record that still stands.

JANUARY 8

TUUKKA RASK GETS FIRST SHUTOUT OF THE SEASON, 2019

It was the longest Tuukka Rask had gone without a shutout. Since joining the Bruins full-time in 2009, the Finnish goaltender had averaged a handful of shutouts every season. But halfway through the 2018–19 campaign, Rask was still looking for his first shutout of the year. The last time he had turned aside every shot he faced was on the road against Tampa Bay on March 17, 2018. Rask had been up and down to start the season, but his game was starting to tighten up.

Heading into a game against the Wild on January 8, 2019, Rask had recorded three straight victories and allowed just five goals in those contests. That night, while Boston kept Minnesota busy by keeping the puck in their end for most of the game, Rask stopped all 24 shots that came his way to notch his first shutout that season. More significant than the shutout was that it was also Rask's 250th career victory, moving him within three wins of passing Cecil "Tiny" Thompson for the most in franchise history.

JANUARY 9

BRUINS RETIRE BOBBY ORR'S JERSEY, 1979

Bobby Orr was back on the ice at Boston Garden, but not as a player. He was there to have his No. 4 jersey retired, becoming just the fifth player in franchise history to receive the honour. Just a few months away from his 31st birthday, Orr should have been out there in his skates joining some of his former teammates as they took on the Soviet Wings in an exhibition game on January 9, 1979, but it was not meant to be.

Orr's battered knees, scarred from surgery after surgery, had finally given out. In the 1975–76 campaign, he managed just 10 games for the Bruins. The following year, he joined the Black Hawks, but he appeared in only 20 games and then missed the rest of the season, along with the following year. Orr attempted a comeback in 1978–79, but after suiting up for just six more games, he hung up his skates. Following a bittersweet celebration, Orr stared up with tears in his eyes as his No. 4 ascended to the rafters.

JANUARY 10

SHAWN THORNTON SCORES SPECTACULAR PENALTY SHOT GOAL, 2012

Shawn Thornton was best known for dropping the gloves, but on January 10, 2012, he had the chance to prove that while he might have had tough knuckles, he still had soft hands. Early in the second period, Thornton stormed out of the penalty box and picked up a loose puck to gain a clear breakaway on Winnipeg goaltender Ondřej Pavelec. But when the Bruins enforcer was fouled up in front of the net, he was awarded a penalty shot.

The hard-hitting Thornton had a well-earned reputation as one of the most effective fourth-liners in the league, but he wasn't known for his goal-scoring prowess. Despite coming off a 10-goal season, his first time hitting double digits, he had notched only three goals to start the campaign. While Thornton later said he was nervous because he hadn't taken a penalty shot since midget hockey, he certainly didn't show it. Skating in on Pavelec, Thornton faked a wrist shot with a nifty leg-kick, toe-drag move before bringing the puck to his backhand and roofing it into the back of the net.

JANUARY 11

BRUINS SCORE FOUR QUICK GOALS, 1927

The Bruins made the most of their first period against the Black Hawks. Just after the halfway mark of the opening frame on January 11, 1927, Boston's Harry Oliver found the back of the net to knot the score at one goal apiece. Twelve seconds later, Frank Fredrickson lit the lamp to give the Bs the lead. Fifty-seven seconds after that, Oliver scored again to extend the lead even further. And then, sixteen seconds later, Oliver completed the hat trick.

All told, the Bruins scored four goals in one minute and 25 seconds, shattering the league record for the fastest four goals originally set by the Toronto Arenas in 1919, when they put four past the Canadiens in one minute and 40 seconds. Almost exactly eighteen years later, on January 21, 1945, the Bruins were at it again. This time, in a match against the New York Rangers that turned into a 14–3 walloping by Boston, they again scored four quick goals, beating their previous benchmark by five seconds, an NHL record that still stands as of this writing.

JANUARY 12

BEP SCORES THREE POINTS, 1943

Armand Guidolin was the youngest in an Italian family, so his mother called him "beppy," which was how she pronounced "baby." The tender moniker, later shortened to "Bep," stuck around and followed him all the way to the big leagues. During the Second World War, with so many players enlisting to serve, there were lineup shortages across the NHL. As part of Boston's efforts to shore up their roster, they called up Guidolin early into the 1942–43 campaign.

Guidolin's nickname was rather fitting because he was now the "beppy" of the league. Making his Bruins debut a month before his 17th birthday, he became the youngest NHL player ever. While Bep was brought up out of necessity, he made the most of his opportunity. On January 12, 1943, he picked up three points in a 3–0 victory over the Black Hawks, further earning consideration for the Calder Trophy. Although Guidolin didn't take home rookie of the year honours, he played three more seasons with the Bruins before returning to Boston as bench boss in the early 1970s.

JANUARY 13

ADAM OATES HITS GOAL-SCORING MILESTONE, 1997

When you think of Adam Oates, you probably don't think of his goal-scoring. If you're like me, you think of his incredible passing. Oates was one of the premier dishers in the history of the game. When Boston managed to pry him loose from St. Louis, his playmaking skills were a boon for the Bruins. In his first full season in black and gold, Oates collected 97 assists, the second most in franchise history, and 142 points.

Although Oates couldn't keep up that kind of production, he was a key contributor for the Bruins over the next four seasons. And while his passing prowess continued to define him in Boston, he also had no problem finding the back of the net. On January 13, 1997, he recorded his 250th career goal, more than half of those with the Bruins, in a loss to the Ottawa Senators. But less than two months after that milestone, following some pointed criticism of Boston's brass, which led to him losing his assistant captaincy, Oates was dealt to Washington as part of a six-player blockbuster trade.

JANUARY 14

ESPOSITO BAGS FIFTH HAT TRICK OF THE SEASON, 1971

"Some nights they go in and some nights they don't," Phil Esposito said. "You just have to keep shooting. Goals will come eventually." Words to live by. And Esposito certainly did. After firing 11 shots on goal against the California Golden Seals and picking up just a single tally, the next game, on January 14, 1971, Esposito kept shooting. He ripped off 10 shots, but this time he picked up a hat trick, along with three assists, in a 9–5 victory against Los Angeles.

And while Esposito was known for scoring in bunches, this three-goal performance was significant. It was his fifth of the season, a modern NHL record for the most in a single campaign. He needed just two more to tie Joe Malone's seven hat tricks from the league's inaugural season. He would need the rest of the schedule, but Esposito matched Malone in the final game of the season. The benchmark stood until Mike Bossy recorded nine hat tricks a decade later, but that standard held for just a year before Wayne Gretzky managed to record double digits.

JANUARY 15

REED LARSON SCORES 200TH GOAL, 1987

Reed Larson had one of the most fearsome slapshots in the NHL. Drafted 22nd overall by the Detroit Red Wings in 1976, the Minneapolis native terrorized opponents with his cannonading shot. Teammate Mark Howe once said that when Larson wound up, players parted like the Red Sea. Those who couldn't get out of the way in time often ended up on the injured list with broken bones. Some were luckier, like Dennis Hextall, who just had one of his skate blades blown off by the impact from one of Larson's blasts.

When Boston acquired the defenceman from Detroit for Mike O'Connell in 1986, he brought his thundering shot to Beantown. So it was only fitting that, on January 15, 1987, he notched his 200th career goal with a clapper from the blue line. With just over two minutes remaining in the first period in a game against the Hartford Whalers, Larson rifled a shot from 45 feet out to reach the milestone, becoming the fifth defenceman in NHL history to do so.

JANUARY 16

BILL COWLEY RECORDS SIX POINTS, 1943

It just was another day at the office for Bill Cowley. On January 16, 1943, Cowley recorded a hat trick and added three assists against the Rangers for his second six-point performance of the season. Cowley, who initially joined the Bruins as a winger in 1935, was eventually moved to centre, where he established himself as one of the game's top players. He helped guide the Bruins to a Stanley Cup in 1939, and two years later, after leading the NHL in scoring, he capped it off with another championship, along with the Hart Trophy.

Cowley finished the 1942–43 season with 72 points, just one back of league-leader Doug Bentley, and took home his second MVP award, but it proved to be one of his last bright spots with the Bs. Although he continued to produce, a few years later, GM Art Ross left him off an exhibition tour of western Canada. He was crushed. Cowley's wife was from Vancouver and was hoping to use it as a honeymoon. Instead, he retired and vowed he'd never return to Boston.

JANUARY 17

PETE PEETERS EXTENDS STREAK, PICKS UP 100TH CAREER VICTORY, 1983

Pete Peeters was unbeatable. In his first season with the Bruins, he was stopping everything that came his way. After picking up a victory against Buffalo on November 13, 1982, Peeters went unbeaten in his next 21 starts, collecting 17 wins and four ties. For Peeters it actually wasn't anything new. During his time with the Flyers, he once racked up a 27-game unbeaten streak. Not bad for a goalie that Philadelphia chose with the 135th overall pick.

With Boston hosting the North Stars on January 17, 1983, Peeters looked to continue his impressive streak. Coming off two straight shutouts, he was also looking for his 100th career victory. Although he allowed a few goals, he reached the milestone and kept his run going. Peeters eventually extended the unbeaten streak to 31 games, falling one match shy of Gerry Cheevers's league record. But Peeters established his own benchmark by becoming the only goaltender in NHL history to have two unbeaten streaks of 25 games or more. Peeters capped off his debut season for the black and gold by taking the Vezina Trophy.

JANUARY 18

WILLIE O'REE MAKES NHL DEBUT, 1958

Willie O'Ree was at his boarding house when he got a telephone call that changed his life. On the other end of the line was his Quebec Aces coach, Joe Crozier, letting him know the Bruins had called him up for a pair of games as an emergency replacement for the injured Leo Labine. O'Ree couldn't believe it. He hardly slept a wink that night. The next morning he took the train to Montreal to meet his new teammates, if only for a few days, and later that day, on January 18, 1958, O'Ree made his Bruins debut.

It was a moment O'Ree had waited for his entire career, but it held even greater significance. As O'Ree skated out onto the ice at the Forum, he became the first Black player to appear in an NHL game. Following the match, O'Ree said it was "the greatest thrill of my life" and a day he would never forget. O'Ree returned to the Bruins three years later, scoring a goal, another milestone that would inspire countless others for years to come.

JANUARY 19

PAT BURNS GETS 400TH CAREER WIN, 2000

"I don't think I'm that bad a coach" was an odd thing for Pat Burns, a three-time Jack Adams Award winner, to say after picking up his 400th career victory, becoming just the 12th bench boss in NHL history to accomplish the feat, but that's the kind of season the Bruins were having. After going winless to start the first nine games of the campaign, things hadn't gotten much better for Boston. The team had just two wins in their last 15 games and just four triumphs since November 24.

Heading into a game in Atlanta on January 19, 2000, the Bruins were stuck with three straight ties. While they couldn't win much, it seemed they couldn't lose either. But with just over four minutes remaining in the game, P.J. Axelsson scored to seal a 4–3 win and give Burns his long overdue milestone. The win didn't turn things around for Burns and the Bs, however. They missed the playoffs, the first time in his career one of his teams didn't qualify for the post-season. Burns was fired eight games into the next campaign.

JANUARY 20

RAY BOURQUE'S ALL-STAR GAME HEROICS, 1996

Ray Bourque stepped out onto the ice at the FleetCenter to a hero's welcome. The ovation was nothing new for the Bruins captain, but this appearance was special. It was January 20, 1996, and Boston was hosting the All-Star Game for the first time in more than two decades. It was the 15th straight time Bourque had suited up for an All-Star Game, but never in front of the home crowd. Although the five-time Norris winner later said he had been nervous because he didn't want to embarrass himself in front of the Bruins faithful, he put on a performance they would never forget.

With time winding down and the game tied 4–4, Bourque's Eastern Conference teammate Pat Verbeek fired a shot at Felix Potvin, who was tending the twine for the Western Conference All-Stars. The puck bounced over to Bourque on the far side, and with just 37.3 seconds left, he backhanded it into the net to seal the victory. For his heroics, Bourque was named All-Star MVP, for the first time in his career. You couldn't have scripted it any better.

JANUARY 21

DEREK SANDERSON PICKS UP FIVE POINTS, 1968

Derek Sanderson had no problem filling the back of the net. In his final season of junior with his hometown team, the Niagara Falls Flyers, he racked up 41 goals in just 47 games. And while goal-scoring came naturally to the young centre, he always preferred setting up his teammates. Following that exceptional season in Niagara, Sanderson joined the Bruins as a regular. He had made a couple of appearances with the club over the past few years, but now he seemed to be in the NHL for good.

Sanderson got off to a solid start but saved his best performance for January 21, 1968. That night he picked up five points in a 6–0 win over Chicago. He had a goal in the rout, but he was most proud of the four helpers he picked up. Sanderson finished his rookie campaign with 24 goals and 49 points and was named rookie of the year in a landslide, giving Boston back-to-back Calder Trophy winners. Teammate Bobby Orr, of course, took it home the year before.

JANUARY 22

BLAINE LACHER PICKS UP FIRST VICTORY, 1995

Blaine Lacher was ready to hang up his goalie pads after graduating high school, but he decided to stay in the crease when he enrolled at Lake Superior State University. It proved to be the right choice. In his third season with the Lakers, Lacher backstopped the team to an NCAA title and then signed with Boston as a free agent. The next year, following the conclusion of the NHL lockout, which shortened the campaign to 48 games, he earned the Bruins' starting job out of a quick training camp.

A few years earlier, Lacher was nearly done with hockey, but on January 22, 1995, he was leading Boston out onto the ice for their final home opener at the Garden. Lacher was practically flawless in his big-league debut, stopping all but one of the 19 shots he faced to record his first NHL victory. The only goal scored against him occurred when the puck and Philadelphia's Dave Brown both went into the back of the net at the same time early in the second period.

JANUARY 23

KEN LINSEMAN GETS 500TH POINT, 1986

In most other professions, being known as "the Rat" could be seen as an insult, but in hockey it's a badge of honour. While most players didn't like playing against rats, they loved having them on their team. Ken Linseman was the perfect rat. So much so that it's what he was known as throughout his career, with some even going as far as saying he looked like one. And while few could get under their opponents' skin as well as Linseman, he was also a darn good hockey player. He once scored 92 points in a season in Philadelphia and played an important part in Edmonton's Stanley Cup victory in 1984.

After that championship he was dealt to Boston, where he continued to solidify his reputation as both a skilled player and a rat. On January 23, 1986, Linseman potted an empty-net goal with 49 seconds left in a game to record his 500th career point. Early into the next season, he was a key antagonist in "the hallway brawl" at the Garden against the Canadiens.

JANUARY 24

JERRY TOPPAZZINI NETS HAT TRICK, 1953

Early into his NHL career, Jerry Toppazzini was not known for his goal-scoring prowess. In his first season with the Bruins, the Copper Cliff, Ontario, native had just three goals through his first 43 games, but on January 24, 1953, Toppazzini recorded three goals, his first career hat trick, in a 9–0 victory against the Rangers. Although Toppazzini, who was affectionately known as Topper, doubled his output, goals were still hard to come by. It was only after he returned to Boston, after brief stops in Chicago and Detroit, that he established himself as a two-way goal scorer.

In his third season back with the Bruins in 1957–58, Toppazzini, now a reliable penalty killer, scored 25 goals, along with eight short-handed goals, a team record that held for more than four decades. He hit the 20-goal mark the next year and provided the Bruins with goal-scoring depth and versatility for another five years. Following his hockey career, Toppazzini returned to Sudbury, a stone's throw from his hometown, where he established the Beef 'n Bird Tavern, which still pays homage to his time with the Bruins.

JANUARY 25

TODD ELIK SCORES 100TH CAREER GOAL, 1996

Todd Elik was making the most of his time in Boston. Following six seasons in the NHL, along with some time in the minors, Elik had signed with the Bruins in the 1995 off-season. Although he was a two-time 20-goal scorer, he had not developed into the second-line centre the Kings hoped he would be when they signed him as an undrafted free agent. But when Elik made it to Boston, his dogged playing style and offensive potential won over head coach Steve Kasper, and he found himself in a prime spot on a line with Kevin Stevens and Joe Mullen out of training camp.

As the season progressed, Elik earned a promotion and was on the Bruins' top line with Cam Neely and Adam Oates. Elik was playing so well that even after Boston had traded for Rick Tocchet, Kasper wasn't sold on demoting him. Elik's strong play continued in the New Year. After ripping off 13 points in nine games, on January 25, 1996, he scored his 100th career goal in a matchup against the Tampa Bay Lightning.

JANUARY 26

LEO BOIVIN'S FIRST GOAL IN 11 MONTHS, 1963

Leo Boivin didn't need to score goals. He was a hard-hitting defenceman whom opposing players feared when they saw him coming down the ice. Although Boston signed Boivin to his first NHL contract in 1950, he wound up starting his career with the Leafs, until the Bruins reacquired him four years later. Back in Boston, Boivin cemented his reputation as one of the league's most formidable blueliners. He delivered thundering hits, and few players could execute hip checks better than him.

And while the big, bad defenceman didn't need to provide offense, he was always good for a few tallies every year. The only season he didn't find the back of the net with the Bruins was the 1957–58 campaign. Five years later, it looked like it might happen again. After scoring against the Rangers on February 21, 1962, Boivin couldn't seem to light the lamp. But finally, after nearly a year, on January 26, 1963, he shot the puck down the length of the ice into an empty Toronto net to end his drought.

JANUARY 27

PIT MARTIN SCORES FOUR GOALS, 1966

Pit Martin proved to be quite the pickup for the Bruins. Acquired from Detroit in exchange for Parker MacDonald on December 30, 1965, Martin made an immediate impact with his new team. After recording eight points through his first 11 games, on January 27, 1966, he collected four goals in a 5–3 victory over Chicago, matching Harry Oliver's record from 1927, shared by seven other Bruins, for the most goals in a regular-season game. After opening the scoring, Martin added goals in each of the next two periods, before picking up his fourth with just over two minutes remaining.

Although Martin didn't rewrite the record books the next campaign, he did reach the 20-goal mark and collected 42 points, both career highs. But his greatest contribution to the club that year would be the role he would play in an off-season transaction. On May 15, 1967, Martin, along with Gilles Marotte and Jack Norris, was traded to the Black Hawks for Phil Esposito, Ken Hodge, and Fred Stanfield. It turned out to be one of the greatest trades in Bruins history, if not the greatest.

JANUARY 28

RON ASSELSTINE DECKS FAN, 1989

As the old adage goes, you never poke the bear. On January 28, 1989, one Bruins fan learned that lesson the hard way. With less than two minutes remaining in a game at the Garden, 22-year-old Frank Baro from Medford, Massachusetts, climbed over the glass behind the visitors' bench and onto the ice to give referee Bill McCreary a piece of his mind. Baro, along with most of the Boston faithful, was upset when the officials missed a high stick on Glen Wesley that left the Bruins defenceman bloodied.

While the home crowd voiced their displeasure from the stands, Baro, probably making the most ill-advised decision of his life up to that point, made his way over the boards. He stuck the landing and actually managed to get within a few steps of McCreary before linesman Ron Asselstine charged and hammered him into the boards. Baro should've known better. Known as "the Bear" for his imposing frame and his stern approach to breaking up fights, Asselstine was one of the last people you'd want to run into on the ice.

JANUARY 29

GLEN MURRAY GETS 500TH POINT, 2004

After more than a decade in the NHL, Glen Murray was an All-Star. Drafted 18th overall by the Bruins in 1991, Murray spent a few seasons in Boston before he was dealt to Pittsburgh, along with Bryan Smolinski, for Kevin Stevens and Shawn McEachern. Following some time with the Penguins and the Kings, Murray returned to Beantown early into the 2001–02 campaign and finished with 35 goals, the most he'd scored at any level since his junior days in Sudbury.

But Murray was just getting started. In his first full season back, he racked up 44 goals and 92 points, both career highs, and was elected to the All-Star Game. The next year, Murray's resurgence continued. In a game against the New York Islanders on January 29, 2004, he scored both of Boston's goals in a 2–1 overtime victory to reach the 500-point milestone. He finished the campaign with 32 tallies, leading the team in goals for the second straight season, but one of his most memorable goals that year was in the playoffs following an Alex Kovalev gaffe.

JANUARY 30

JOHNNY BUCYK SCORES 1,200TH POINT, 1975

Johnny Bucyk was aging like a fine wine. Sixteen years into his NHL career, Bucyk, a Ukrainian Canadian who was nicknamed "the Chief" because his darker complexion made a Boston cartoonist assume he was Indigenous — an assumption so problematic that we don't have enough room to unpack it — was playing the best hockey of his life. More than a decade after his tenure with the Bruins began, Bucyk collected 116 points in the 1970–71 campaign.

Even when he entered his 20th season a few years later as a 39-year-old, Bucyk showed no signs of slowing down. In a game against the Golden Seals on January 30, 1975, Bucyk opened the scoring to net his 1,200th career point, becoming the sixth player in league history to reach the milestone. He finished the year with 81 points, behind only Bobby Orr and Phil Esposito on the Bruins. The next year, the greying Bucyk somehow did even better, recording 83 points. The only player to record more points as a 40-year-old was another ageless wonder, Gordie Howe.

JANUARY 31

JACK NORRIS PLAYS FIRST NHL GAME, 1965

It was the last time Jack Norris let his equipment out of his sight. After the Bruins called him up from the minors to replace regular netminder Eddie Johnston, who was feeling under the weather, he left his goaltending gear with a bellhop at a Toronto hotel. When Norris couldn't find his equipment before the team took on the Leafs, Johnston had no choice but to get between the pipes. Although he was suffering from the flu, he put in a valiant effort but was shelled in a 6–1 loss.

Worse still was that he had suffered a broken right hand in the game and wouldn't be available, snapping an incredible streak of 160 straight starts, when Boston hosted the Maple Leafs the next night at the Garden. So on January 31, 1965, wearing borrowed skates and equipment from Johnston, Norris suited up for his first NHL game, stopping 27 shots in a 4–2 loss. His debut didn't go as planned, but he learned an important lesson: "I'll sleep with my equipment from now on," he told reporters.

FEBRUARY

FEBRUARY 1

MIKE WALTON RETURNS FROM FREAK ACCIDENT, 1973

Mike Walton was lucky to be alive. When he was in St. Louis with the Bruins, his road roommate, Bobby Orr, tried to play a practical joke on him. Walton was out on the balcony outside their hotel room when Orr shouted something out. Walton, startled by the superstar defenceman, stumbled and wound up crashing through the glass door. According to reports, Walton needed upwards of 200 stitches to close up all the lacerations he sustained in the freak accident.

Walton's agent, Alan Eagleson, went as far as saying a piece of glass came within a quarter of an inch of slicing his jugular vein. At the time of the injury, Walton was sitting at 21 goals and was on pace for his best season to date. He missed an entire month of the campaign, 12 games in all, while he recuperated. Walton returned to action on February 1, 1973. Although he didn't get on the scoresheet that night, a little over a week later, he picked up a hat trick, his first in more than five years.

FEBRUARY 2

RICK MIDDLETON RACKS UP BACK-TO-BACK FOUR-POINT NIGHTS, 1980

Rick Middleton came by his nickname, "Nifty," honestly. He was highly skilled, and many of his plays were exactly that, nifty. Middleton actually started his career in New York, but after just a couple of seasons on Broadway, he was traded to Boston for Ken Hodge. It was a move that the Rangers would come to regret. Middleton had reached the 20-goal mark in each of his first two seasons with the Blueshirts, but by his third campaign with the Bruins, he was approaching 40 goals and was the team's leading scorer.

The next year, Middleton built on his breakout season with even more nifty performances. On February 2, 1980, he picked up two goals and four points in a game against the Quebec Nordiques, his second straight four-point outing, giving him 14 points in his previous five matches. He finished the season with a team-leading 40 goals, marking the first of five straight 40-goal campaigns, which included a 51-goal effort that made Middleton just the fourth player in Bruins history to reach the milestone.

FEBRUARY 3

BRUINS TRADE KRIS VERSTEEG, 2007

Kris Versteeg never got to wear a Bruins sweater. Selected 134th overall by Boston in the 2004 NHL Entry Draft, Versteeg turned pro with Providence in the American Hockey League, so technically he did sport a Bruins sweater, but before he had the opportunity to wear the spoked *B* for the big club, he was traded. On February 3, 2007, the Bruins sent Versteeg, along with future considerations, to the Blackhawks for Brandon Bochenski.

At the time, Bochenski was lighting up the AHL with the Norfolk Admirals, racking up 66 points in 35 games. While he collected 22 points down the stretch for Boston, Bochenski was dealt to Anaheim after notching just six points through 20 games the next year. Meanwhile, Versteeg made his NHL debut the next season. It took him another year to become a regular, but he became a solid contributor in Chicago, winning a Stanley Cup in 2010. Although Versteeg was jettisoned after that championship as part of a salary cap crunch, he returned to the Blackhawks a few years later and won another title.

FEBRUARY 4

BRUINS LOSE TO SNOWBOUND RANGERS, 1961

The Bruins haven't always had the best luck with winter travel. Three decades after Eddie Shore had to hire a team of horses to pull him out of a ditch so he could finish his treacherous overnight snowy journey to Montreal, a pair of Bruins almost missed a game during a winter storm. On February 4, 1961, amid a raging nor'easter, Johnny Bucyk was on his way to pick up Jerry Toppazzini for their game at home against the Rangers when his car stalled.

Bucyk ended up hitchhiking to Toppazzini's place, and the duo reportedly had to bum rides, six in total, to make it to the Garden. There was so much snow on the road that they had to hop out and shovel to keep the vehicles going. But the two made out better than their opponents. The train from New York took eight hours, twice as long as the usual schedule, and the game was delayed by two hours. Despite their gruelling journey, the weary Rangers picked up a 2–1 victory.

FEBRUARY 5

WOODY DUMART SCORES 200TH GOAL, 1952

When Woody Dumart was last in Chicago, he thought for sure he had scored his 200th career goal. The tally would've given the Bruins a 1–0 victory, but referee Bill Chadwick waved it off because Boston defenceman Jack McIntyre was in the crease. So they had to settle for a scoreless tie, and the Bruins captain would need to wait for his milestone goal. He didn't have to wait too long.

Less than a week later, on February 5, 1952, the Bs hosted the Black Hawks at the Garden. Early in the third period, Dumart backhanded the puck through Harry Lumley's pads to notch his 200th goal, becoming the 22nd player in league history to accomplish the feat. Although Dumart was miffed he hadn't reached the benchmark when he was in the Windy City, he was more than happy to do it at home in front of the Boston faithful. "What a feeling," he told reporters. Dumart retired a couple of years later with 211 goals to his name, then the third most in Bruins history.

FEBRUARY 6

BRAD MARCHAND SCORES PENALTY SHOT WINNER IN OT, 2016

Rasmus Ristolainen should have kept a tighter grip on his stick. Halfway through overtime in a game against the Bruins on February 6, 2016, the Buffalo defenceman tried to break up a Brad Marchand breakaway. But when Ristolainen put his stick over top of Marchand's twig, the feisty Bruins winger popped the blueliner's lumber into the air and out of his hands. As the stickless Ristolainen tried to stay with the play, he pawed and pushed Marchand off the puck. Referee Brad Watson penalized him by awarding Marchand a penalty shot.

It was admittedly a questionable call, especially in sudden death, but Marchand certainly didn't mind. With the game on his stick, he skated in on Sabres goalie Robin Lehner and backhanded the puck into the net to pick up the victory. It was the first time in Bruins history that the club won an overtime game on a penalty shot. Marchand, who already had two penalty shot goals to his name, matched Woody Dumart for the most by a Bruins player, and has since taken sole possession with seven.

FEBRUARY 7

BRUCE "BUTCH" CASSIDY NAMED INTERIM HEAD COACH, 2017

After more than a decade, Butch was a big-league bench boss again. On February 7, 2017, after the Bruins fired Claude Julien, Bruce Cassidy was named interim coach. Following his dismissal from Washington early in the 2003–04 campaign, Cassidy became an assistant in Chicago for a season before leaving the NHL to take a junior coaching gig. After a couple of years in the Ontario Hockey League, he joined Boston's AHL affiliate in Providence as an assistant until he became head coach in 2011.

After guiding the Baby Bs to four straight seasons with at least 40 wins, Cassidy was promoted to the Bruins as an assistant in 2016. Over the next five years, he led the Bruins to a Stanley Cup Final appearance and the Presidents' Trophy, taking home the Jack Adams Award along the way. But after a first-round exit in 2022, Boston fired Cassidy. Butch, however, wasn't out of work for long. Eight days later, he was hired by Vegas, where he'd win a championship at the end of his first season behind the bench.

FEBRUARY 8

HARRY LUMLEY NOTCHES 300TH CAREER WIN, 1958

For a while it seemed like Harry Lumley might never reach the 300 career wins mark. Lumley, who was known as "Apple Cheeks" for his rosy complexion, was five victories shy of the achievement when the Leafs traded his rights to the Black Hawks at the end of the 1955–56 campaign. But rather than reporting to the Windy City, Lumley, who was only a few years removed from a Vezina, opted to play in the minors.

In 1957, it was rumoured that the Bruins were interested in his services, but many felt the club wouldn't be comfortable meeting Chicago's asking price. A year later, however, with Boston in desperate need of goaltending, they managed to pry Lumley loose for cash. After initially reporting to the team's AHL affiliate in Springfield, he returned to the NHL for his first regular-season game in almost two years. A few weeks later, on February 8, 1958, after racking up a series of wins, Lumley finally reached the 300-win milestone, becoming just the second goaltender in league history to accomplish the feat.

FEBRUARY 9

KEN HODGE BAGS SIX ASSISTS, 1971

It was just another night for hockey's most potent line. On February 9, 1971, in a 6–3 victory against the Rangers, the line of Phil Esposito, Ken Hodge, and Wayne Cashman combined for 14 points. The rest of the heavy lifting was done by Bobby Orr and Johnny Bucyk. When the final buzzer sounded, Cashman had two goals and an assist, Esposito had a tally and four helpers, and Hodge had six assists, establishing a new franchise record for the most assists in a game.

Hodge was acquired in the same trade that brought Boston Esposito, and the pair, along with Cashman, would form one of the most dominant lines in hockey history a few years later. Not only could they seemingly score at will, but they were tough to play against. There was no moving Esposito from in front of the net, and good luck moving any of them off the puck. Hodge finished the year with 105 points, the most ever by a right winger at that time, and finished fourth in scoring behind Esposito, Orr, and Bucyk.

FEBRUARY 10

KRAUT LINE CARRIED OFF THE ICE, 1942

Some things are bigger than the game. After the Bruins walloped the Canadiens 8–1 on February 10, 1942, the Habs put the lopsided score aside to honour three of their adversaries: Milt Schmidt, Woody Dumart, and Bobby Bauer of Boston's vaunted Kraut Line. The trio, all of German heritage and hailing from Kitchener, Ontario, had combined for 11 points in their last game of the season before heading off to serve in the Royal Canadian Air Force during the Second World War.

When the match was over, the three courageous players were presented with gold identification bracelets, watches, and their salaries for the rest of the year. But the greatest gift they received was when they were hoisted onto the shoulders of their teammates, and even some of the opposing Montreal players, and carried off the ice while the Boston Garden faithful serenaded them with "Auld Lang Syne." The touching moment, undergirded by the respect and camaraderie the sport was founded on, was a poignant reminder of why hockey is the greatest game on earth.

FEBRUARY 11

ROSS BROOKS GETS FIRST SHUTOUT, 1973

Ross Brooks never gave up. Even when it seemed like his dream of playing in the NHL had passed him by, he kept playing and persevered. Finally, after more than a decade in the minors across four different circuits, Brooks made his big-league debut for the Bruins just a week after turning 35 years old, making 34 saves in a tie with the Buffalo Sabres. A few nights later, he recorded his first victory. And then something remarkable happened. Although Brooks ceded the net back to Eddie Johnston, he couldn't lose.

On February 11, 1973, Brooks stopped all 22 shots he faced against the Kings to record his first career shutout and his seventh straight start without a loss. He extended his improbable undefeated streak to 14 games, matching Bill Durnan's record from the 1943–44 campaign for the longest undefeated streak from the start of a career, until he finally lost in Boston's last game of the season. Brooks's benchmark held for more than two decades until Patrick Lalime surpassed it with the Pittsburgh Penguins.

FEBRUARY 12

CAM NEELY NETS QUICK HATTY, 1994

Cam Neely may have had a bad knee and was nursing a groin injury, but that didn't slow him down any. On February 12, 1994, in the first period of a game against the New Jersey Devils, Neely scored a natural hat trick in just over four minutes. Although it was his 11th career three-goal effort and his third hat trick that season, it was reportedly the first time Neely had notched three goals in the same period at any level of hockey.

After opening the scoring for the Bruins with a quick wrister following a Joe Juneau feed, less than three minutes later Neely wired a slapshot from 40 feet out that found its way through Martin Brodeur's pads. A little over a minute later, he forced his way to the net on a power play and tapped in a loose puck to complete the hat trick and give Boston a 3–1 lead. Neely's performance gave him 39 goals in just 35 games that season, an exceptional pace for a healthy player let alone one with a nagging knee.

FEBRUARY 13

BRONCO HORVATH EXTENDS SCORING LEAD, 1960

Bronco Horvath was leading the charge in the NHL's scoring race. On February 13, 1960, in a high-scoring affair against Montreal, he picked up two goals and an assist to give him 72 points on the season. Jean Béliveau trailed by six, and Bobby Hull was nine points back. Horvath, who was claimed from the Canadiens in the NHL Intra-League Draft a few years earlier and became an integral part of Boston's famed Uke Line alongside Johnny Bucyk and Vic Stasiuk, was having a breakout season.

The Bruins still had 15 games remaining on the schedule, but Horvath's 72 points was already the third most by a Bruins player in a single season. He kept collecting points down the stretch, but Hull managed to close the gap. In the final game of the season, which pitted the two against each other at Boston Garden, the Chicago sniper was just one point behind. While Horvath was held off the scoresheet that night, Hull recorded a goal and an assist to take the Art Ross Trophy by a single point.

FEBRUARY 14

BRAD MARCHAND BEATS FLEMING MACKELL FOR FASTEST GOAL, 2016

History doesn't repeat itself, but it often rhymes. When the Bruins hosted the Rangers on Valentine's Day in 1953, Fleming Mackell, known for his swift skating and two-way skills, broke the Blueshirts' hearts when he opened the scoring just nine seconds into the contest. It was the fastest any Bruin had scored after puck drop in franchise history. The benchmark held for more than six decades. That is, until exactly 63 years later to the day, when Brad Marchand made short work of Petr Mrázek.

Just eight seconds into a matchup against the Red Wings, Marchand wristed the puck past the Detroit netminder to surpass Mackell's mark by a single second. Mackell had passed away just a few months earlier, but if anyone was going to bump his name out of the top spot in the record books, I don't think he would've minded that it was Marchand. Like Mackell, Marchand endeared himself to the fans with his offensive and penalty-killing abilities and, like Mackell, has always found a way to elevate his game in the playoffs.

FEBRUARY 15

BRUINS ACQUIRE CHRIS KELLY, 2011

When Chris Kelly spoke with reporters after he learned he had been traded to the Bruins following a game against the Islanders, he was, ironically, wearing a shirt that said "Property of Senators." Kelly, who had been drafted 94th overall by Ottawa in 1999, had been with the organization his entire career until he was traded to Boston on February 15, 2011, in exchange for a second-round draft pick.

A skilled two-way player, especially in the faceoff circle, Kelly was exactly what the Bruins were looking for as they prepared for a deep playoff run. And with the Senators at the bottom of the Eastern Conference, Kelly was only too happy to be heading to a contender. A few nights later, he was back in familiar territory, making his Bruins debut in Ottawa, but was held off the scoresheet against his former team. He picked up five points down the stretch and was an important contributor in the post-season, recording 13 points in 25 games, to help Boston hoist its first Stanley Cup in nearly four decades.

FEBRUARY 16

JEAN RATELLE RECORDS 1,220TH POINT, 1980

If Jean Ratelle hadn't broken a bone in his ankle and missed the last 15 games of the season, he would've given Phil Esposito a run for his money for the 1972 Art Ross. When Ratelle went down, he had 109 points in 63 games, a Rangers record that held for more than three decades, and was just six points back of Esposito. But with Ratelle out for the rest of the regular season, Esposito finished with 133 points to win his third Art Ross Trophy, while Ratelle returned for the Stanley Cup Final, only to come up short to Esposito and the Bruins.

A few years later, they crossed paths again when Ratelle, along with Brad Park and Joe Zanussi, was traded to Boston for Esposito and Carol Vadnais. Although the deal marked the end of the famed GAG (Goal-a-Game) Line on Broadway, Ratelle continued scoring and dishing in Beantown. Even as his career wound down, he still produced. On February 16, 1980, he recorded his 1,220th career point, passing Jean Béliveau for the seventh most in NHL history.

FEBRUARY 17

RÉAL CHEVREFILS SCORES FIRST NHL GOAL, 1952

It was probably the longest Réal Chevrefils had gone without tickling the twine. But finally, in a matinee game against the Black Hawks on February 17, 1952, Chevrefils, who was playing in his 17th game for the Bruins, found the back of the net twice to record his first NHL goals. He also added an assist in the third period for good measure as Boston skated to a 5–2 victory over Chicago.

Following a 52-goal campaign with the Barrie Flyers of the Ontario Hockey Association and a Memorial Cup championship in 1951, Chevrefils drew comparisons to former Bruins legend Milt Schmidt when he broke into the league. And while it was a lofty estimate, Chevrefils was considered one of the top talents in junior hockey, behind only Jean Béliveau. While Chevrefils showed flashes of brilliance in his rookie campaign, within a few years he was traded to the Red Wings as part of a nine-player trade that included Terry Sawchuk and Vic Stasiuk. But Chevrefils wasn't gone long. He returned after 38 games. A year later, he put together a 31-goal campaign, a career best.

FEBRUARY 18

BRUINS TRADE BLAKE WHEELER, 2011

It was a busy day of dealing for the Bruins. On February 18, 2011, a few days after acquiring Chris Kelly from the Senators, Boston continued making moves, well in advance of the trade deadline, in preparation for what it hoped would be a deep playoff run. Looking to add a veteran presence to the blue line, the Bruins acquired Tomáš Kaberle, a power-play specialist, from the Leafs in exchange for prospect Joe Colborne and a pair of draft picks. Later that same day, the Bruins sent impending restricted free agent Blake Wheeler and Mark Stuart to Atlanta for Rich Peverley and Boris Valábik.

It's tough to argue with the results: Kaberle and Peverley hoisted the Stanley Cup with Boston, and Valábik finished out the campaign in the minors, but the club lost a top talent in Wheeler. While you will always take a championship over what might have been with a player, over the next eight seasons, only a handful of NHLers scored more points than Wheeler, and none of them were on the Bruins.

FEBRUARY 19

JUSTIN BRAZEAU SCORES FIRST NHL GOAL, 2024

This story was actually supposed to be about the Bruins playing an exhibition game in the hometown of the famed Kraut Line, in 1952, with Bobby Bauer coming out of retirement for just one night, but as I watched Boston's 2023–24 season unfold, I had a change of heart. That's a great yarn, but I've got a soft spot for players scoring in their NHL debut. And while Justin Brazeau's lighting the lamp in his first game for the Bruins on February 19, 2024, certainly meets that criteria, there was more to it.

Brazeau, who hails from the tiny northern Ontario community of New Liskeard, took the long way to the big leagues. A late-round pick of the North Bay Battalion of the Ontario Hockey League, the six-foot-six winger went undrafted to the NHL, even after putting together a 61-goal campaign in his final year of junior. But Brazeau didn't give up. He spent the better part of the next five years in the minors until he got the call he had been waiting for.

FEBRUARY 20

HAPPY BIRTHDAY TO PHIL ESPOSITO, 1942

One of the greatest Bruins ever grew up in the same town as my mother, and yet, somehow, she didn't cheer for the Bs. On February 20, 1942, Phil Esposito was born in Sault Ste. Marie, Ontario. Before he came around, the city was known for producing steel, but by the 1970s it was firmly entrenched as the place where Esposito, along with his brother Tony, were from. And while this story could've been just about celebrating Esposito, he actually achieved a number of milestones, other than just making another trip around the sun, on his birthday in a Bruins sweater.

In 1971 he recorded his first 50-goal campaign, becoming just the fourth player in NHL history to reach the benchmark. Exactly a year later, on his 30th birthday, he accomplished the feat again, making him just the second player to do it in back-to-back seasons. And a couple of years after that, in 1974, Esposito somehow hit the 50-goal mark on his birthday once again. He also added two more tallies that game to record his 22nd career hat trick.

FEBRUARY 21

BRUINS PLAY ON LAKE TAHOE, 2021

It was the most picturesque background for a hockey game. On February 21, 2021, with snow-capped mountains in the distance, the Bruins took on the Flyers on the shores of Lake Tahoe. While the NHL had been doing outdoor games regularly for more than a decade, this brought the game out of the stadiums and truly into the great outdoors.

And while it made for a better backdrop, it wasn't without its hitches. When the Avalanche and Golden Knights kicked off the festivities the day before, the match was halted and significantly delayed because the mild weather had wreaked havoc on the ice. By the time the playing surface was suitable enough to resume the game, the Nevada sun had long set. Conditions were better for the Bruins, but their contest was still delayed because of the glare coming off the ice. But David Pastrňák was prepared. He rocked a pair of sunglasses with hot-pink trim in the warm-up. He ditched the shades for the game, but his vibe continued. He scored a hat trick in a 7–3 rout of Philly.

FEBRUARY 22

HITCH GETS HIS DUE, 1934

Lionel Hitchman may be one of hockey's greatest unsung heroes. A stalwart on the Boston blue line for a decade, it was his steady play on the back end that gave his formidable defence partner, Eddie Shore, the confidence to run and gun down the ice. That job, of course, came with its share of occupational hazards. During a game against the Ottawa Senators in March 1930, Hitchman caught some friendly fire from Shore in the second period. The puck broke his jaw, but he finished the game. Hitchman didn't even bother seeing a physician until the next day. His jaw was wired shut for three weeks, but he returned for the final game of the regular season, sporting an iconic leather helmet.

Off the ice, Hitch was described to me as a "Renaissance man" by his granddaughter Pam Coburn, who wrote a book advocating his induction in the Hockey Hall of Fame. He played piano, he set fly-fishing records, he wrote poetry, he kept a pet bear, and on February 22, 1934, he became the first player to have his number retired by the Bruins.

FEBRUARY 23

BRUINS TRADE REGGIE LEACH, 1972

Reggie Leach didn't have to wait too long to face his former team. On the morning of February 23, 1972, it was announced that the Bruins had traded him to the California Golden Seals, along with Rick Smith and Bob Stewart, for defenceman Carol Vadnais and minor-leaguer Don O'Donoghue. Later that same day, the two teams squared off at the Coliseum in Oakland. By the end of the second period, the Seals were up 6–3, with Leach assisting on the third goal, but the Bruins stormed back, scoring five unanswered goals in the final frame to take it 8–6.

Although Vadnais struggled in his Bruins debut (he was on the ice for five of California's goals), he would indeed provide the defensive depth Boston was looking for and was rewarded with a Stanley Cup. Leach got his own championship a few years later with the Flyers and narrowly missed out on a repeat but was awarded the Conn Smythe, becoming the first skater to earn the trophy in a losing effort, after scoring a record-setting 19 goals in 16 playoff games.

FEBRUARY 24

EDDIE SHORE RECORDS HAT TRICK, 1931

Whenever I think of Eddie Shore, one of the first things my mind drifts to is the classic film *Slap Shot*. Shore is referenced throughout the movie, including one scene in which the team's frugal manager, Joe McGrath, tells player-coach Reggie Dunlop, played by Paul Newman, about the time Shore sent him a player who had a salacious habit I won't repeat here, chiefly because he embodied the type of play revered by the Hanson brothers. "Yeah, old-time hockey. Like Eddie Shore," they exclaim. Shore would have fit in nicely with the Chiefs with his aggressive, hard-nosed style of play, but he was much more than a bruiser.

Before Bobby Orr brought Bruins supporters out of their seats, Shore dazzled the Boston faithful with his sensational end-to-end rushes. Once, during a game against the lowly Philadelphia Quakers on February 24, 1931, Shore blew past his opponents so many times that he scored his first and only career hat trick. While Shore would later be remembered for the Ace Bailey incident, it was his "old-time hockey" that captivated fans.

FEBRUARY 25

LINUS ULLMARK SCORES A GOAL, 2023

Every goalie dreams of scoring a goal. And on February 25, 2023, Linus Ullmark made his dream come true. With 48 seconds remaining in a game against the Canucks, the Boston netminder corralled the puck and ripped it up high and down the length of the ice into the vacant Vancouver cage. Ullmark became the eighth goaltender in NHL history to score a goal and just the first Bruin to accomplish the feat.

Even better than scoring the goal was that, after being mobbed by his teammates on the ice, Ullmark skated over to the bench and led the high-five procession. As he paraded by his teammates, giving them fist bumps with his trapper, you could see how excited his fellow Bruins were that he scored. They all had smiles as wide as a goalie crease, and it was tough to tell who was having more fun, them or Ullmark. But of course it was Ullmark. He capped off the night with his 30th win of the season, continuing his career year and Vezina candidacy.

FEBRUARY 26

STEVE KASPER PICKS UP FOUR POINTS, 1987

There's a saying that cooler heads prevail. One night in Boston, Steve Kasper put that old adage to the test. On February 26, 1987, the Bruins hosted the Nordiques in a chippy affair at the Garden. Just before the halfway mark of the second period, a bench-clearing brawl erupted, resulting in nine ejections. When the final buzzer sounded, the officials had doled out 231 penalty minutes.

Late in the session, after the dust had settled, Quebec's David Shaw tried to stir things up again. He went after Kasper along the boards and tried to goad him into a fight by punching him in the face. But instead of retaliating, Kasper just stared him down. He knew better. Shaw received two minutes for roughing and was sent to the penalty box. The power play carried over into the final frame, and while Shaw watched from the sin bin, Kasper converted, picking up his fourth point of the night, matching a career high. Kasper stayed calm and was rewarded for keeping his composure, a lesson that's just as valuable off the ice.

FEBRUARY 27

GEOFF COURTNALL RECORDS FIRST HAT TRICK, 1988

Geoff Courtnall was going to be a 30-goal scorer; it was just a matter of when. After signing with the Bruins as an undrafted free agent out of junior, he reached the 20-goal mark in his second full year. His production dropped off the next season — he scored just 13 goals — but Courtnall knew he had more in him. In the 1987–88 campaign, he sailed by the 20-goal mark before the new year and was a few tallies ahead of Cam Neely for the team lead.

Courtnall's pace slowed down a bit when the calendar flipped, but on February 27, 1988, in a game against the Minnesota North Stars, he recorded his 30th goal and added two more to collect his first career hat trick. Courtnall would become a regular 30-goal scorer in the NHL, but it wouldn't be in Boston. A month later, he was traded to the Oilers, along with Bill Ranford, where they'd win the Stanley Cup against their former club that spring. Courtnall reached the 30-goal mark four more times during stints in Washington, Vancouver, and St. Louis.

FEBRUARY 28

TOM JOHNSON SUFFERS CAREER-ENDING INJURY, 1965

The Bruins' casualty list was mounting. Five minutes into the second period in a game against the Black Hawks on February 28, 1965, defenceman Tom Johnson collided with Chicago's Chico Maki near the Boston net. During the dust-up, Johnson, a former Norris Trophy winner, sustained a gash to his left leg and was rushed to hospital. A few days later, the full prognosis was revealed. Johnson had severed one of the muscles near his knee and was out for the rest of the season. He joined an infirm crew that included Eddie Johnston with a broken finger, Dean Prentice with a broken back, Bobby Leiter with a broken arm, and Forbes Kennedy with a fractured shoulder.

While those broken bones healed, Johnson never played again. Unable to recover from the injury, the veteran blueliner hung up his skates at the start of the next campaign, but stayed on with the Bruins in a scouting and player-development role. Johnson later found himself behind the Boston bench, guiding the team to a Stanley Cup in 1972.

FEBRUARY 29

RAY BOURQUE HITS 1,000 POINTS, 1992

Ray Bourque had a hunch. Before leaving for a game against the Washington Capitals on February 29, 1992, the Bruins captain told his wife he was going to reach the 1,000-point mark. For most players, especially a defenceman, it was a lofty forecast. Bourque was still three points away, but he wasn't just any player, so it certainly wasn't out of the question. Boston was held off the scoresheet in the first period, but early in the second frame, Bourque assisted on a Brent Ashton goal to inch closer to the mark.

Before the session came to a close, Bourque scored on the power play to put the milestone in his sights. Toward the end of the final stanza, Bobby Carpenter thought Bourque might have gotten a piece of another Ashton goal to give him 1,000, but the superstar blueliner made another bold bet. He said he was going to reach it on a Carpenter goal. Less than five minutes later, he made good on both predictions that day: assisting on Carpenter's 21st goal of the season and reaching the 1,000-point mark.

MARCH

MARCH 1

DIT CLAPPER RECORDS HAT TRICK, 1932

As far as hockey names go, it doesn't get much better than Dit Clapper. His birth certificate says Aubrey Victor, but when the young Clapper tried to pronounce Vic, it sounded more like Dit, and so from that point on, he was known as Dit. Originally a defenceman, when he joined the Bruins in 1927, Art Ross shifted him to the wing. The move quickly paid off. Clapper scored his first goal in his NHL debut.

The next season, he found a fit with Cooney Weiland and Dutch Gainor, forming what would become known as the explosive Dynamite Line. In the 1929–30 campaign, Clapper racked up 41 goals. The only player with more that year was Weiland, his linemate. Clapper had no problem filling the net, but hat tricks seemed harder to come by. He managed a couple, but he wasn't known for scoring in bunches. At the tail end of his fifth season in Boston, on March 1, 1932, Clapper bagged just his third career three-goal performance in a game against the Canadiens.

MARCH 2

PHIL ESPOSITO HITS 100, 1969

Phil Esposito joined a pretty exclusive club. On March 2, 1969, he scored a goal early in the third period of a game against the Penguins to record his 100th point of the season, becoming the first player in NHL history to reach the milestone. Esposito may have been the only standing member of the Century Club, but its ranks would swell a few weeks later when Bobby Hull punched his ticket. Esposito, however, was probably more welcoming when teammate Bobby Orr was admitted to the group the next year.

Following the match, reporters asked him what else he wanted to accomplish that season. "Win some more games, score some more, win the scoring title, then get the Cup," Esposito said. He managed to get it nearly all done. The Bruins won more games. He finished with 49 goals and 126 points to win the Art Ross, but the championship eluded his grasp. But Esposito wouldn't have to wait too long. The next year, he led the Bruins to their first Stanley Cup in nearly three decades.

MARCH 3

BRUINS ACQUIRE SERGEI GONCHAR, 2004

The Bruins won the Sergei Gonchar sweepstakes. Leading up to the 2004 NHL trade deadline, teams were lining up for his services, but it was Boston that managed to pry him out of Washington. On March 3, they acquired the Russian defenceman for Shaone Morrisonn and first- and second-round picks in the upcoming draft. Gonchar immediately added significant firepower to the Bruins' blue line.

One of the league's premier offensive defencemen, he was at the top of his class that season with 49 points in 56 games. Even if you excluded Gonchar's 31 points from the Capitals' power play, one of the best that year, he still nearly had more points than Nick Boynton, who was leading the Bruins' back end with 22. Down the stretch Gonchar recorded nine points in 15 games and another five points in the playoffs. The Boston faithful might have hoped to see Gonchar in black and gold a little longer, but after the NHL lockout wiped out the 2004–05 campaign, he returned from playing in Russia and signed a five-year deal in Pittsburgh.

MARCH 4

BILL COWLEY PICKS UP SIX POINTS, 1944

Bill Cowley had already bagged a scoring title and narrowly missed out on lassoing another. Known as Cowboy, Cowley earned his bona fides with the Bruins, leading the team to a Stanley Cup in 1939, capturing the most NHL points in 1941, and earning two Hart trophies along the way. At the opening of the 1943–44 season, he was poised to notch the most points and be in contention for a third Hart.

Through the first 26 games, Cowley had collected 19 goals and 52 points, 12 more than the next closest player, Herb Cain. But a shoulder injury in early January put Cowley on the infirm list. Despite missing nearly two months, just a few days after his return, on March 4, 1944, he racked up six points, matching a career high. The offensive eruption brought him within five points of Cain, who leapfrogged him while he was on the shelf, but the Cowboy ran out of trail. Cain finished atop the league with 82 points while Cowley wasn't too far behind, with 71 points in just 36 games.

MARCH 5

BOBBY BAUER RECORDS LAST NHL HAT TRICK, 1947

Bobby Bauer was going out with a bang. The Bruins captain had announced it would be his final NHL season, but with the way the 32-year-old was playing, it certainly seemed like he had plenty of hockey still left in him. After notching his first career hat trick early in the campaign in a game against the Leafs, on March 5, 1947, Bauer had another three-goal performance, once again against Toronto. After setting up Milt Schmidt, who was celebrating his 29th birthday, just before the halfway mark of the first period, Bauer then collected a natural hat trick on two sets of power plays.

Bauer finished the year with 30 goals and 54 points, his most productive campaign with Boston by a significant margin. He'd pick up two more points in the playoffs before hanging up his jersey. But it wouldn't be the last time he'd wear black and gold. Five years later, as part of a celebration of Schmidt and Woody Dumart, Bauer joined his long-time linemates for one last game in Boston.

MARCH 6

ROGIE VACHON PICKS UP FINAL SHUTOUT, 1982

Harry Sinden had had his eye on Rogie Vachon for quite some time. After the Kings goaltender turned in a spectacular performance at the 1976 Canada Cup, the Boston GM had been trying to get him in a Bruins sweater. Sinden missed out when Vachon signed with the Wings a couple of years later, but when things didn't work in Detroit, he was finally able to swing a deal.

Eager for a fresh start, Vachon requested a trade and offered up Boston as a potential destination. And so, on July 15, 1980, the Bruins acquired Vachon from the Wings in exchange for netminder Gilles Gilbert. In his first season in Beantown, Vachon played 53 games and served as a mentor to Olympic hero Jim Craig, who was playing in his first NHL campaign after backstopping Team USA to gold at Lake Placid. The next year, playing behind Marco Baron, Vachon recorded his final NHL shutout on March 6, 1982, turning aside all 24 shots he faced from the Kings, one of his former teams, in a 4–0 victory.

MARCH 7

EDDIE SHACK AND LARRY ZEIDEL JOUST, 1968

Eddie Shack left the ice with a splitting headache. Just before the halfway mark of the first period in a game against the Flyers, on March 7, 1968, the Bruins winger got into a stick-swinging duel with Larry Zeidel. After taking whacks at each other's helmetless noggins, they were both tossed from the match. They were lucky they didn't each wind up in the hospital. Instead, they received repairs in the medical room at Maple Leaf Gardens — the game was being played in Toronto because the roof of the Spectrum in Philadelphia had been damaged in a windstorm.

While the two had their scalps stitched up, Zeidel, the feisty Flyer, had to be removed from the game when he tried to go after Shack again. The pair had a history of bad blood. A decade earlier, when Shack was a rookie with the Rangers and Zeidel was playing for the Hershey Bears of the AHL, they got into their first jousting match during an exhibition game that later spilled over into the stands when they fought each other in street clothes after they had been ejected.

MARCH 8

RAY BOURQUE PICKS UP HAT TRICK, 1983

When coach Gerry Cheevers was asked to describe Ray Bourque, he needed only one word: *awesome.* The assessment came after the Bruins' budding star picked up his first career hat trick in a lopsided 11–5 defeat of the Quebec Nordiques on March 8, 1983, becoming the first Boston blueliner since Bobby Orr to record three goals in a game. The bench boss was quick to heap praise on the youthful defenceman but resisted the urge to compare him to the eight-time Norris Trophy winner. And if anyone could make the comparison, it was Cheevers, who played behind Orr for seven seasons in Boston.

But the bench boss knew that few could live up to those expectations, and however compelling Bourque's bourgeoning track record might have been, the young player didn't need that kind of pressure. Other coaches, however, weren't as hesitant. Oilers GM and coach Glen Sather, who played a pair of seasons with Orr in Beantown and many more against him, said Bourque was as close to Orr as anyone he'd seen. It was hard to argue with that.

MARCH 9

GREGG SHEPPARD SCORES TWO QUICK SHORTIES, 1975

They might have been two of the easiest goals Gregg Sheppard scored at the start of his tenure with the Bruins. On March 9, 1975, with a minute to go in a game against Boston, the Flames, trailing by a goal and on the power play, pulled their goalie for even more firepower. But Atlanta was running out of time. With just 22 seconds remaining, Sheppard scored a short-handed empty-netter to put the game out of reach.

He wasn't done just yet. Twenty-one seconds later, with time on the clock about to expire and Flames goalie Dan Bouchard still on the bench, Sheppard buried another short-handed tally. The swift shorties gave Sheppard his 25th and 26th goals of the season, establishing a new career high for the North Battleford, Saskatchewan, native, who was playing his third campaign in black and gold. The next game, he was back at it again, scoring another short-handed goal, but this time there was a goalie in the net. Sheppard finished the year with 30 tucks, the first of three consecutive 30-goal seasons with Boston.

MARCH 10

DENNIS O'BRIEN FINDS A HOME IN BOSTON, 1978

Dennis O'Brien had been practically living out of his suitcase. After starting the season with the North Stars, where he began his NHL career nearly a decade earlier, he was dealt to Colorado just 13 games into the campaign. He was settling into the Mile High State when he got word the Rockies were sending him to the Barons. When O'Brien's wife called him to say that the movers were back at their home in Minnesota, he had to tell her to instruct them to send the furniture to Cleveland instead of Denver. She wasn't impressed.

But O'Brien wasn't long for Ohio, either. After playing 23 games for the Barons, he was placed on waivers. It almost looked like he would finish up the season in the minors, but on March 10, 1978, the Bruins put in a late claim for his services. Boston wound up being his fourth stop that year, a league record that was later matched by Dave McLlwain in 1991–92, Mark Arcobello in 2014–15, and Jussi Jokinen in 2017–18.

MARCH 11

Bs NOTCH 50TH WIN, 1971

No team had won more games in a season than the Bruins. After eclipsing the Canadiens' record of 46 victories from the 1968–69 campaign in early March 1971, the Bruins kept on rolling. Arriving at the Great Western Forum in Los Angeles on March 11, the club was just one victory shy of 50. The Kings opened the scoring, but the Bruins responded with seven unanswered tallies to record their 50th victory.

The Bruins finished the season with 57, but that number meant nothing if it wasn't followed by 12 more wins in the playoffs (there weren't four rounds yet). Unfortunately, Boston came up short to Montreal in the opening round. Not only would the Habs go on to win the Cup that year, but a few years later, they surpassed Boston's benchmark, notching 58 victories in the 1975–76 season. The Bruins eventually took the record back nearly five decades later, but after picking up 65 regular-season wins, the Presidents' Trophy winners were upset by the Florida Panthers in the first round — but we'll get to that.

MARCH 12

CRAIG JANNEY BAGS FIRST NHL HAT TRICK, 1988

Like many young American hockey players, Craig Janney was inspired by Team USA's improbable Olympic gold medal win on home soil at Lake Placid in 1980. Eight years later, Janney himself donned the stars and stripes at the Winter Games, but there would be no miracle; the U.S. finished seventh. The silver lining, however, was that a few weeks later the Enfield, Connecticut, native signed a contract with the Bruins, who drafted him 13th overall a couple of years earlier.

On March 12, 1988, Janney recorded his first NHL hat trick in a game against the Quebec Nordiques. He completed the three-goal effort with just over a minute remaining to secure the victory. The next year, playing in his first full campaign with the black and gold, Janney had a breakout season, scoring 16 goals and 62 points in 62 games and finishing in the top five for Calder Trophy voting as the league's most outstanding rookie. But a few years later, not long after notching 92 points, Janney was traded to the Blues, along with Stéphane Quintal, for the silky-smooth passer Adam Oates.

MARCH 13

BRAD MARCHAND COLLECTS HAT TRICK IN VANCOUVER, 2017

Vancouver fans booed Brad Marchand at their own peril. The pesky winger had been public enemy number one since the Bruins defeated the Canucks on home ice to hoist the Stanley Cup in 2011. Whenever Marchand returned to Rogers Arena, he was taunted every time he touched the puck. But here's the thing: Marchand feeds off that kind of energy. So when the Canucks hosted the Bruins on March 13, 2017, he responded to the usual welcome in a way only he can. Just under a minute into the final session, he scored the game-tying goal.

Later in the frame, after stealing the puck from captain Henrik Sedin, he deked his way to the net and put it past Ryan Miller. It held up as the game-winner, but before regulation came to a close, Marchand added an empty-netter to complete the hat trick. Following the game, he acknowledged that he embraced the booing, but he had an even better line for the Canucks faithful: "Lots of great memories in this building ... when you have a night like that it just adds to those."

MARCH 14

RICK TOCCHET RECORDS FIRST BRUINS HATTY, 1996

Rick Tocchet put his team on his back against some familiar opponents. Early in the third period in a game against the Penguins, on March 14, 1996, Tocchet, who won a Stanley Cup with Pittsburgh four years earlier, scored on the power play to give the Bruins a 2–1 lead. Just after the halfway mark of the frame, he found the back of the net again. Tocchet might have had himself a natural hat trick if it wasn't for his former teammate Jaromír Jágr, who scored a few minutes later to cut into the deficit.

The "natty" was off the table, but the hatty was still up for grabs. Less than 30 seconds after Jágr's tally, Tocchet notched his third of the night to record his first hat trick in black and gold. Exactly one week later, he recorded another three-goal performance. Tocchet, who joined Boston a couple of months earlier via trade from Los Angeles, finished the campaign with 16 goals in 27 appearances for the Bruins, one of the better goals-per-game stretches in his career.

MARCH 15

BOBBY ORR HITS 100, 1970

Bobby Orr punched his ticket to the Century Club in a way that only he could. Early in the second period of a game against Detroit on March 15, 1970, with the Bruins short-handed, Orr caught a pass from Derek Sanderson and then made a brilliant rush down the length of the ice. After making his way around several Wings, he put the puck past goaltender Roy Edwards to record his 100th point of the campaign, becoming the first blueliner in NHL history to reach the milestone.

While Orr and his teammates celebrated, the Garden crowd rose to their feet, giving the superstar a standing ovation. Those who weren't clapping pelted the ice with debris that took 10 minutes to clear off. While the two teams waited for a clean sheet, Gordie Howe reportedly ribbed Orr for holding up the game. Better that than taking a signature Howe elbow to the chops. Orr finished the season with 120 points, taking home the Art Ross. He still remains the only defenceman to earn the award.

MARCH 16

GARNET BAILEY SCORES FIRST NHL POINTS, 1969

With Eddie Shack and Eddie Westfall on the shelf with injuries, the Bruins called up Garnet Bailey from the minors. Bailey played a couple of games for Boston to start the campaign but was sent back to the American Hockey League. He went scoreless in those first two contests, but when he got the call again later in the year, he made the most of his opportunity. On March 16, 1969, in his third game back with the Bruins, Bailey notched two goals and added three assists.

But more than the points, Bailey proved he had what it took to stay in the NHL. He'd go on to play nearly a decade in the big leagues, making stops in Detroit, St. Louis, and Washington before hanging up his skates. Bailey later went on to serve as director of professional scouting for the Kings, but his life was tragically cut short when he was killed on United Airlines Flight 175 as part of the September 11 terrorist attacks. To honour his memory, the Kings named their mascot, Bailey, after him.

MARCH 17

BRUINS RALLY TO WIN, 1968

The Bruins needed a win to keep their position in the standings. They were in a battle for second place in the East Division against the Rangers and Black Hawks, and had one less game to play. With just a handful of matches left, the Bruins couldn't afford to leave any points on the board. On March 17, 1968, with New York already picking up a victory and Chicago cruising to one of its own against Oakland, Boston needed a win to avoid dropping to fourth place.

It didn't look promising. Late in their game against the Canadiens at the Garden, the Bruins trailed 1–0. But with time winding down on the clock, the black and gold scored three goals in exactly two minutes to take the game and cling to their position. Boston managed to rattle off just two more victories down the stretch and wound up dropping to third place in the division. They matched up against Montreal in the opening round of the playoffs and were swept aside in four games.

MARCH 18

JACK NORRIS FACES DETROIT BARRAGE, 1965

Jack Norris did the best he could. On March 18, 1965, in a game against the Red Wings, the rookie netminder was hung out to dry by his teammates in a 10-goal barrage by the Motor City rivals. Detroit struck early in the first period, and just over the halfway mark of the frame, they were already up 5–0. Although Reg Fleming got the Bruins on the board before the session came to a close, the game was all but out of reach. The Wings added two more in the second and three more in the final stanza.

Norris, who had been called up to replace the ailing Eddie Johnston, had endured a couple of stinkers already in his short tenure with the Bruins but never double digits. While the league had not yet started tracking shots officially, newspapers reported that Norris faced 57 shots — an admirable performance. But it proved to be one of his final appearances for Boston. A couple of years later, he was sent to Chicago as part of the trade for Phil Esposito.

MARCH 19

TINY THOMPSON GETS FIRST SHUTOUT, 1929

Tiny Thompson wasn't actually so tiny. Growing up, he was always one of the tallest players on his team, so he was jokingly referred to as "Tiny." The nickname followed him all the way to the big leagues when he started tending the twine for the Bruins. Personally, as someone who is only an inch taller than Thompson's reported height of 5 foot 10, I'm glad that's how he got his moniker. Regardless of his stature or sobriquet, one thing is clear: Thompson's first season for Boston was big. He played every regular-season game, picking up 12 shutouts.

In the playoffs Thompson continued his strong play between the pipes. On March 19, 1929, in his first post-season appearance, he turned aside every shot he faced, becoming just the second goaltender in NHL history to record a shutout in his playoff debut. Thompson picked up two more shutouts that spring, backstopping the Bruins to their first Stanley Cup. The following year, after winning all but six of Boston's 44 games, he earned his first of four Vezina trophies.

MARCH 20

BOBBY ORR SCORES 21ST GOAL OF THE YEAR, 1969

Bobby Orr couldn't find much to be happy about in a 5–5 tie, but there was plenty to celebrate that day. On March 20, 1969, Orr turned 21 years old, making him legal to buy a beer in Boston, but he was also closing in on some hockey history that day. Heading into a game against the Black Hawks, Orr was sitting at 20 goals on the campaign, tied for the league record for the most goals in a season by a defenceman.

It looked like Orr was going to be held off the scoresheet that match, but with just a single second remaining on the clock, he bulged the twine to force a draw and pick up his 21st of the year, on his 21st birthday no less, to establish a new benchmark for defencemen. Orr, of course, would push that standard further, eventually getting to 46 tallies in the 1974–75 season, a mark that would hold for more than a decade until Paul Coffey surpassed it with the Oilers.

MARCH 21

BRUINS BARRAGE RON TUGNUTT, 1991

Ron Tugnutt was playing so well that even Cam Neely told him to take a bow. On March 21, 1991, the Nordiques netminder stopped nearly everything the Bruins threw at him. Although he allowed a few goals, he stopped 70 shots through regulation and a period of overtime. While the NHL didn't officially start tracking saves until the 1955–56 season, Tugnutt's performance was deemed the most saves by a goaltender in NHL history, although Detroit's Normie Smith, who made 92 saves in a marathon playoff game in 1936, might like to have a word.

It was just one of those nights in which Tugnutt was seeing the puck perfectly. Ray Bourque managed to get one by him, but Tugnutt stopped the other 18 shots the Bruins captain fired at him, a league record as well, including a last-ditch effort with just eight seconds remaining that Tugnutt snared with his glove. But Bourque couldn't solve him again, and the match ended in a 3–3 tie. An exasperated Bourque called it the best performance he had ever witnessed by a goaltender.

MARCH 22

DOUG MOHNS SCORES TWO GOALS, 1964

They called him "Diesel." Hailing from Capreol, Ontario, a railway hub just outside of Sudbury, Doug Mohns had powerful skating strides that would have rivalled the locomotives pulling out of his hometown. Mohns joined the Bruins for the 1953–54 season and was a fixture on the team's blue line for more than a decade, creating a formidable pair with Fern Flaman. While Flaman was more of a shutdown defenceman, Diesel could join the rush and contribute offensively.

On March 22, 1964, in the final game of the season, Mohns potted two goals against the Black Hawks. They would be his final tallies with Boston. A few months later, he was traded to Chicago, where he would actually be moved up front to left wing, becoming a key part of the Scooter Line with Stan Mikita and Ken Wharram. Mohns earned his moniker for his power, but he also proved as durable as a diesel engine. He played another decade in the NHL before finally hanging up his skates with 1,391 games under his belt, the sixth most in league history at the time.

MARCH 23

GERRY CHEEVERS EARNS 20TH CAREER SHUTOUT, 1977

Gerry Cheevers had earned a milestone shutout, but all he wanted to do was talk about his horse. On March 23, 1977, after stopping all 29 shots he faced against Detroit to earn his 20th career shutout, good enough for fifth place on the Bruins' all-time list, Cheevers was more interested in chatting with reporters about the prospect of his colt, Royal Ski, running at the Kentucky Derby later in the spring. Cheevers hoped his young horse, one of the top earners the year before, could give Seattle Slew a run for his money, but Royal Ski ended up getting sick and wasn't able to compete in "the Run for the Roses."

And if that wasn't bad enough for the Bruins netminder, the Derby was the same day as the opening game of the Stanley Cup Final between Boston and Montreal. Far from a shutout performance, Cheevers allowed seven goals in a drubbing. Although his game tightened up as the series wore on, Cheevers didn't get much offensive support, and the Bruins were swept by the defending champions.

MARCH 24

ZDENO CHARA HITS 1K, 2012

When Zdeno Chara was growing up in the Czech Republic, he was told he would have been better off playing basketball instead of hockey. While Chara, who ended up growing to six foot nine, would have handled himself well on the hardwood, Boston fans are thankful he never heeded that advice. Making his NHL debut for the Islanders in 1997, Chara became the tallest player in league history. And despite towering over, and probably terrifying, his opponents, he was insanely agile and athletic, instantly making him one of the most formidable players on the circuit.

After eventually joining the Bruins via free agency in 2006, Chara took the team to new heights, literally. He guided the club to a Stanley Cup in 2011, hoisting the silver chalice high above his head. The next season, on March 24, 2012, the monstrous defenceman played in his 1,000th career game. Chara clearly made the right call. Whoever told him he shouldn't bother with hockey might be shocked to learn he's running marathons, and running them well, in retirement.

MARCH 25

BRAD MARCHAND GETS EIGHTH GAME-WINNER, 2018

Brad Marchand has always been a big-game player. From his clutch performances in the playoffs to ending games in the regular season, he is exactly who you want on the ice in the final seconds of any contest. And the 2017–18 campaign proved to be no exception. On March 25, just 28 seconds into overtime against the Minnesota Wild, Marchand buried his 33rd of the season, and his eighth winning tally of the year, matching a career high. Earlier in the month, he scored three straight game-winning goals, piling up five markers in that stretch.

The next season, Marchand continued to prove how clutch he was, racking up nine game-winners, a new career high. Although he was still a country mile behind Phil Esposito's mark of 16 in a single campaign, he was making a solid run at the record for the most in franchise history. While I was editing this book, however, Marchand was traded to Florida on March 7, 2025, leaving him stuck just six tallies behind Johnny Bucyk for the all-time milestone.

MARCH 26

BRIAN ROLSTON SETS SHORT-HANDED GOAL RECORD — OR DOES HE?, 2002

If there's one thing I won't stand for, it's Jerry Toppazzini erasure. Sure, I might be a little biased. Toppazzini grew up in Copper Cliff, not far from Sudbury, where I'm writing these words, and in retirement he founded a watering hole called the Beef 'n Bird that I spent many Friday nights in during my younger days. Topper, as he was affectionately known, played the game hard and was a penalty-killing specialist. In fact, for many decades, he held the Bruins' record for the most short-handed goals in a season with eight.

But when Brian Rolston recorded his eighth short-handed tally of the year on March 26, 2002, some coverage didn't even mention Topper, instead citing Don Marcotte, Ed Westfall, Derek Sanderson, and Gregg Sheppard, who each had seasons of seven short-handed goals. It could have been that Toppazzini was later credited with eight when the NHL digitized its game sheets in 2017, but either way, Rolston officially got the record just over a week later when he notched his ninth in a game against the Flyers.

MARCH 27

DAVID PASTRŇÁK TRIUMPHANT IN RETURN, 2019

David Pastrňák had missed five weeks with a bum thumb, but he certainly didn't play like it. After making his return to the lineup, Pastrňák collected six points in his first four games back. When the Bruins hosted the Rangers on March 27, 2019, he kept the hot streak going, putting up the best offensive night of his career. The Czech winger, who injured his thumb leaving a team function in February, picked up his fourth career hat trick and added two assists in a 6–3 victory against New York.

It was Pastrňák's third three-goal performance of the year, making him the first Bruin since Cam Neely to record a trio of hat tricks. The goal-scoring effort also gave him 36 goals on the campaign, a career high. And despite missing 16 games with the busted digit, Pastrňák finished the season with 81 points, another career milestone. The next year, before the world was turned upside down by the Covid-19 pandemic, Pastrňák racked up 48 goals, tying him with Alex Ovechkin to share the Rocket Richard Trophy.

MARCH 28

RICK MIDDLETON HITS MILESTONES, 1981 AND 1982

March 28 seemed to agree with Rick Middleton. On that day in 1981, in a game against the Black Hawks, he recorded three assists, including a helper on Peter McNab's game-winning tally, to reach the 100-point mark for the first time in his career, becoming just the fifth Bruin to reach the mark and the first to accomplish the feat since Phil Esposito.

Exactly one year later, less than two minutes into a contest against the Sabres, Middleton found the back of the net to record his 50th goal of the campaign, the first time he hit the vaunted goal-scoring benchmark. Although the Bruins would've liked to forget about that game (they ended up losing 9–5 to Buffalo), it was another milestone match for Nifty. It would prove to be the only time he would rack up 50 goals in a season with Boston — he narrowly missed the mark the next year, finishing with 49. The following season, he was just a few tallies shy of reaching it again but ended up with 105 points, a career high.

MARCH 29

BRUINS WIN FIRST STANLEY CUP, 1929

It was the ultimate sibling rivalry. For the 1929 Stanley Cup Final, there was more at stake than a championship between the Bruins and Rangers, the league's first all-American battle for the rights to Lord Stanley's mug; there was bragging rights at the family dinner table for the Thompson brothers. Between the pipes for Boston was rookie netminder Cecil "Tiny" Thompson, who we have already determined was not so tiny, and at the other end of the ice, playing on the wing for New York, was his younger brother Paul. It marked the first time that a goalie–forward brother combination squared off in the post-season.

In the first game, on March 28, Tiny stopped every shot he faced, staking the Bruins to a 2–0 lead in the best-of-three series. The very next day, Boston closed out the series with a 2–1 victory, earning the first Stanley Cup in franchise history. Decades later, when asked about facing off against Paul in the Final, Tiny answered the question as only an older brother could: "It was really no contest."

MARCH 30

BRUINS SCORE THREE QUICK GOALS, 1952

It wasn't necessarily a must-win game for the Bruins, but it was absolutely a can't-lose game. Down 0–2 in their semifinal series against the Canadiens, Boston was in jeopardy of falling into an insurmountable deficit. At that point in NHL history, only one team had managed to recover from falling behind 0–3 in a best-of-seven series. Looking to avoid testing those odds, on March 30, 1952, the Bruins stepped up. Early in the second period, the bespectacled Hal Laycoe, who was one of the few players of his era to wear glasses on the ice, opened the scoring.

Within just over a minute, the black and gold managed to notch two more goals to take a 3–0 lead. The Bruins added another in the final frame to take a 4–1 victory and get back into the series. Following the gutsy performance, the Bruins won the next two games to climb into the driver's seat. But after losing the next game in a double-overtime heartbreaker, they lost the seventh and deciding match in Montreal.

MARCH 31

BRUINS' FIRST PLAYOFF SERIES, 1927

After trouncing the Black Hawks 6–1 in their playoff debut, the Bruins pretty much had it in the bag two nights later on March 31, 1927. It was a two-game total-goals series, so as long as they didn't lose 6–0 to Chicago, they'd be moving on to the next round. Neither team managed to light the lamp in the opening frame, but early in the second period the Bruins struck first when rookie Percy Galbraith opened the scoring.

Boston notched two more that session, including another from Galbraith. The Black Hawks put two on the board late in the stanza, but early in the final frame Galbraith bulged the twine again to record Boston's first-ever post-season hat trick. Chicago managed two more, but it was too little, too late. The Bruins were off to face the Rangers, winners of the American Division. In another two-game total-goals series, it all came down to the second match after neither scored in the first contest. Boston wound up winning 3–1 and went on to the Stanley Cup Final, but faltered to Ottawa.

APRIL

APRIL 1

30TH OT GAME, 2004

No team has played as many overtime games in a single season as the Boston Bruins. On April 1, 2004, after giving up a lead midway through the third period in a game against the Washington Capitals, the Bruins headed into their 30th overtime session of the campaign, extending their NHL record. A couple of years earlier, the Colorado Avalanche played additional hockey 28 times, a mark Boston had surpassed a few days before with a comeback OT victory at home against Montreal.

It was one of the few times the Bruins had pulled off a win in extra time. They had won only eight times when pushed to overtime, instead leaving dozens of points on the board with 13 ties and eight losses. Remember, this was in the era before the shootout, so they might have had a more favourable record with the gimmicky exhibition, but that was still a lockout and a lost season away. Neither the Bruins nor the Caps managed to score again on April Fool's Day, giving Boston its final draw.

APRIL 2

"SUDDEN DEATH" MEL HILL, 1939

Mel Hill struck again. Eight minutes into the third overtime period against the Rangers, on April 2, 1939, Mel Hill, who had already earned the nickname "Sudden Death" with his overtime heroics throughout the series, notched the deciding goal in the seventh game, adding to his legend. Hill opened the series with a triple-OT goal, along with another in the first extra session in the second game, so it was rather fitting that he closed it out with another triple-overtime heartbreaker to send the Bruins to the next round.

But with so much adrenalin flowing through his veins and the game ending well past midnight, the story goes that instead of heading home to go to sleep, Hill walked the beat with a Brookline, Massachusetts, police officer for hours until the sun crested the horizon. It was only then that the sudden death–hardened Saskatoon native finally turned in. Hill would rest easier as the playoffs wore on — his remaining goals were scored in regulation, including the opening tally in what would prove to be Boston's championship-clinching game against the Maple Leafs.

APRIL 3

FERN FLAMAN SCORES TWICE, 1958

Fern Flaman hadn't scored all season. While the Bruins captain wasn't exactly known for his goal-scoring abilities, he was coming off a six-goal, 31-point campaign, both career highs. Through more than a decade in the NHL, the only time the blueliner didn't find the back of the net in a full season was when he spent two years in Toronto. Enough said. But after failing to light the lamp through 66 games in the 1957–58 season, Flaman couldn't have found a better time to break out of his slump.

On April 3, early in the second period of Boston's fifth semifinal game against the Rangers, Flaman scored his first tally since March 7, 1957, to give the Bruins a 4–0 lead. But Flaman wasn't done just yet. Five minutes later, the rugged defenceman from Dysart, Saskatchewan, fired a shot from long range that went off New York rearguard Bill Gadsby and in to notch just his second career multi-goal effort. Flaman's pair of tallies would prove to be his final playoff goals for the Bruins.

APRIL 4

BARRY PEDERSON PUTS SEVEN ON THE BOARD, 1982

Barry Pederson found himself in some pretty illustrious company. On April 4, 1982, in the final game of the season, the rookie picked up a hat trick, along with four assists, factoring in on every single Boston goal in a 7–2 victory over the Hartford Whalers. Pederson's performance tied the team record for most points in a game, forever linking him with Bobby Orr and Phil Esposito as the only other Bruin to accomplish the feat. The offensive tour de force capped off an incredible campaign for Pederson, who finished with 44 goals and 92 points.

Before the season began, Pederson's goal for himself was to collect 20 tallies, stay out of the minors, and firmly establish himself with the Bruins. He certainly did that and more. Pederson was named a finalist for the Calder Trophy but finished runner-up to Winnipeg's Dale Hawerchuk, the top rookie point scorer that year. The next season, Pederson proved his first-year production was no fluke. He racked up 107 points, tied for the fifth most in the NHL, and his first of back-to-back 100-point campaigns with the Bruins.

APRIL 5

DON MCKENNEY GETS FIVE APPLES, 1958

Following his first season as a professional hockey player in 1954, Don McKenney was at a crossroads. He could either continue his career on the ice or give it up for the diamond. A talented winger from Smith Falls, Ontario, McKenney was also quite the baseball player. He had the opportunity to join the Brooklyn Dodgers organization but decided to stick with hockey. McKenney felt it was his best shot at making the big leagues. He was proven right the next year, when he made his NHL debut for the Bruins. He quickly established himself as a consistent 20-goal scorer, later reaching the milestone in six consecutive seasons, and earned the nickname "Slip" for his uncanny ability to slip the puck past goaltenders.

And while McKenney could light the lamp, he could also be a great set-up man. On April 5, 1958, he assisted on five of Boston's goals in an 8–1 shellacking of the Rangers, establishing a franchise record for the most helpers in a playoff game, a benchmark that still stands as of this writing.

APRIL 6

PETER MCNAB GETS 40TH GOAL WITH HAT TRICK, 1980

Peter McNab was already a 40-goal scorer. Nobody could ever take that away from him. But a couple of years after first reaching the milestone, he would have missed out on it again if it wasn't for one of his teammates. Following the final game of the regular season on April 6, 1980, McNab, who had two goals in the contest, was sitting at 39 tallies. The final goal of the match had been credited to Terry O'Reilly, but some reporters thought McNab might have gotten a piece of it.

When they asked O'Reilly about it, he said they should go look at the tape. He marched into the office of general manager Harry Sinden, who was also serving as interim head coach, where they became convinced that it was indeed McNab's goal. Sinden brought it to the attention of official scorer Ed Sandford, and after he examined the footage, he, too, determined the tally belonged to McNab and awarded him his 40th of the season. And while O'Reilly didn't get an assist on that one, it wouldn't have been possible without him.

APRIL 7

ANDREW RAYCROFT MAKES PLAYOFF DEBUT, 2004

Andrew Raycroft was perfect in his Stanley Cup Playoffs debut. On April 7, 2004, the rookie netminder stopped all 31 shots he faced in a 3–0 win over the Canadiens. Although it was Raycroft's first brush with the playoffs, he wasn't nervous. "Experience isn't that important," he told reporters. "If you're playing well, you're playing well." And Raycroft had every reason to expect he would play well in the post-season.

He had put together a stellar freshman campaign that included 29 wins and a sterling .926 save percentage, one of the best in the NHL that year among all full-time goaltenders. His regular-season performance would earn him the Calder as the league's most outstanding rookie, making him the first Bruins goaler in more than five decades to take home the award. Raycroft's confidence carried into the next matchup. He continued his shutout streak until late in the second period and stopped everything else in a 2–1 overtime victory. But as the series wore on, the Bruins were outshot and outscored by the Habs, eventually losing 2–0 in Game 7.

APRIL 8

BOB MILLER'S 20TH FOR THE RECORD, 1978

Peter McNab, Terry O'Reilly, Bobby Schmautz, Stan Jonathan, Jean Ratelle, Rick Middleton, Wayne Cashman, Gregg Sheppard, Brad Park, Don Marcotte, and Bob Miller. That's how many Bruins reached the 20-goal mark in 1977–78. Eleven of them. That mark has not been matched since then, and it likely never will. On April 8, 1978, the penultimate game in the regular season, Bob Miller, from nearby Medford, Massachusetts, potted an empty-netter with just six seconds remaining to become the 11th Boston player to reach the milestone, surpassing the record belonging to the Canadiens from the 1970–71 and 1974–75 campaigns.

Together, they scored 283 of Boston's 333 goals, the third most in the NHL that year. The 20-goal brethren actually outscored most of the league that year. The only teams with more tallies than them were the Canadiens, Islanders, Flyers, and Sabres. Forty years later, the Bruins honoured the group before a game on February 13, 2018. To put things in perspective, the club would finish that season with just three 20-goal scorers: David Pastrňák, Brad Marchand, and Patrice Bergeron.

APRIL 9

BRUINS TAKE NEWFOUNDLAND, 1956

It was the Bs versus the b'ys. On April 9, 1956, the Bruins continued their barnstorming tour of Newfoundland. They had played their first game a couple of days earlier at Corner Brook but almost didn't make it to their next game in Bay Roberts, when the flight they were on to St. John's was rerouted because of fog. They ended up landing in Gander, an airport town, and then had to board a train to the provincial capital before hopping on a bus.

They arrived at Bay Roberts just a few hours before puck drop for a game in the community's new outdoor rink. It wasn't the first outdoor game featuring an NHL team — that distinction belongs to the Red Wings, who played outside at a prison a couple of years earlier — but it was the first one that featured ticket-holding fans. Four teams from the town each played a frame against the Bruins, but then at one point every player from the squads swarmed the ice to try to get the puck by Terry Sawchuk.

APRIL 10

GILLES GILBERT RECORDS FIRST PLAYOFF SHUTOUT, 1974

Nothing was getting by Gilles Gilbert. On April 10, 1974, in Boston's opening playoff game against the Leafs, the Bruins netminder was flawless. Gilbert turned aside all 35 shots he faced to record his first career post-season shutout. Even when Toronto added pressure in the third period, he stood tall. At one point, Paul Henderson ripped a shot off the right side of Gilbert's mask that sent the goaltender to the ice. He might have been dazed, but he got back up on his skates just in time to block a shot from Eddie Shack. The Bruins were only up by a goal, so Gilbert had to stay sharp until the final buzzer sounded.

It was the beginning of an impressive playoff run for Gilbert. Not only would he collect three assists, the most by a goaltender in a single post-season, but he was integral to Boston's return to the Stanley Cup Final. Although the Bruins came up short to the Flyers, they wouldn't have gone as far as they did without Gilbert's brilliant play between the pipes.

APRIL 11

BOBBY SCHMAUTZ NETS PLAYOFF HATTY, 1977

When Bobby Schmautz strolled into the Garden on April 11, 1977, he had a surprise for his teammates. Under his arm was a seven-pound Hershey bar. His brother-in-law worked for the chocolate company and had brought the gigantic treat to Boston as an Easter gift. Knowing he'd never be able to make his way through the bar on his own without sustaining a couple of cavities, Schmautz brought it to the rink. He broke off pieces and passed them around the dressing room while they waited for the start of their playoff series against the Kings.

The chocolate must have hit the spot. Less than two minutes into the game, Schmautz had the Bruins on the board. A few minutes later, after Brad Park extended the lead, Schmautz got another one. And then before the frame came to a close, he completed the hat trick, giving the Bruins a 5–0 lead heading into intermission. Boston went on to handily take the match 8–3, but all Schmautz could think about was where had his brother-in-law been all season.

APRIL 12

BRUINS WIN STANLEY CUP, 1941

The Bruins brought their brooms to Detroit. On April 12, 1941, Boston defeated the Red Wings 3–1 to complete a four-game sweep and clinch the Stanley Cup for the second time in three years. Boston's dismantling of Detroit was actually the first time in NHL history that a team won four straight games in the Final to hoist the trophy. The ultimate best-of-seven series was introduced only a couple of years earlier, when the Bruins were also the first team to win the chalice under that format.

With their backs against the wall, the Red Wings opened the scoring in the opening frame, but with Jimmy Orlando — I really just wanted to write his name — in the box for Detroit, Boston's Flash Hollett notched the equalizer just before the halfway mark of the second period. With Orlando still in the sin bin serving the full two minutes of his minor penalty, a practice that held until 1956, Bobby Bauer lit the lamp. The Bruins added another before intermission to put the game and championship out of reach.

APRIL 13

MARC SAVARD BURIES GAME-WINNER, 2008

Marc Savard was known for his silky-smooth playmaking, but when the Bruins needed it, he delivered a big goal. Down 2–0 in their opening-round series against the Canadiens on April 13, 2008, another loss would've put the Bs in a hole that few teams have been able to dig out of. Boston opened the scoring, but after the Habs tied it early in the second period, regulation ended in a tie. But just before the halfway mark in overtime, with the Bruins buzzing in Montreal's zone, the Canadiens were assessed a delayed penalty.

Savard hopped over the boards as the extra attacker and joined his teammates in the onslaught. After Peter Schaefer made a short pass to Dennis Wideman, the defenceman made a nifty backhand no-look dish to Savard on the right side, and he wired it past Carey Price. TD Banknorth Garden erupted, and Savard jubilantly leapt into Wideman's arms. The Bruins were suddenly back in the series. Although they'd lose the next match, Boston won two straight elimination games to force Game 7.

APRIL 14

JOE JUNEAU TIES ROOKIE ASSIST RECORD, 1993

In pretty much any other season, Joe Juneau would have won the Calder. On April 14, 1993, the Bruins rookie collected his 70th assist of the campaign, matching Peter Stastny's mark for the most in a debut season, a mark they both still hold, by the way. Juneau, who graduated from Rensselaer Polytechnic Institute with a degree in aeronautical engineering and was a star for Canada at the 1992 Olympics before joining the Bruins, finished the year with 102 points, becoming just the fifth player in NHL history to reach the milestone.

Only three rookies had scored more points in a season than him, but one of those happened to be in his class that year: Teemu Selanne. The Finnish Flash recorded a first-year performance for the ages: 76 goals, a mark that will likely never be matched, and 132 points. So it was no surprise that when it came to the voting, Selanne garnered every first-place vote, with Juneau finishing runner-up. As of this writing, Juneau's totals for assists and points remain the gold standard for Bruins rookies.

APRIL 15

STAN JONATHAN BULLDOGS KINGS WITH GOAL, 1977

Don Cherry saw something in Stan Jonathan that every other NHL team had missed. During the 1975 draft, the undersized winger from the Six Nations reserve near Brantford, Ontario, had been passed over in every round, until Cherry made a case to his boss, Boston GM Harry Sinden, that they should take a chance on Jonathan. Cherry had seen him play that year in junior and had a feeling he was a perfect fit for the Bruins. A year after the draft, Jonathan made the Bruins squad full-time, proving Cherry right.

Cherry was apparently so smitten with Jonathan that he hung a picture of his beloved bull terrier, Blue, above Jonathan's stall, a fitting tribute for the player known as "Bulldog" because of his fierce tenacity. Following a solid first full regular season, Jonathan made his playoff debut. After scoring in each of his first two post-season games, on April 15, 1977, with just 13 seconds remaining in regulation, he scored to give the Bruins a 7–6 victory over the Los Angeles Kings and a 3–0 series stranglehold.

APRIL 16

BRUINS WIN SECOND STANLEY CUP, 1939

When Flash Hollett scored to give the Bruins a 3–1 lead, the Boston Garden faithful celebrated the Stanley Cup championship by lighting off firecrackers in the stands and raining programs down onto the ice. There was just one problem. There were still 37 seconds left to play. The match was halted while the playing surface was cleared off so the game could be completed. When the final buzzer sounded more than a half-minute later, fans were able to celebrate a second time, littering the ice once more, officially commemorating Boston's second-ever title on April 16, 1939.

The club made history by becoming the first NHL team to earn the trophy in a best-of-seven series, a format that was introduced that year. After league president Frank Calder presented the silver chalice to captain Cooney Weiland, the celebrations continued in the Bruins' dressing room, where Art Ross reportedly shouted at his troops that they were the greatest hockey team he had ever seen. It was tough to argue. Two years later, with largely the same squad, they hoisted the Cup again.

APRIL 17

RENE RANCOURT HELPS DELIVER UNFORGETTABLE ANTHEM, 2013

It was one of the most stirring renditions of "The Star-Spangled Banner" at a hockey game, and perhaps anywhere. On April 17, 2013, just two days after terrorists detonated a pair of bombs at the finish line of the Boston Marathon, killing three people and injuring 500 others, the Bruins were back on the ice. While the community was still reeling, the city proved that "Boston strong" was more than just a slogan: It was a way of life.

When Rene Rancourt began singing the anthem, he quickly realized the significance of the moment. He lowered his microphone and invited the fans to take over the rest of the way. The Garden faithful came together in a beautiful chorus to finish the ballad, delivering an unforgettable moment in Boston sports history. Even more than a decade later, I still get chills watching the video. While the Bruins wound up losing 3–2 in a shootout, some things are bigger than the game, and the fans that night demonstrated how strong a community can truly be when it comes together.

APRIL 18

RICK MIDDLETON RECORDS SIX POINTS, 1983

A day earlier and Rick Middleton could have been an NHL record holder — for a few hours, anyway. On April 18, 1983, he got in on every Bruins goal against the Sabres, scoring twice and collecting four assists in a 6–2 victory. Middleton's six points tied him with Dickie Moore, Phil Esposito, Darryl Sittler, Guy Lafleur, and Mikko Leinonen for the most in a single playoff game. But the day before the Bruins trounced Buffalo, a player by the name of Wayne Gretzky — you might have heard of him — racked up seven points against the Calgary Flames, establishing a new league benchmark.

Following the game, Middleton said he hadn't heard about the Great One's performance but noted that with how chances were going his way that night, a couple more points wouldn't have been out of the question. And while Gretzky denied Middleton's shot at having his name at the top of a league record, Nifty still tied Esposito for the most playoff points in a game by a Bruin, a mark that has since been matched by David Pastrňák but not yet surpassed.

APRIL 19

PHIL ESPOSITO'S REVENGE HAT TRICK, 1970

Three years after the Black Hawks traded him to the Bruins, Phil Esposito finally had the chance to play against his former team in the playoffs. Although Chicago already regretted the deal, with Esposito earning the Art Ross and Hart in just his second campaign with Boston, he really made them pay for it that post-season. On April 19, 1970, the Bruins opened their semifinal series against the Black Hawks. By the first intermission, Esposito had already quieted the Chicago Stadium faithful with a pair of goals to give the Bruins a 2–0 lead.

The Hawks got on the board in the middle frame, but Boston added two more, with Esposito completing the hat trick against his younger brother, Tony, to put the game out of reach. Esposito would collect two more goals and six more points that series as Boston swept Chicago to punch their ticket to the Stanley Cup Final. A couple of weeks later, with the Black Hawks watching from the sidelines, Esposito added another trophy to his growing collection.

APRIL 20

BRAD PARK PICKS UP FOUR POINTS, 1976

For a while it looked like Brad Park's season might have been over. After injuring his left knee when his skate caught a rut in a game in late February 1976, the recently acquired Bruins defenceman underwent surgery a couple of weeks later to repair some torn cartilage. Losing Park for the playoffs would have been devastating for Boston. Since arriving from the New York Rangers a few months earlier, Park had collected 53 points in 43 games and certainly looked like the much-needed successor to Bobby Orr, who hadn't played since November.

Seeing how knee injuries had ravaged Orr, the Bruins faithful held their collective breath. But just seven weeks after going under the knife, Park was back in the lineup. Although he was not 100 percent, he had made a remarkable recovery and was feeling better with every game he played. On April 20, 1976, Park scored two goals and added two assists in a 7–1 shellacking of the Kings and was suddenly the Bruins' leading scorer with six points in four games.

APRIL 21

ANDREW FERENCE FLIPS MONTREAL THE BIRD, 2011

“Andrew Ference, you better get ready to open up your wallet.” CBC analyst Glenn Healy wasn’t making a prediction — he was stating a fact. On April 21, 2011, just before the midway mark of the second period of Boston’s fourth game against the Canadiens, Ference bulged the twine to bring his trailing team within one. After scoring his first playoff goal in a decade, Ference looked directly into the Montreal crowd at the Bell Centre and flipped the bird.

Ference might as well have just made out a cheque to the NHL during the intermission. He tried unconvincingly to argue it was unintentional and that his finger got stuck in his glove, but nobody was buying it. The next day, following Boston’s 5–4 overtime victory to knot up the series at two games apiece, he was indeed fined $2,500. Upon return to his home in Boston’s North End neighbourhood, Ference found an envelope stuffed with cash taped to his door. It seemed some of the Bruins’ boosters wanted to chip in and help pay for the infraction.

APRIL 22

BOB SWEENEY SCORES SHORTY AGAINST MONTREAL, 1988

Bob Sweeney got into hockey because of the Big Bad Bruins. Growing up an hour away from the Garden in Boxborough, Massachusetts, Sweeney was first drawn to the club during the championship run in 1970. That Stanley Cup victory, punctuated by Bobby Orr's gravity-defying goal, led to an explosion of interest in hockey in the Boston area. Sweeney daydreamed about suiting up for the Bruins, but he never thought it would be a reality. But after finishing high school hockey, he was selected by the Bruins in the sixth round of the 1982 NHL Entry Draft.

Sweeney made it to Boston the next year but with the NCAA, playing for Boston College and winning Beanpot tournament MVP honours as a freshman. After finishing college he made his big-league dreams come true. Following the 1987–88 season, his first full campaign with the Bruins, Sweeney played a key role in the playoffs. On April 22, he scored a short-handed goal in a 3–1 victory against the Habs, giving Boston a shot at vanquishing Montreal in the post-season for the first time in decades.

APRIL 23

SEAN KURALY SCORES BIG GOAL AGAINST TORONTO, 2019

I've made it no secret that I'm a Leafs fan writing a Bruins book. Sometimes that has made my job challenging as an author. You wouldn't necessarily want to read these stories if I had written them from my fan perspective, but I'll bet you won't have a problem knowing how much anguish your team has put me through. Take this next one, for instance.

On April 23, 2019, I decided to watch Game 7 alone in my basement. That way I wouldn't be caught scream-crying in public. Early in the third period, Boston was up by just one goal and I still had reason to be hopeful, but then Sean Kuraly quickly extinguished any optimism. After dangling through nearly every Toronto player on the ice, he ripped a shot past Freddie Andersen. There was plenty of time left, but in that moment I knew it was over. And, of course, I was right. The Bruins added two more to take a 5–1 victory, eliminating the Leafs in a Game 7 for the second straight year.

APRIL 24

BRAD PARK SCORES GAME 7 OVERTIME WINNER, 1983

Brad Park was playing the best hockey of his life. Although his arthritic knees, battered by a handful of operations, had long since betrayed him, he was still a valuable contributor for the Bruins. Heading into the club's seventh and decisive game against the Sabres on April 24, 1983, Park had already picked up six points in that series. He may not have been able to keep up in a foot race anymore, but he could still produce.

After Boston fell behind by a pair of goals, Park scored on the power play just before the halfway mark of the second period to tie the game. When neither team scored in the final frame, they went to sudden death. Early in the extra session, Park rifled a shot that Bob Sauve initially stopped, but after a rebound squirted out amidst a pile of bodies in front of the net, Park fired the puck again, this time beating the Buffalo netminder. The Garden erupted. Park, who had never before scored in overtime, was Boston's Game 7 overtime hero.

APRIL 25

JAKE DEBRUSK SCORES TWICE IN GAME 7, 2018

Jake DeBrusk was in his first-ever post-season, but he was already developing a playoff reputation. He was a Leafs killer. DeBrusk, who had just finished his first full campaign with the Bruins, was playing beyond his years against Toronto. He had picked up a few goals already as the opening-round series went the distance. The seventh game was back home at TD Garden on April 25, 2018. After the Leafs opened the scoring, just over a couple of minutes later, DeBrusk knotted it up.

While Toronto went into the final frame with a lead, just as they had in Game 7 five years earlier, it didn't take long for Torey Krug to tie it. A few minutes after that, who else but DeBrusk scored again to make it 5–4 and seal the victory. In the years since, DeBrusk's reputation as a Leafs killer has only grown. He scored the game-winning goal to force Game 7 in 2019, and in 2024 he set the tone for the series, collecting a pair of goals in the opening game.

APRIL 26

BRUINS END 45-YEAR LOSING STREAK AGAINST HABS, 1988

The last time the Bruins had defeated the Canadiens in the playoffs, President Franklin Delano Roosevelt was in the Oval Office. In the time it took Boston to beat Montreal in the post-season again, the United States had dropped an atomic bomb, passed the Civil Rights Act, and landed on the moon. Forty-five years. That's how long it took the Bruins. The team had suffered 18 consecutive playoff defeats at the hands of their archrivals.

But finally, after more than four decades, the Bruins vanquished the Canadiens on April 26, 1988. Playing at the Forum, the site of so much Bruins' futility, it was only fitting that Boston finally got over the hump with the help of some players who grew up in La Belle Province. Réjean Lemelin from Sherbrooke stopped all but one of the 29 shots he faced; Steve Kasper, who grew up not far from the Forum, scored twice; and another Montreal native, Ray Bourque, may not have gotten on the scoresheet but was just as integral to the victory.

APRIL 27

BRUINS KNOCK OUT MONTREAL, 2011

The Bruins faithful were on their feet. It was Game 7 overtime against the Canadiens on April 27, 2011, so there was no way they were sitting down for that. Just under six minutes into the extra session, Boston had Montreal hemmed into its own zone. After defenceman Adam McQuaid did a great job of keeping the Habs from clearing the puck, he got it to Milan Lucic. Protecting the biscuit, Lucic dished it over to Nathan Horton, who was at the top of the Stanley Cup Playoffs logo on the ice — something I wish the league would bring back — just inside the blue line.

Horton, who scored the double-overtime winner two games earlier, once again played the hero. He ripped a shot through traffic, beating Carey Price to give Boston a 4–3 victory, their third sudden-death triumph of the series. While TD Garden erupted in celebration, NESN broadcast commentator Jack Edwards screamed into his headset, "The Bruins knock out Montreal!" Next it was on to Philadelphia to avenge the previous year's historic collapse.

APRIL 28

RICK MIDDLETON WOWS COACH, 1983

Gerry Cheevers was running out of adjectives to describe Rick Middleton. "We're going to have to start inventing words," the Bruins' head coach said. "He's out there in the ultra-somewhere." Middleton was already known as "Nifty" for his playmaking, but maybe Cheevers was onto something. The way Middleton was playing in the 1983 Stanley Cup Playoffs, he had reached the ultra-nifty stratosphere. On April 28, he picked up three assists, including two on short-handed goals, to guide the Bruins to a 4–1 victory over the Islanders in the second game of the Wales Conference Final.

Middleton's three assists gave him 29 points, tying him with Wayne Gretzky for the playoff scoring lead and surpassing Phil Esposito's mark of 27 points in 1970, for the most by a Bruin in the post-season. Those three helpers also brought him up to 21 assists, vaulting over Bobby Orr's mark of 19 assists in 1972. Although both those milestones were established in title runs, despite his incredible play, Middleton wasn't able to bookend his performance with a championship.

APRIL 29

BRUINS STORM EUROPE, 1959

The Bruins were invading Europe. On April 29, 1959, Boston took on the Rangers at the Empire Pool arena in London, England, as part of a 23-game tour that would take the two NHL teams through six countries across Europe, marking the first time the league had returned to the continent in more than two decades. In the opening match, the Bruins were trailing 5–1 to the Blueshirts in the middle of the second period. It certainly seemed like victory was beyond their grasp. But Boston rallied, scoring six unanswered goals to take the game 7–5.

The improbable comeback might have had something to do with the pucks. Before the tour began, the clubs agreed to experiment with a new puck design that featured an orange coating on one side. The idea was that it would help fans better track the puck, but it was a flop. Rangers GM Muzz Patrick complained that the players couldn't see the puck. They hauled 288 across the pond, and both teams were only too happy to leave them behind.

APRIL 30

ANSON CARTER SCORES OVERTIME WINNER, 1999

Anson Carter figured that with the way the game was going, it would take an ugly goal for the Bruins to win. Carolina goaltender Artūrs Irbe was playing so well that Carter figured if they were to get another one by him, it would have to be a garbage goal. But unlike the kind of goals I'm known for in my men's league, it was anything but ugly. It was a beauty.

With just over five minutes remaining in the second overtime on April 30, 1999, Joe Thornton dished the puck to Carter deep in the Hurricanes' zone. With no one between him and Irbe, Carter pulled the puck from his right over to his left. As the Latvian netminder sprawled across the crease, the winger tucked the biscuit behind him with a nifty backhander. After raising his arms in celebration, Carter dove to the ice where his Bruins teammates jumped on top of him, forming a dogpile. Boston was just one more win away from advancing past the opening round for the first time in five years.

MAY

MAY 1

MARC SAVARD SCORES IN OT, 2010

Marc Savard was overcome with emotion. The slick playmaker had missed the tail end of the regular season and the first round of the playoffs while he recovered from a concussion. It wasn't clear when he would be able to return, but when the Bruins hosted the Flyers on May 1, 2010, for the opening game of their semifinal series, Savard was in the lineup. It was his first game in almost two months. As soon as he hit the ice, he received a roaring ovation from the TD Garden faithful that nearly moved him to tears. But the best was yet to come.

With just over six minutes remaining in overtime, Savard got the puck from Dennis Wideman and absolutely wired it from the right faceoff circle, beating Philadelphia goaltender Brian Boucher. As Savard skated toward the opposite boards to celebrate with his teammates, he exuberantly pumped both fists and then whacked his stick several times on the ice before chucking it over the glass and into the crowd. He couldn't have scripted his return any better.

MAY 2

SEAN KURALY SCORES AGAINST HOMETOWN TEAM, 2019

It was a piece of hockey history that the Blue Jackets could've done without. Just before the halfway mark of the third period in Columbus's fourth playoff game against the Bruins, on May 2, 2019, Boston's Sean Kuraly scored his second of the post-season to further silence the home crowd. Kuraly, who grew up not far from Nationwide Arena, in Dublin, became the first Buckeye State native to score a playoff goal against the Blue Jackets.

A product of the Ohio AAA Blue Jackets system, he would have had many supporters in the rink that night, but most of them had put aside those allegiances for the playoffs. But Kuraly was able to count on some Bruins boosters. After scoring he spotted a pair of Boston fans standing along the boards. He made a beeline for them and threw himself into the glass in celebration. The Blue Jackets would have preferred Kuraly scoring for them in the playoffs, so a couple of years later they signed him as a free agent. Kuraly spent four years with Columbus but never made it to the post-season with his hometown team. On July 1, 2025, Kuraly returned to Boston, inking a two-year deal.

MAY 3

VLADIMÍR RŮŽIČKA SCORES OVERTIME WINNER, 1991

When Chris Nilan, posing as a journalist, asked teammate Vladimír Růžička why he kissed his stick, the Czech centre, who was known as "Rosie" and was still mastering his command of English, had a simple answer: because. Without missing a beat, Nilan then asked if he wanted to kiss his (Nilan's) stick next game, drawing a hearty laugh from Růžička. Nilan had every reason to ask. He had only a couple of points in the playoffs, while Růžička was coming off a five-point performance, a career high, against the Penguins on May 3, 1991.

In the second game of Boston's conference-final matchup against Pittsburgh, Růžička had assisted on all four of the Bruins' goals in regulation. Early in overtime, he nearly scored against a stickless Tom Barrasso, but Ron Francis cleared the puck away before he could strike. After that moment Růžička gave his stick some love, kissing it on a hunch he'd eventually find the back of the net. His lips did not betray him. A few minutes later, Růžička scored to give the Bruins a 5–4 victory and a 2–0 series lead.

MAY 4

BRUINS SCORE BACK-BREAKER AGAINST COLUMBUS, 2019

Artemi Panarin was no match for the Big Bad Bruins. With the score tied 3–3 with less than two minutes remaining on May 4, 2019, the Columbus forward was trying to make a play to keep the puck in the offensive zone. But Panarin was simply overmatched by a trio of Bruins, particularly blueliner Brandon Carlo, who managed to muscle him out of Boston's end.

Panarin ended up losing the puck when the Blue Jackets were forced to tag up to avoid going offside. Carlo recovered it and then got it up to Brad Marchand at centre ice, and the Bruins took off the other way. Breaking into the Columbus zone with Ohio native Sean Kuraly and David Pastrňák, Marchand managed to slip the puck between a handful of Blue Jackets and over to the Czech winger. Pastrňák made no mistake. He buried it past a sprawling Sergei Bobrovsky, who couldn't get over in time to cover that side of the net. It had looked like overtime was looming, but Pastrňák ended the game with a back-breaker in regulation.

MAY 5

DEAR BRAD, PLEASE STOP LICKING YOUR OPPONENTS, 2018

It was a memo the NHL probably thought it would never need to send. But on May 5, 2018, the league informed Brad Marchand that if he didn't stop licking opposing players, he would be subject to supplemental discipline. Reading that in a post–Covid-19 world just makes my skin crawl. I mean, it was disgusting then, but it's even more disgusting now. It all started in the opening round of the playoffs that year when Marchand licked Toronto forward Leo Komarov's face.

When the Bruins took on the Lightning in their next series, Marchand was at it again, licking Tampa Bay's Ryan Callahan during the fourth game. That's when the league stepped in. Marchand got the message. He didn't lick anybody else that post-season. And as much you kind of have to admire his inventiveness in finding new ways to antagonize his opponents, I think we can all agree that even he went too far with this tactic. Besides, even as the league's pre-eminent pest, he was always at his best when he focused on his skills.

MAY 6

BRUINS STOMP DEVILS, 1988

The Bruins made the Devils pay. In the final moments of the first period in the third game of the Prince of Wales Conference Final on May 6, 1988, New Jersey's Pat Verbeek and Kirk Muller took some extra penalties. It had been a rough series so far, punctuated by Boston's Willi Plett chucking knuckles with rookie Brendan Shanahan, who showed how tough he was, on two separate occasions, but New Jersey's infractions would prove to be the devil in the details.

With the pair still in the box to start the second session, the Bruins didn't waste the opportunity. After Ken Linseman scored just over a minute into the period, they notched another power-play goal less than a minute later. And then just 15 seconds after that, they scored another to chase Sean Burke from his net. Boston had scored three goals in 73 seconds, with Ray Bourque assisting on all of them. They added two more and another in the third to take a 6–1 victory and a 2–1 edge in the series.

MAY 7

BRUINS FAIL TO KNOCK OUT PHILLY, 2010

The Bruins had the chance to put the Flyers away. On May 7, 2010, Boston was up 3–0 in its semifinal series against Philadelphia. One more victory and they would make it to the conference final for the first time in nearly two decades. Although they were on the verge of clinching, the fourth game is always the hardest one to close. Former Flyer-turned-Bruin Mark Recchi opened the scoring, but the Flyers answered back a few minutes later.

After Philadelphia took the lead in the second period, the black and gold tied it up early in the final frame, only for the Flyers to pull ahead again. But with just 32 seconds left, Recchi notched his second of the night to force overtime. In the latter half of the extra session, Simon Gagné, who was back in the lineup after breaking his toe in the opening round, scored to give Philadelphia a 5–4 victory and keep their playoff hopes alive. It was a tough blow for the Bruins, but surely they'd close it out in the next game at home, right? Right?

MAY 8

DAVID KREJČÍ WINS IT IN OVERTIME, 2013

Nathan Horton got the assist on David Krejčí's sudden-death dagger on May 8, 2013, but they may as well have given it to Maple Leafs defenceman Dion Phaneuf. Just over the halfway mark of overtime, Horton was working to move the puck out of the Bruins' end when the Toronto captain, who was known for big hits but also his defensive blunders, tried to lay him out. Phaneuf caught a piece of the Bruins winger, but instead of pinching off the advance, he pinballed into Phil Kessel, drafted fifth overall by the Bruins seven years earlier, taking him out of his skating lane.

Meanwhile, Krejčí retrieved the loose puck and headed down the ice with Milan Lucic on his far side. While the Leafs may have been thinking Krejčí was going for the cross-ice pass, the Czech centre patiently and methodically held on to the puck. Seemingly slowing down time, Krejčí waited for his moment and then put it past James Reimer to notch his fifth goal of the series and give the Bruins a commanding 3–1 lead.

MAY 9

BRUINS TAKE OPENER AGAINST 'CANES, 2019

The Bruins had a lethal power play. So before the Hurricanes squared off against them in the first game of the Eastern Conference Final on May 9, 2019, Carolina coach Rod Brind'Amour had a simple message for his players: Stay out of the box. For the most part, they seemed to heed the warning from their bench boss — that is, until the third period came around. With the Hurricanes up 2–1 with 20 minutes to play, it was probably the most inopportune time to get undisciplined.

Early into the final frame, Jordan Staal was sent to the sin bin for boarding. Just as his infraction was winding down, Marcus Johansson scored to tie it up. But what really hurt the 'Canes was that 15 seconds after the tying goal, Dougie Hamilton, taken ninth overall by the Bruins in 2011, took an ill-advised roughing penalty. Just 13 seconds after he was whistled to the box, Boston bulged the twine again, scoring their second power-play goal in a 28-second span, to take the lead and the first game of the series.

MAY 10

BOBBY ORR LEAPS INTO HOCKEY LORE, 1970

There wasn't much that Bobby Orr couldn't do, and on May 10, 1970, he proved he could fly. After putting the puck past Blues goaltender Glenn Hall to clinch Boston's first Stanley Cup in nearly three decades, Orr took flight. With a little help from the stick of St. Louis blueliner Noel Picard, Orr leapt into the air to celebrate the championship. He may have been above the ice for only a split second, but in that moment, you could swear the superstar defenceman was soaring.

Before Orr hit the ice and returned to earth, the flashbulb and shutter of Ray Lussier's camera captured the sequence and immortalized it. It is arguably the most iconic image in hockey history, but there's also some incredible symbolism behind it. Orr, who wore No. 4, scored Boston's fourth goal of the game, in the fourth game of the Stanley Cup Final, in the fourth period (overtime), to give the Bruins their fourth championship in franchise history. And then was tripped up by Picard, who also sported No. 4.

MAY 11

BRUINS WIN SECOND CUP IN THREE YEARS, 1972

Bobby Orr did it again. For the second time in three years, he scored a Stanley Cup–clinching goal. On May 11, 1972, Orr opened the scoring in the sixth game of the Final against the Rangers. It would be all the Bruins needed. Wayne Cashman added two more in the final frame, but Gerry Cheevers stopped every shot he faced, backstopping Boston to another title. Although Orr's clincher this time around was not nearly as exciting as his overtime and gravity-defying goal from two years earlier, it held some extra significance.

"This is even better than the last time because the Rangers were a top contender and we beat them on the road," Orr told reporters. A couple of nights earlier, the Bruins had champagne chilled and ready to go at the Garden, but after they came up short in a 3–2 loss, they left the bubbly behind when they headed back to New York. Instead, Orr and the Bruins had to settle for sipping Budweiser out of the Cup, but I have no doubt the beer tasted just as sweet.

MAY 12

BRUINS STOMP 'CANES 6–2, 2019

The Bruins had no shortage of playoff scoring depth. When Connor Clifton scored his first of the post-season early in the second period against Carolina on May 12, 2019, he became the 19th player on the team to register a tally, tying a club record from 1988 for the most goal scorers in the playoffs. Clifton's goal held up as the game-winner in a 6–2 victory that gave Boston a 2–0 series lead, but the onslaught that night further demonstrated the team's formidable depth. Two of the goals came from Matt Grzelcyk, a third-pairing defenceman who had scored just three times in the regular season.

Few teams could match the offensive support the Bruins were getting throughout their lineup. When Boston's deep playoff run came to a close, 21 different players had found the back of the net, a franchise record that will be tough to match again. Besides the goaltending battery, the only player without a goal was John Moore, and he managed to suit up for just 10 games. Now that's depth.

MAY 13

IT WAS 4–1, 2013

My two buddies and I made the mistake of watching this game with one of our friends who didn't root for any NHL team in particular but was decidedly anti-Leafs. With Toronto up 4–1 against the Bruins in Game 7 on May 13, 2013, things were going well. But as the Leafs' third-period lead evaporated, our pal, who is admittedly a bit of a troll (sorry, Marsh), became increasingly more animated as he watched us shrink into our seats.

When Patrice Bergeron scored six minutes into overtime to complete the improbable comeback that continues to live in infamy as the yardstick for playoff collapses, our buddy, whom we probably should have kicked out of the house before sudden death started, began cackling. While I was devastated the Leafs blew it, I could feel my anger rising as the taunting continued. I don't think it's a stretch to say all three of us probably had the same thought, if only for a moment, that we may just have to murder our dear friend and bury him in the backyard.

MAY 14

BRUINS BLOW 3–0 SERIES LEAD, 2010

All right. You may just want to skip ahead to the next page. I get it. And since this book is now yours just as much as it is mine, you can choose your own adventure. I won't go as far as encouraging you to tear this page straight from the spine. Trust me, it's not going to give you that cathartic relief you're looking for. Since there's nothing I can say to make this moment any better, let's just cut to the chase. On May 14, 2010, the Bruins blew a 3–0 series lead to the Flyers, becoming just the third team in NHL history to squander that kind of stranglehold in a best-of-seven series.

The Bruins were actually up 3–1 after the first period, but Philadelphia scored four straight goals, including another game-winner from that pesky Simon Gagné with time to spare in regulation, to complete the unlikely comeback. It will forever live in infamy in hockey history, but winning a Stanley Cup the next year helps you have a short memory.

MAY 15

BRUINS ACQUIRE PHIL ESPOSITO, 1967

After the Bruins acquired Phil Esposito, along with Ken Hodge and Fred Stanfield, from the Black Hawks for Gilles Marotte, Pit Martin, and Jack Norris, on May 15, 1967, the centre from Sault Ste. Marie, Ontario, reflected on the trade. He told reporters that it "could be a big break for me." Esposito also felt that the timing was right for him and his former Chicago compatriots to head to Boston. "The Bruins are an up-and-coming hockey team," he noted. "We could help them work their way right to the top of the league."

Esposito's words proved to be prophetic. Although he had played well in the Windy City on a line with Bobby Hull and Chico Maki, his big break would come in Beantown. In his second campaign with the Bruins, Esposito racked up 49 goals and 126 points, both career highs that he would shatter in a couple more years, to win his first of five scoring titles. As for leading the Bruins to the promised land, he would do that in just three years.

MAY 16

BRUINS SWEEP 'CANES, 2019

The Bruins were off to the Stanley Cup Final for the first time in six years. On May 16, 2019, Boston defeated Carolina 4–0, completing the sweep of the Eastern Conference Final. Following a scoreless first period, David Pastrňák got the Bruins on the board early in the second frame. It would prove to be all they'd need to oust the 'Canes. Although Patrice Bergeron added two more tallies, along with an empty-netter from Brad Marchand, Tuukka Rask was flawless, stopping all 24 shots that came his way.

In defeating Carolina, who were also swept out of the conference final a decade earlier — coincidentally, the last time they were in the playoffs — Boston picked up its seventh straight victory that post-season, their longest playoff winning streak since they collected nine in a row in 1972. Those who remembered their history recalled how those playoffs ended and hoped Boston could add four more victories to its run. But for now, they had to wait. By the time the Cup Final commenced, the Bruins had been off for nearly two weeks.

MAY 17

TYLER SEGUIN HAS BREAKOUT PERFORMANCE, 2011

There was no doubt about it: Tyler Seguin had arrived. On May 17, 2011, after spending most of the playoffs watching from the press box, Seguin, who was drafted second overall by Boston a year earlier, drew into the lineup for his second game. Less than a minute into the middle frame against Tampa Bay, the Seguin show began. After getting the puck from Michael Ryder, the Bruins rookie took off through the neutral zone, blowing past defencemen Victor Hedman and Randy Jones. With nothing between him and Dwayne Roloson, Seguin deked out the Lightning goalie with a nifty backhander to tie the game.

Less than six minutes later, after David Krejčí made it 3–2 for the Bruins, Seguin extended the lead, whistling a shot past Roloson's glove. Before the session came to a close, Seguin also picked up two assists. His four points matched the club record held by Peter McNab, Barry Pederson, and Ken Linseman for the most points in a single playoff period. Seguin proved convincingly he belonged and became a regular for the rest of the post-season.

MAY 18

GERRY CHEEVERS RECORDS EIGHTH, AND FINAL, PLAYOFF SHUTOUT, 1978

The Garden faithful were chanting for Gerry Cheevers, but the Bruins netminder didn't pay much attention to the chorus. "My wife's yelling at me all the time at home like that anyway," he later told reporters. Maybe so, but the Boston fans had every reason to be screaming. On May 18, 1978, Cheevers stopped every shot he faced against the Canadiens in the third game of the Stanley Cup Final, backstopping the Bruins to a 4–0 victory to get their first win of the series. It was the eighth playoff shutout of Cheevers's career, and it was also the first time that Montreal had been blanked in the Final in seven years.

Cheevers may not have been tested much that night — he faced only 16 shots — but it was an important milestone. He shook off the previous two losses in Montreal, and it got the Bruins back in the series. Following the game, when his teammates were asked about his performance, Wayne Cashman told the press corps that Cheevers wasn't a star, "he was a saint."

MAY 19

FIVE BRUINS BEAT KING HENRIK, 2013

It was a rough afternoon for Henrik Lundqvist. On May 19, 2013, the Bruins got five goals by the Rangers netminder in a 5–2 matinee victory to take a 2–0 lead in their semifinal series. It was actually the first time since March 9, 2011, that the reigning Vezina winner had given up more than four goals in a game. Rookie Torey Krug opened the scoring early in the first period, with Gregory Campbell and Johnny Boychuk getting on the board in the second. In the final frame, Brad Marchand and Milan Lucic both scored to put the game out of reach.

As Omar Little once said in *The Wire*, arguably the finest TV show ever made, "If you come at the king, you best not miss." The Bruins did not. Five different goal scorers contributed to the win. And while it may not have been a regal performance for Lundqvist, at the other end of the ice, Tuukka Rask played brilliantly, especially when the Rangers outshot the Bruins heavily in the second period, making 35 saves.

MAY 20

TAZ CALLS IT A CAREER, 1985

It was a day that Harry Sinden had been dreading. "I kind of live in fear of the time when we'd have to face an NHL season without Terry O'Reilly," the Bruins GM told reporters. Well, that reality set in on May 20, 1985, when O'Reilly announced he was hanging up his skates. For Sinden and the Bruins faithful, it wasn't simply a retirement — it was the end of an era. For more than a decade, the hard-nosed winger had been the heart and soul of the team, setting the standard for what it meant to be a Boston Bruin.

Nicknamed "Taz" by Phil Esposito for his relentless play that reminded teammates of the cartoon character the Tasmanian Devil, O'Reilly gave his all on every shift and approached each game as though it might be his last. But injuries finally caught up to him. After missing 100 games in the previous three seasons to knee and shoulder issues, O'Reilly felt he had to call it. He finished his career with the Bruins with 2,095 penalty minutes, a record that will likely stand the test of time.

MAY 21

STAN JONATHAN PUMMELS PIERRE BOUCHARD, 1978

On paper it was a serious mismatch. Pierre Bouchard had six inches and more than 30 pounds on Stan Jonathan, but the scrappy Bruins winger was not afraid of anyone. And on May 21, 1978, he proved that, pound for pound, he was one of the toughest fighters in the league. Six minutes into the fourth game of the Stanley Cup Final, the two dropped the gloves. Once things got started, Bouchard might have wished he had kept his cool and skated away.

As they traded punches, it was clear that Jonathan was getting the better of his much taller opponent. After switching to his left hand, Jonathan landed a few more haymakers before knocking Bouchard down to the ice. When it was all said and done, Jonathan barely had a scratch on him, while Bouchard's face was covered in blood. Following the scrap, legendary Toronto sportswriter Frank Orr wrote that "Bouchard's nose resembled a hubcap that had been beaten with a hammer and one eye had a deep blue race track around it."

MAY 22

BRUINS ACQUIRE GILLES GILBERT, 1973

The Bruins needed help in goal. After Gerry Cheevers bolted to the World Hockey Association for a lucrative contract in 1972, the club was left with an aging goaltending battery. Looking to shore up the crease, on May 22, 1973, Boston made a trade with Minnesota, acquiring young netminder Gilles Gilbert in exchange for Fred Stanfield. With the North Stars, Gilbert had been the backup to Cesare Maniago, and occasionally to veteran Gump Worsley, but with the Bruins he would be given the opportunity to become a No. 1 starter.

If they hadn't traded Gilbert to Boston, it's likely the North Stars would have lost him to a competing WHA contract that they wouldn't have been able to match. The Bruins immediately signed Gilbert to a six-year deal following the trade. He made an immediate impact in his first campaign. He picked up 34 wins in the regular season, the most by a Boston goalie in the modern era, and then played brilliantly in the playoffs, backstopping the team to a run to the Stanley Cup Final.

MAY 23

TIM THOMAS MAKES INCREDIBLE SAVE, 2011

It was some of Tim Thomas's finest work of the playoffs. Just before the halfway mark of the third period on May 23, 2011, the Bruins had a precarious 2–1 lead over the Lightning, with a chance to take a 3–2 advantage in their conference-final series, when Eric Brewer uncorked a shot from the blue line. But Brewer wasn't aiming for Thomas. Instead, he directed his shot to the left of the goaltender, looking to get a deflection off the end boards. The play worked perfectly. The puck bounced out to a wide-open Steve Downie, who had nothing but a yawning cage to shoot at.

But Thomas flung himself over to the post and managed to stop the puck with the outstretched paddle of his stick, preventing a sure goal. It was the kind of save the Bruins faithful had come to expect from Thomas, but even the goaltender admitted he had gotten a little lucky. Hey, even the best netminder in the world, and that's what Thomas was during that run, needs a little luck from time to time.

MAY 24

LIGHTS GO OUT AT THE GARDEN, 1988

The fog appeared like a bad omen. On May 24, 1988, with the Bruins on the brink of being swept in the Stanley Cup Final, a haze rose off the Garden ice in the second period, brought on by the heat that night in Boston. Play was halted multiple times to contend with the fog. During the stoppages, the benches cleared and all the players skated around the rink to try to dissipate the uninvited mist. But the fog would prove to be the least of their problems.

Not long after Craig Simpson tied the game 3–3 for the Oilers late in the frame, the power went out. The NHL was forced to call the game and reschedule it for after the next match in Edmonton. The Bruins were still alive, but like the lights at the Garden, their playoff hopes were dim. They wouldn't get the chance to replay the game in Boston. Two nights later, the Oilers completed the sweep with a convincing 6–3 victory to hoist the Cup on home ice.

MAY 25

DAVID KREJČÍ NETS HAT TRICK, 2011

David Krejčí was ready to move on to the Stanley Cup Final. On May 25, 2011, the Czech centre scored a hat trick in the sixth game of the Eastern Conference Final against the Lightning, but it wasn't enough to get the job done. Tampa Bay won to force a seventh and decisive game. Although his team came up short, Krejčí made some history, becoming the first Bruin since Cam Neely in 1991 to record a three-goal performance in the playoffs.

With a few minutes remaining in the first period, Krejčí fired a quick wrister over the glove of Dwayne Roloson to give Boston a 2–1 lead. Nearing the halfway mark of the third period, with the Bruins down by a pair of goals, Krejčí tapped in a marvelous pass from Nathan Horton on the power play to make it a one-goal game. Even after Boston gave up another one, Krejčí wouldn't quit. A few minutes later, he got the puck past a sprawling Roloson to make it 5–4, but that's as close as he and the Bruins would get that night.

MAY 26

BRUINS ACQUIRE RICK MIDDLETON, 1976

Rangers GM John Ferguson deemed Rick Middleton expendable. The New York executive felt that the team had enough young talent coming up through its ranks, so on May 26, 1976, he sent the 22-year-old winger to the Bruins for Ken Hodge, who was a decade older than Middleton. Boy, was Ferguson wrong. Hodge played just one full season on Broadway, collecting 62 points in 78 games, before finishing his career in the minors a few years later. Meanwhile, in Boston, Middleton picked up a hat trick in his Bruins debut, a preview of things to come.

Over the next 12 years, Middleton established himself as one of the greatest players in franchise history. He reached the 40-goal mark in five consecutive seasons, including a 51-goal effort, and hit the 100-point mark twice. While he certainly racked up points, Middleton also honed his two-way game in Boston and became a reliable player on both sides of the puck. When he hung up his skates in 1988, he had earned 898 career points as a Bruin, behind only Phil Esposito and Johnny Bucyk.

MAY 27

TOREY KRUG LAYS OUT HELMETLESS HIT, 2019

It was vintage playoff hockey. In the third period of the first game of the Stanley Cup Final, on May 27, 2019, Torey Krug had his helmet ripped off by David Perron while the two skirmished in front of the Boston net. Rather than retrieving his bucket, Krug skated down the length of the ice and caught Robert Thomas going for a loose puck in the St. Louis end. Skating in full stride with the wind blowing through his hair, Krug absolutely nailed Thomas with a bone-crunching bodycheck.

TD Garden erupted into a raucous chorus of cheers. Just writing about it right now makes me want to run through a wall. Spoiler alert: Had Boston gone on to win the championship that year, the hit undoubtedly would have been one of the defining moments of the series. Even more so because the following season, the NHL passed a new rule requiring that players must reasonably return to the bench in the event that their helmet comes off during play.

MAY 28

JEAN RATELLE RETIRES, 1981

Jean Ratelle was calling it a career. On May 28, 1981, the stately centre announced that his time had come and he was hanging up his skates. While Ratelle's playing days were over, he was staying in the game as an assistant coach with the Bruins. An NHL veteran of 20 years, Ratelle broke into the league with the Rangers before he was traded to the Bruins in 1975 as part of the trade for Phil Esposito. At the end of his first campaign in Boston, Ratelle was awarded his second Lady Byng Trophy for sportsmanship and gentlemanly conduct, becoming the first player in league history to win it with two teams.

Over the course of his Hall of Fame career, he never earned a major penalty and frequently finished the season with penalty minutes in the single digits. But Ratelle was known for more than just his grace on the ice. During his era he was one of the NHL's top point-getters, and there were few skaters, if any, who were swifter and smoother than Gentleman Jean.

MAY 29

BRUINS BEAT ISLANDERS IN FRONT OF PLAYOFF CROWD, 2021

For the first time in more than two years, it felt like playoff hockey had truly returned to TD Garden. On May 29, 2021, the Bruins hosted the New York Islanders for the opening game of their semifinal series, marking the first time the arena had been full since the Covid-19 pandemic turned the world upside down. The previous year, when the NHL resumed operations in late summer, Boston played all of its post-season games in the Toronto "bubble" with zero spectators. The next post-season, Bruins fans were back in attendance, but only in a limited capacity throughout the first round.

So when David Pastrňák scored a power-play goal at the end of the first period to get the Bruins on the board, the Garden literally shook. He added two more to notch his second career playoff hat trick, powering Boston to a 5–2 victory. Following the match, Pastrňák reflected on the raucous ovation from the crowd: "It's a different sport with them in the building. Definitely warms your heart and reminds you why you play this sport." Well said.

MAY 30

DON CHERRY HEADS TO COLORADO, 1979

Don Cherry wasn't out of work for too long. A week after getting fired by the Bruins, he was named head coach of the Rockies on May 30, 1979. At a news conference, Cherry divulged that he had received offers from Atlanta, Toronto, and Buffalo but landed in the Mile High State. In the five years he had been the Bruins' bench boss, he had guided the club to the conference final four times and reached the Stanley Cup Final in back-to-back years.

But despite his sterling record, Cherry's most recent playoff exit was the infamous "too many men" call in Game 7 against the Canadiens. On the ensuing power play, Montreal tied the game, forcing overtime, and then eventually won in the extra session. As Cherry himself admitted: "Any time you get too many men on the ice, it's the coach's fault." While Cherry's boisterous attitude might have made him a fan favourite in Boston, it didn't necessarily endear him to the Rockies' ownership group. Despite reportedly signing a five-year deal, he lasted just one season before he was canned.

MAY 31

BRUINS ACQUIRE JUNIOR LANGLOIS, 1965

Do you know who was the last player to wear No. 4 on the Bruins before Bobby Orr made it iconic? Albert "Junior" Langlois. On May 31, 1965, Boston acquired Langlois, along with Parker MacDonald, Ron Harris, and Bob Dillabough, from Detroit for Ab McDonald, Bob McCord, and Ken Stephanson. Langlois played just one season with the Bruins before finishing out his career in California in the minors. Although Langlois's time in Boston was brief, it was not as short-lived as MacDonald's stint.

After just 29 games with the Bruins, he was traded back to Motor City in exchange for the up-and-coming Pit Martin. In his first full campaign with the black and gold, Martin reached the 20-goal mark for the first time in his career, but he would prove to play a much more valuable role in the off-season. He ended up being one of the key pieces that went to Chicago in the deal for Phil Esposito. While it ultimately proved to be a lopsided trade, Martin played with distinction for the Black Hawks and even served as captain.

JUNE

JUNE 1

BURROWS BITES BERGY, 2011

The Canucks took a bite out of the Bruins. On June 1, 2011, Vancouver took the first game of the Stanley Cup Final with a 1–0 victory, but the storyline that left a mark was that Alex Burrows appeared to have bitten one of Patrice Bergeron's fingers. Near the end of the first period, the two were involved in a scrum behind the Boston net. When Bergeron got his glove in front of the Vancouver agitator, Burrows seemingly chomped down.

Following the game, Bergeron, whose reputation on and off the ice was as unimpeachable as it gets, alleged that Burrows had bitten him so hard that he left a mark on his finger through his glove. When Bergeron asked him why he did it, Burrows reportedly explained in French that because his fingers were near his mouth he had to, which is the kind of response you'd get from your toddler after they're caught biting their sibling. It looked like Burrows might face supplemental discipline from the NHL, but the league could not find conclusive evidence.

JUNE 2

JIM CRAIG BECOMES A BRUIN, 1980

For Jim Craig, 1980 showed him that miracles are real and dreams really do come true. He was acquired by his hometown Bruins on June 2, just a few months after backstopping Team USA to an improbable victory over the Soviet favourites in the medal round of the men's hockey tournament at the Lake Placid Winter Games, then leading his team to gold against Finland. Craig, who had grown up in North Easton, Massachusetts, had played in net for Boston University before Atlanta drafted him in 1977.

Following his golden performance at the Olympics, Craig made his NHL debut for the Flames. So when he got the call in the off-season that he was being sent to Boston for a pair of picks, it really felt like a dream. But Craig wasn't able to bring the magic from Lake Placid to the big leagues. He made just 23 appearances for the Bruins. Following a year in the minors and a return to the U.S. national team, he played three games for the North Stars, his final NHL outings, before hanging up his goalie pads in 1984.

JUNE 3

BRUINS TROUNCE PENS, 2013

It was not the start Sidney Crosby was looking for. Just 28 seconds into Game 2 of Pittsburgh's Eastern Conference Final series against Boston, on June 3, 2013, the Penguins captain made an uncharacteristic error at the offensive blue line. He tried to flip the puck across the ice to Kris Letang, but Brad Marchand was able to bat it out of the air and took off the other way. No one was catching Marchand at that point. He turned on the afterburners and had a clear lane to goaltender Tomáš Vokoun. Marchand put the puck over his glove to give the Bruins an early lead.

Although Crosby gave his netminder a tap on the pads to acknowledge his mistake, things didn't get any better. Boston added two more goals toward the end of the period to chase Vokoun from the crease. Marc-André Fleury entered the net in relief, but he gave up another to Marchand before intermission, along with two more in the final frame as the Bruins cruised to a 6–1 victory and 2–0 series lead.

JUNE 4

RICK BOWNESS NAMED COACH, 1991

Rick Bowness's long journey behind an NHL bench started in Boston. On June 4, 1991, Boston announced that he had been named head coach. Bowness, who answers to "Bones" except on a tax return, had spent nearly a decade in the professional ranks as a player, including 173 games in the NHL, and transitioned into a coach while he was still playing. Following four years with the Winnipeg Jets organization, including a brief stint at the helm, Bowness joined the Bruins as a full-time bench boss, guiding the club's AHL affiliate in Maine for a pair of seasons.

After mentoring the team's young talent in the minors, Bowness was the obvious choice to replace Mike Milbury. Although Bowness led the Bruins to the Wales Conference Final, where they lost to the eventual Cup champion Penguins, he was not back for another campaign. Instead, he went to Ottawa to lead the expansion Senators, continuing on with a career in coaching at the NHL level that would span more than three decades and see Bowness behind the bench of nine different teams in various capacities.

JUNE 5

PATRICE BERGERON WINS FIFTH SELKE, 2022

Death, taxes, and Patrice Bergeron winning the Frank J. Selke Trophy. There aren't too many guarantees in life, but those are a few of the assurances you can count on. Even as he approached the twilight of his career, Bergeron remained one of the best two-way players in the league, and arguably in the game's history. On June 5, 2022, he was awarded his fifth Selke, breaking a tie with Bob Gainey for the most all-time wins.

While bagging the trophy for a fifth time is pretty impressive, for me what's more notable is that it was Bergeron's 11th consecutive season as a finalist, the longest streak in NHL history, somehow surpassing Wayne Gretzky's decade-long run as a finalist for the Hart. At the time of his record-breaking win, it wasn't clear if Bergeron would be coming back for a 19th season, but he eventually did, capping off his career with one last Selke. By the time this book is published, Bergeron will be just a year away from being named a first-ballot Hall of Famer, but until then, we should also be talking about renaming the Selke after him.

JUNE 6

CANUCKS TRADE CAM NEELY, 1986

This date is a double whammy. Or, better yet, dare I say a double Cammy? If you haven't closed the book yet, I don't blame you if that's the line that puts you over the edge. But for real, not only is June 6 Cam Neely's birthday — he was born in 1965 in Comox, British Columbia — it is also the date on which the Bruins acquired him, along with a first-round draft pick that turned out to be Glen Wesley, from the Canucks, for Barry Pederson.

Pederson was only a couple of years removed from recording back-to-back 100-point seasons, but the Bruins' brass believed that, following a series of injuries, his production would continue to drop off. But with Neely, who just turned 21 years old, Boston saw the future. "Cam's potential is enormous," said Bruins GM Harry Sinden. And he was right. Neely would break out offensively in Boston, and would eventually notch consecutive 50-goal campaigns. Beyond filling the net, Neely brought the Bruins faithful out of their seats with his potent blend of hard-nosed play and skill, immediately endearing himself as a fan favourite.

JUNE 7

Bs SWEEP PENGUINS, 2013

When the Penguins went down 0–2 to the Bruins in the 1991 Prince of Wales Conference Final, they recovered, winning the series in six games, and then went on to win their first-ever Stanley Cup. But more than two decades later, history wasn't on their side. After dropping the first three games of the Eastern Conference Final to Boston, Pittsburgh was on the verge of being swept on June 7, 2013. Five minutes into the final frame, Adam McQuaid, who scored just one goal during the lockout-shortened regular season, notched what would prove to be the only goal of the game.

As the boisterous TD Garden crowd chanted "We want the Cup," the Penguins scrambled for the equalizer, but it wouldn't come. Boston completed the sweep with a 1–0 victory, earning a berth in the Stanley Cup Final for the second time in three years. It was the first time the Penguins had been swept in the playoffs since 1979. The team that did it that year? I'll give you three guesses, but you'll only need one: the Bruins.

JUNE 8

BRUINS ROLL AT HOME, 2011

It was another command performance by Tim Thomas. On June 8, 2011, the Bruins netminder stopped all 38 shots he faced to record his first shutout in the Stanley Cup Final, and his third of the post-season, backstopping Boston to a 4–0 victory, which knotted up the series at two games apiece. After dropping the first two matches in Vancouver, the Bruins had now made it a best-of-three for the chance to hoist Lord Stanley's mug, and a big part of that was Thomas's sterling play.

Two nights earlier, when Boston shellacked Vancouver with eight goals, Thomas still withstood a Canucks onslaught, stopping all but one of the 41 shots that came his way. At the other end of the ice, Roberto Luongo hung in for all eight goals, but two nights later the Bruins chased him from his net. A few minutes into the final frame, Rich Peverley scored his second of the night to make it 4–0, and Luongo, who had given up four goals on 20 shots, was yanked for Cory Schneider.

JUNE 9

BRUINS FORCE GAME 7, 2019

The *St. Louis Post-Dispatch* jumped the gun. Just a few hours before puck drop of Game 6 of the Stanley Cup Final on June 9, 2019, readers got a glimpse of celebratory championship ads that the newspaper had put together for its online edition, in the event the Blues won the Stanley Cup that night. As a historian, it immediately made me think of the infamous photo of President Harry S. Truman holding up an edition of the *Chicago Daily Tribune* with the erroneous headline "Dewey Defeats Truman," in reference to the 1948 election in which many thought Republican Governor Thomas E. Dewey would oust Truman from the Oval Office.

But of course, Truman actually won that election, earning his first full term as president. More than seven decades later, the Bruins had the chance to take a page from Truman's book. They ended up defeating the Blues 5–1 and forcing Game 7, the 17th time in NHL history the Cup Final would go the distance … while the *Post-Dispatch* had to tweet out an apology.

JUNE 10

CANUCKS CLAIM GARY DOAK, 1970

It says a lot about Gary Doak that the Canucks made him their first selection in the 1970 expansion draft. On June 10, Vancouver nabbed the hard-nosed blueliner from the reigning Stanley Cup champions. Although Doak had not played a full season in Boston — his first few campaigns were curtailed by injuries — he had a well-earned reputation as a tough, stay-at-home defenceman. He played just one full season with the Canucks before making stops in New York and Detroit, then heading back to Boston in 1973 as part of a trade for Garnet "Ace" Bailey and future considerations.

On his second tour of duty with the Bruins, Doak epitomized what it meant to wear the spoked B and became a fan favourite for the better part of the next decade. At the end of the 1976–77 campaign, he earned the Seventh Player Award, given to the Bruin who played above and beyond expectations, as voted by the fans. As far as what Doak meant to the franchise, that award says it all.

JUNE 11

BRUINS AND SABRES SWAP PLAYER RIGHTS, 1976

When the Bruins were unable to come to terms with André Savard, whom they had drafted sixth overall a few years earlier, they traded his rights to the Sabres, on June 11, 1976, for the rights to Peter McNab, who was also unable to reach a new deal with his club. Not long after the swap, McNab signed a contract with the Bruins, while it took Savard a week to come to terms with Buffalo.

McNab immediately made an impact with the Bs. Over the next six straight years, he recorded no fewer than 35 goals and 75 points and was consistently one of the team's top scorers. Although Savard was a strong two-way player, the Bruins clearly got the better of the deal. Perhaps that's why it took more than three decades for the two teams to make another trade, when the Sabres sent Dan Paille to Boston for a third-round draft pick, marking the first time they made a deal involving an active roster player. They certainly take their division rivalry seriously.

JUNE 12

TIM THOMAS REBUKES ROBERTO LUONGO, 2011

Tim Thomas's CV was pretty clear. University of Vermont graduate. Bruins goaltender. Vezina Trophy winner. Olympic silver medallist. What wasn't listed was Roberto Luongo's tire pumper. Following Boston's third loss in the Stanley Cup Final, the Canucks goaltender had some choice words about his counterpart. The next day, before the team departed for Beantown, Luongo walked back some of his comments when speaking to members of the media at the Vancouver airport. The netminder noted he had been "pumping [Thomas's] tires ever since the series started. I haven't heard one nice thing he had to say about me."

When Thomas met with reporters in Boston on June 12, 2011, the day before Game 6, he responded by saying, "I guess I didn't realize it was my job to pump his tires." Instead of worrying about how Thomas felt about his performance, Luongo should have focused on his own game. The next day, he gave up three goals on eight shots and was pulled for the second time that series as Boston won 5–2 to force Game 7.

JUNE 13

BRUINS FORCE GAME 7, 2011

It was do or die. The Bruins were on the verge of elimination in the Stanley Cup Final. To keep their championship dreams alive, they needed to play the game of their lives at home against the Canucks on June 13, 2011. They delivered in short order. After Brad Marchand opened the scoring just over five minutes into the first, the Bruins scored three more goals in quick succession: four minutes and 14 seconds to be exact.

The third marker, a tally by Andrew Ference on the power play, sent Roberto Luongo to the bench for Cory Schneider, and the fourth established a new league record for the fastest four goals by one team in a Cup Final game, surpassing the previous mark by more than a minute (set by the Canadiens more than five decades earlier). Although the Canucks got two goals in the final frame, the Bruins added another to take a 5–2 victory and send the series back to Vancouver for the ultimate showdown for the right to hoist Lord Stanley's mug.

JUNE 14

STEVE BÉGIN'S BIRTHDAY, 1978

If there was one word to describe Steve Bégin, it would be perseverance. Born in Trois-Rivières, Quebec, on June 14, 1978, Bégin had a difficult childhood but was determined to make the NHL. He was drafted 40th overall by the Flames in 1996 and then went on to spend more than a decade in the league, including the 2009–10 season in Boston, where he played 77 games, the most of any campaign. But injuries forced Bégin to retire not once but twice. He initially hung up his skates in 2011 because of an ailing hip, but after undergoing surgery, he made a comeback, returning to Calgary, where he closed out his career.

Following hockey, Bégin started a civil engineering firm but knew there was something he still needed to accomplish: completing his secondary education. After some encouragement from his friend Georges St-Pierre, UFC champion and spokesperson for ChallengeU, Bégin enrolled in online classes, and just a few months after his 40th birthday, received his diploma in a ceremony at the Bell Centre in Montreal.

JUNE 15

BRUINS WIN CUP, 2011

The Stanley Cup had never been higher. Sure, maybe on an airplane during its travels around the world for celebrations, but when Zdeno Chara, the tallest player in NHL history, lifted it high above his six-foot-nine frame on June 15, 2011, he had literally taken the trophy to new heights. The towering celebration marked the first time in nearly four decades that the Bruins were on the top of the hockey world. Although the Bs had struggled to score on the road throughout the series, they managed to snuff out the Canucks in Game 7, notching four goals and blanking their opponents.

It must have been something in the water. Before the game, Nathan Horton, who had been knocked out of the series by a vicious hit from Aaron Rome, poured out a water bottle filled with the melted ice from TD Garden in front of the Bruins' bench. The "home" ice may have ignited the offense, but it was Tim Thomas who sealed the victory. He recorded his second shutout of the series, solidifying his easy case for the Conn Smythe Trophy.

JUNE 16

BOURQUE AND NEELY WIN AWARDS, 1994

Only two players had won the Norris more times than Ray Bourque: Doug Harvey and Bobby Orr. Harvey earned the trophy seven times with the Canadiens and Rangers, while Orr won it an incredible eight years in a row during his legendary career with the Bruins. On June 16, 1994, Bourque earned his fifth Norris, narrowly beating out Scott Stevens for the bragging rights. Bourque received 26 first-place ballots from the voters of the Professional Hockey Writers Association, two more than Stevens.

But Bourque wasn't the only Bruin to take home some hardware that day. Cam Neely, who scored 50 goals that year after missing most of the previous two seasons with knee injuries, was awarded the Bill Masterton Memorial Trophy for best exemplifying the qualities of perseverance, sportsmanship, and dedication to hockey. While Neely certainly fit the bill, the league should also have awarded him an official 50 goals in 50 games record. But because Neely didn't accomplish the feat in Boston's first 50 games of the season, it doesn't count — but it should, especially after his incredible comeback.

JUNE 17

KINGS SIGN KEITH CROWDER, 1989

Keith Crowder was beloved in Boston. He was a lunch-pail player who wasn't afraid to do the dirty work. He excelled in digging the puck out of the corners but was just as good at getting it into the back of the net. During his tenure with the Bruins, Crowder was a three-time 30-goal scorer and was in contention for the Seventh Player Award every season, bestowed annually by the fans to the player who exceeds expectations; he took it home in the 1984–85 campaign.

And while Crowder could seemingly do it all, the pressure to produce was weighing on him. Following the 1988–89 season, Crowder was looking for a change of scenery. After the club released him, he signed a contract with the Kings on June 17. The way Crowder looked at it, there would be no lofty expectations to score in Los Angeles with Wayne Gretzky there. But despite having the Great One to alleviate some of that offensive pressure, Crowder had his least productive season, notching just four goals, before injuring his knee and hanging up his skates.

JUNE 18

BOBBY ORR WINS EIGHTH CONSECUTIVE NORRIS, 1975

When Harry Howell won the Norris Trophy as the league's top defenceman at the end of the 1966–67 season, he told his colleagues at the NHL's awards luncheon "I'm glad I won it this year, because I think some other guy is going to win it for the next decade." That other guy he was talking about was Bobby Orr, who had just finished his rookie season. Howell might have gotten a few laughs, but it was no joke; he was right.

The next year, Orr won his first Norris and would keep a tight grip on the hardware. On June 18, 1975, he took home the trophy for an incredible eighth straight season. No other player in NHL history had won any award that many times, let alone in a row, although Frank Boucher came close, winning the Lady Byng seven times in eight years with the Rangers. Howell's prediction was almost bang on. And had Orr's battered knees not betrayed him, it's quite possible he would have won it for a decade.

JUNE 19

BRUINS FALL SHORT TO HAWKS IN OT, 2013

There were more goals in the second period than there had been in each of the previous two games of the Stanley Cup Final. On June 19, 2013, the Bruins and Blackhawks combined for five goals in the middle frame. Heading into the second session, the score was 1–1. Before the halfway mark of the period, Chicago added two more tallies to take, and extend, their lead. Milan Lucic cut into the Blackhawks' advantage, but less than a minute later, Marcus Krüger restored Chicago's two-goal lead.

But the Bruins wouldn't go away. A couple of minutes later, Patrice Bergeron scored. He added another in the third to tie it up, but Patrick Sharp later lit the lamp on the man advantage to take back the lead. The Bruins, however, answered once again when Johnny Boychuk slapped one in to force overtime. And while Boston had proved all game they could rally, you need to score first in overtime, and Brent Seabrook did just that to give the Hawks a 6–5 victory and tie the series.

JUNE 20

BRUINS TRADE JOZEF STÜMPEL TO L.A. (AGAIN), 2003

From 1997 to 2003, the Bruins made only three trades with the Kings, and they all involved Jozef Stümpel. Originally drafted 40th overall by Boston in 1991, the Slovakian centre became a full-time Bruin during the lockout-shortened season. A couple of years later, after racking up 48 points in 39 games at the Garden, Stümpel earned the Elizabeth C. Dufresne Trophy, bestowed annually to the Bruin who is considered the most outstanding in home games. But a few months after taking home the award, Stümpel was traded to the Kings, along with Sandy Moger and a draft pick, for Byron Dafoe and Dmitri Khristich.

After four seasons in Los Angeles, nine games into the 2001–02 campaign, Stümpel was sent back to Boston with Glen Murray for Jason Allison and Mikko Eloranta. Stümpel, however, wasn't back in Beantown for too long. The Kings acquired him again on June 20, 2003. I wish I could tell you why Jozef had to be included in every Bruins and Kings trade during that six-year period, but I'm Stümpeled. If you just groaned, it's because my editor let me keep that bad joke.

JUNE 21

BRUINS TAKE JOE THORNTON FIRST OVERALL, 1997

When the Bruins landed the first overall pick in 1997, there was no question who they were taking. Joe Thornton, a six-foot-four centre, was the consensus number one pick. He drew comparisons to Eric Lindros for his physical presence and scoring touch, and NHL Central Scouting director Frank Bonello went as far as calling him "a complete player at 17, if there is such a thing." So on June 21, the Bruins opened the NHL Entry Draft by calling his name.

Thornton, who was known as "Big Bird," a nickname that would serve him well in Boston, was still a month away from turning 18, making him just the second 17-year-old selected No. 1. The other was Pierre Turgeon. Although Thornton was expected to make an immediate impact, Bruins fans would have to wait. He fractured his left arm in the pre-season and was expected to be sidelined for up to two months. But just over three weeks after the injury, Thornton incredibly made his NHL debut on October 8 against the Phoenix Coyotes.

JUNE 22

BRUINS DRAFT PATRICE BERGERON, 2003

The 2003 NHL Entry Draft was arguably the deepest in league history. There was no shortage of top talent available. So much so that Patrice Bergeron wound up being a second-round pick. On June 22, the Bruins took him 45th overall. Think about that for a second. That means every team in the NHL, including Boston, passed on him, with a handful letting him slip by twice. It's easy to look back and say that teams should've selected players higher, but this is definitely one of those times.

You can honestly make a case that Bergeron should have been selected first overall. No disrespect to any of the players who were taken ahead of him, but few if any made the type of impact on their franchises that Bergeron did with Boston. Mind you, as a Bruins fan reading this book, you probably wouldn't have wanted that outcome, because Bergeron would have wound up in Pittsburgh. Luckily for you, that didn't happen, and he went on to have a Hall of Fame career in Boston.

JUNE 23

BRUINS HIRE SULLY, 2003

Almost exactly six years after the Bruins acquired Mike Sullivan from the Calgary Flames for a seventh-round pick, he was back in Boston, but behind the bench. On June 23, 2003, the team announced that Sullivan had been named head coach. It was the perfect fit. Sullivan, who was better known as "Sully," was a hometown boy. He grew up in Marshfield, Massachusetts, just outside Boston and had one of his most productive NHL seasons with the Bruins.

While he didn't have much coaching experience, aside from a season at the helm of the club's AHL affiliate in Providence, he was a quick study. Sullivan's first season with the Bruins was solid. Boston finished atop the Northeast Division with 41 victories but lost to the Canadiens in seven games in the playoffs. But following the 2004–05 lockout, the Bruins missed the post-season and Sullivan was fired. After more than a decade as an NHL assistant or bench boss in the minors, he became an NHL head coach again in 2015, leading the Penguins to the first of two straight Stanley Cups.

JUNE 24

BRUINS ACQUIRE TUUKKA RASK, 2006

Tuukka Rask was at a midsummer party in Finland. The sun was not going down, and the beers were flowing over the course of what he remembers as a three-day bender. Somewhere after midnight, Rask got a phone call from his agent. He had been traded to the Bruins. Rask, a little fuzzy from the brews, acknowledged the news and put his phone back in his pocket. He would deal with it after the weekend festivities. While that was how Rask later recounted it on the *Spittin' Chiclets* podcast, on June 24, 2006, he was sent to Boston from Toronto in exchange for fellow netminder Andrew Raycroft.

Rask had been drafted 21st overall by the Maple Leafs the year before, while Raycroft was struggling after winning the Calder Trophy as the league's top rookie a couple of seasons earlier. Although Rask admitted he did not know much about the Bruins at the time of the trade, he would go on to become one of the best goaltenders in franchise history, racking up 308 victories, a club record that will be tough to beat.

JUNE 25

BRUINS TRADE ANDY MOOG TO STARS, 1993

Andy Moog saw the writing on the wall. Despite recording a 37-win season, a career high, he knew he wasn't long for Boston. It was no secret that he and head coach Brian Sutter didn't exactly see eye to eye. During the 1993 Stanley Cup Playoffs, when the Bruins were down 2–0 in their series against the Sabres, Sutter started rookie John Blue for the third game. "That was a pretty good sign Brian wasn't really in my corner, that he'd use just about anybody instead of me," Moog later said. Sutter did go back to Moog for the fourth matchup, but by then it was already too late. Boston lost 6–5 in overtime and was swept out of the playoffs.

So when Harry Sinden called Moog on June 25, 1993, to inform him he was being dealt to Dallas for fellow goaltender Jon Casey, Moog wasn't necessarily surprised. The trade had been in the works for a little while, but the teams delayed making it official because Moog's father lost his battle to cancer a week earlier.

JUNE 26

RAY BOURQUE RETIRES, 2001

Ray Bourque went out on top. Just a couple of weeks after finally winning the Stanley Cup with the Avalanche, on June 26, 2001, the long-time Bruins captain and defenceman was retiring. After 22 seasons in the NHL, Bourque was hanging up his skates and calling it a career. And what a career it was. Over the course of two decades in Boston, Bourque took home the Norris five times as the league's top defenceman and established himself as one of the best blueliners in franchise history, which is saying something when his predecessors included Eddie Shore and Bobby Orr.

At his retirement press conference, Bourque was asked if he had considered a ceremonial return to Boston to retire as a Bruin, but it hadn't crossed his mind. "I am a Colorado Avalanche, and I am retiring as one. I'll always be a Bruin in my heart," he said. It didn't matter whose colours Bourque was wearing when he retired. The Bruins faithful knew how much he bled black and gold and how important he was to the organization.

JUNE 27

BRUINS DRAFT PASTA, 2014

Looking back, it might have been one of the biggest steals of the draft. On June 27, 2014, Boston selected David Pastrňák 25th overall. The Bruins had the Czech forward much higher on their board and debated trading up to take him earlier, but they decided to wait and hope he fell to their position. The gambit paid off. While it's easy to say now that Pastrňák should've probably gone second overall behind only maybe Leon Draisaitl, at the time it wasn't so clear. Even long-time respected hockey journalist Kevin Allen, who covered the game longer than most, whiffed on his prognostication. Writing for USA Today Sports, Allen said Pastrňák "could eventually develop into a second-line NHL player."

As we know now, he developed into a top-line goal scorer that every team wishes it had in its lineup. Within a few years, Pastrňák, who is affectionately known as "Pasta" by the Bruins faithful, became one of the league's premier snipers, sharing the Rocket Richard with Alex Ovechkin in 2019–20 with 48 tallies and reaching the vaunted 60-goal mark a few years later.

JUNE 28

BRUINS TRADE KEN DRYDEN, 1964

It barely made the newspapers, but it was a move that would come back to haunt the Bruins. On June 28, 1964, Boston traded Alex Campbell and the rights to goaltender Ken Dryden to their archrivals, the Canadiens, for Guy Allen and Paul Reid, neither of whom ended up seeing any NHL action. It was only a few weeks earlier that the Bruins had selected a soon-to-be 17-year-old Dryden 14th overall in just the league's second-ever draft.

The Bruins didn't think about it again until the 1971 playoffs. Making his post-season debut, the rookie netminder and the Canadiens vanquished the Bruins in the first round, thwarting Boston's chances to repeat as Stanley Cup champions. Dryden and the Habs would go on to win it all, with the cerebral goaltender earning the Conn Smythe. Later in the decade, Dryden backstopped Montreal to back-to-back victories in the Final against the Bs. As America's foremost hockey historian Stan Fischler would tell you, the Bruins really blew it with that trade, but then again so did the Hawks when they sent Esposito to Boston. That's hockey!

JUNE 29

RICK SMITH'S BIRTHDAY, 1948

Rick Smith never thought he would make it to the big leagues. Born in Kingston, Ontario, on June 29, 1948, he was taking courses at McMaster University (one of my alma maters; go Marauders!) during his junior days in Hamilton, with the goal of becoming a dentist. But in 1966, the Bruins selected him seventh overall in the amateur draft. Although Smith was one step closer to the NHL, he wasn't convinced it would be the right path for him. He figured he would need to pay his dues for Boston's farm team in Oklahoma City, which seemed a little too far away for a kid from Kingston.

A fellow Kingstonian by the name of Wayne Cashman, however, convinced him to give it a shot and even drove him to the team's training camp that year in London, Ontario, just over four hours west down Highway 401. Instead of being sent to Oklahoma, Smith made the Bruins out of camp. He went on to play eight seasons in Boston as part of a pro career that lasted more than a decade.

JUNE 30

HAPPY BIRTHDAY TO ANDREW ALBERTS, 1981

Andrew Alberts looked back at his coach and said, "Sully, I've never played left wing before." The Bruins' bench boss gave him a concise response: "Get your ass on the ice." So Alberts, a career defenceman, dutifully hopped over the boards in a game against Ottawa. He remembers his brief experiment as a forward, chiefly because of who he was up against that night: Zdeno Chara. Alberts survived but later said Chara had killed him a few times, which puts him in good company.

After managing to make it to his next birthday on June 30, Alberts was relieved that the next time he saw Big Z, it wasn't as an opponent, but rather a teammate; in 2006, Chara signed with the Bruins as a free agent. Alberts, who was back on defence, turned out to be his partner for the 2006–07 campaign. Not many players can say they lined up against Chara as a forward and lived to tell the tale, only to go on and patrol the blue line with him, but Alberts can.

JULY

JULY 1

BRUINS SIGN BIG Z, 2006

It was the biggest free-agent signing in Bruins history and not just because Zdeno Chara is a gigantic human being and the tallest player to ever patrol NHL ice. On July 1, 2006, Boston announced it had signed Chara, the most coveted player available in free agency that year, to a five-year deal worth $37.5 million. Chara had been in the league for nearly a decade with the Islanders and Senators and had already established himself as one of the premier defencemen, but he would truly cement his legacy in Boston. He was named captain a few months later, and during his tenure he would win the Norris Trophy and lead the club to its first Stanley Cup in nearly four decades.

Looking back, the Chara signing was so notable that it dwarfed another significant Bruins signing. That same day, the club inked Marc Savard, who was coming off a career-high 97 points in Atlanta, to a four-year contract. Savard would lead the Bruins in scoring by a country mile in his first season in black and gold.

JULY 2

SEAN O'DONNELL SIGNS IN BOSTON, 2001

It had been a rough few weeks for Sean O'Donnell. Early in the second period of Game 7 of the Stanley Cup Final against the Avalanche, the Devils defenceman took a high-sticking penalty. While he watched anxiously from the box, Colorado captain Joe Sakic scored on the power play, making it 3–0 and putting the game, and the Cup, out of reach for New Jersey. Things, however, picked up for O'Donnell during free agency.

On July 2, 2001, he signed a three-year deal with the Bruins that was reportedly worth $7.5 million. Boston would be O'Donnell's fourth team in the last three years, but he would find a home in Beantown, adding some toughness to the blue line. But he added more than just grit to the back end. In his first season with the black and gold, he notched 22 assists and 25 points, both career highs. He stayed with the Bruins for his entire contract but joined the Coyotes as a free agent following the 2004–05 lockout. O'Donnell did eventually get his Stanley Cup in 2007 with the Anaheim Ducks.

JULY 3

MIKE KNUBLE LEAVES FOR PHILLY, 2004

Mike Knuble will always have a special place in the hearts of Bruins fans. On Valentine's Day 2003, Knuble scored two quick goals in 27 seconds to open a matchup against the Florida Panthers, establishing an NHL record for the fastest two goals from the start of a game by one player. He finished that season with 30 goals and 59 points, both career highs by significant margins. Knuble played one more campaign for the black and gold before signing a three-year deal with the Flyers on July 3, 2004. But he didn't play in Philadelphia the next year.

With the league locked out by the owners, Knuble went to Sweden, where he played for Linköping in the Swedish Hockey League. Following the lockout, he officially became a Flyer. Playing on a line with Simon Gagné and Peter Forsberg, which became known as "the Deuces Wild Line," because they each had a two in their respective jersey numbers, Knuble racked up 34 goals and 65 points, establishing new personal bests in the NHL that would go unmatched.

JULY 4

TYLER SEGUIN TRADED TO DALLAS, 2013

The Bruins didn't think Tyler Seguin was a fit. Not long after the Bs lost the Stanley Cup to the Blackhawks, the club's upper management was weighing his future. He had been drafted second overall just three years earlier, but with concerns about his off-ice partying (I mean, he was only 21, and I remember what I was doing at that age) and his desire to win, it appeared he was not long for Boston. In an episode of *Behind the B*, director of player personnel Scott Bradley lauded Seguin's talent but felt there were too many red flags. The Bruins' brass agreed and decided to trade the young centre.

On July 4, 2013, they dealt Seguin as part of a seven-player deal with the Stars. It would prove to be a poignant reminder of the risk of giving up on players too early. In Dallas Seguin became the type of player the Bruins hoped he would become. In his first six seasons with the Stars, Seguin scored no fewer than 26 goals and led the team in scoring three times.

JULY 5

BRUINS SIGN IGGY, 2013

Jarome Iginla was a Bruin. Finally. A few months after it seemed he was going to Boston at the trade deadline, only to wind up with the Penguins — whom the Bruins had swept out of the Eastern Conference Final to punch their ticket to the Stanley Cup Final — Iginla finally signed on the dotted line. On July 5, 2013, he inked a one-year contract worth $6 million. With Nathan Horton not returning and Jaromír Jágr looking like he was going elsewhere, GM Peter Chiarelli was keen to bolster the right side of his forward corps.

Iggy, who could still fill the back of the net and was arguably the best power forward of his generation, was the perfect fit for the Bruins. Finding a spot on Boston's top line alongside David Krejčí and Milan Lucic, Iginla scored 30 goals, tied for the team lead with Patrice Bergeron, and 61 points in what would be his only campaign with the Bruins. The next year, Iginla signed a three-year deal with the Avalanche, before finishing out his Hall of Fame career in Los Angeles.

JULY 6

BOSTON SIGNS ROB ZAMUNER, 2001

Rob Zamuner is the only player in NHL history to be traded for a GM. Sort of. After seven seasons with the Lightning, where he had established himself as a strong two-way player, particularly in the faceoff circle — so much so that he earned himself a spot on Team Canada's roster for the 1997 World Championship, where he earned a gold medal, and the 1998 Nagano Winter Olympics — Zamuner was sent to the Senators as part of the compensation for Tampa Bay's hiring of Rick Dudley, who still had two years on his contract as Ottawa's general manager.

A couple of years after that historic and unconventional move, Zamuner made his way to Boston. On July 6, 2001, he signed a three-year deal with the Bruins. Zamuner continued his solid defensive play in Beantown, but it would be his last NHL stint. Following the 2004–05 lockout, he was unable to secure another big-league deal and ended up finishing his playing career in Europe and, finally, in Australia for the Brisbane Blue Tongues. I really just wanted to put their name in this book.

JULY 7

GERRY CHEEVERS BECOMES COACH, 1980

Gerry Cheevers was hanging up his blocker and trapper, but he wasn't going very far. At a press conference on July 7, 1980, the Bruins goaltender announced his retirement and also that he was going to become the team's next head coach, the 14th in franchise history. Although Cheevers, who was turning 40 in five months, wanted to keep playing, like fellow Boston legend Bobby Orr, his knees just wouldn't allow it. Following a pair of procedures on both joints, Cheevers said it was difficult just to get out of bed in the morning, so playing would have been next to impossible.

While the Bruins filled the spot behind their bench — GM Harry Sinden had fired coach Fred Creighton with seven games to go in the 1979–80 campaign — Cheevers's appointment left a question mark in the crease. Gilles Gilbert was still recovering from a back injury, and Jim Craig, while an improbable Olympic champion, had appeared in only four NHL contests. Boston, however, found its answer later in the off-season when it inked veteran Rogie Vachon.

JULY 8

BRUINS AT THE 1995 DRAFT

As much as teams try, drafting is never an exact science. Sometimes first-round picks don't pan out, and other times, you can strike gold in a later round. Case in point is how the Bruins made out at the 1995 NHL Entry Draft on July 8. With the ninth overall pick from Hartford, Boston selected hard-nosed defenceman Kyle McLaren. McLaren spent seven years patrolling the Bruins' blue line, but they could've had Jarome Iginla, who was taken two spots later. In that same round, the club took Sean Brown 21st overall. But before Brown ever suited up in black and gold, he was traded to Edmonton. Brown, however, eventually made it to Boston; the Oilers sent him back in 2002.

But it was their seventh-round pick that worked out best. The Bruins drafted Swedish winger P.J. Axelsson 177th overall. Axelsson, who was known as "Potatoes," spent more than a decade with the Bruins. Known for his strong two-way play, he finished with the 14th-most career points from his draft class. Not bad for a seventh-round pick.

JULY 9

JIM HARRISON'S BIRTHDAY, 1947

Jim Harrison was a Bruins legend before he even came to Boston. Born in Bonnyville, Alberta, on July 9, 1947, Harrison played junior for the Estevan Bruins in Saskatchewan. During a game against the Regina Pats on December 4, 1966, he scored a natural hat trick in an incredible 24-second span in the final minute to cap off a 6–5 comeback victory. It still stands as a club record for the quickest three-goal effort. A year later, Harrison was instrumental in the Bruins' Memorial Cup run, racking up 19 goals and 34 points in 14 games.

The next year, he made his big-league Bruins debut but spent most of the season in the minors in Oklahoma. Harrison suited up for another 23 games for Boston before he was traded to Toronto, where he became a regular NHLer. Following a few seasons with the Leafs, Harrison bolted for the World Hockey Association, where his legend grew. In a game on January 30, 1973, he notched 10 points, becoming the first player in pro hockey history to accomplish the feat.

JULY 10

TUUKKA RASK SIGNS EIGHT-YEAR EXTENSION, 2013

Boston was reeling after coming up short in the Stanley Cup Final, but there was still business to take care of: locking up restricted free agent Tuukka Rask. A couple of days after the loss to Chicago, GM Peter Chiarelli said he was confident a deal would be inked in short order. Sure enough, a couple of weeks after stating that, on July 10, 2013, the club announced it had signed the goalie to an eight-year, $56 million contract extension. Rask, who had been playing under a one-year contract, was just coming off his first campaign as Boston's starter in the lockout-shortened season. In the playoffs he posted a sterling .940 save percentage, the best in the post-season, backstopping the Bruins to just two wins shy of a title.

Not that there was any doubt, but Rask quickly demonstrated he was worth the investment. He finished the 2013–14 season with 36 victories, a career high, and a .930 save percentage, the best among starters that year, to earn the Vezina Trophy as the league's top netminder.

JULY 11

BRUINS SIGN LANE MACDERMID, 2012

Lane MacDermid proved he was a tough customer. In his Bruins debut, he dropped the gloves against heavyweight Mike Rupp. MacDermid played just four more games in the NHL that season, spending most of the year in Providence for Boston's AHL affiliate, but figuring the 22-year-old left winger could push for fourth-line duty and add some sandpaper to the lineup, the Bruins re-signed him to a one-year two-way deal on July 11, 2012.

MacDermid managed to suit up for a few games in the lockout-shortened season but was traded to Dallas at the tail end of the campaign, along with Cody Payne and a conditional second-round draft pick, for Jaromír Jágr. Although being the return in a Jágr trade would have been an interesting enough footnote in NHL history, the next day in a game against the Ducks, MacDermid scored his first NHL goal. But what truly made it a milestone goal was that he accomplished the feat exactly 31 years to the day after his father, Paul, scored his first NHL goal as a member of the Hartford Whalers.

JULY 12

BRUINS EXTEND BERGY, 2013

It was one of the easiest contracts the Bruins ever inked. On July 12, 2013, just two days after locking up goaltender Tuukka Rask, Boston signed Patrice Bergeron, who was still recovering from playoff injuries that included a broken rib, separated shoulder, and punctured lung, to an eight-year, $52 million extension that was set to kick in at the end of the following season when his laughably affordable three-year, $15 million deal expired. While the new contract would give Bergeron a notable salary increase, it would soon become one of the best deals in the NHL.

Bergeron was already a pillar of the team, a future captain, and was only getting better with age. The next season, he reached the 30-goal mark for the first time in nearly a decade and earned his second Selke Trophy as the league's top defensive forward. Under his new contract, Bergeron managed to take his play to the next level. The faceoff specialist established career highs in goals and points, several times over, while finishing each season as a Selke finalist.

JULY 13

BRUINS ACQUIRE PAVEL ZACHA, 2022

The Bruins got a nice Haula for Erik. I'm sorry. I know you have come to expect better from me at this point, but you really shouldn't — this is who I am. Anyway, on July 13, 2022, the Bruins traded Erik Haula to the Devils for Pavel Zacha. Zacha, who was drafted sixth overall by New Jersey in 2015, was headed to arbitration, but a few weeks after the trade, they avoided adjudication and agreed to a one-year, $3.5 million contract.

Finding a new fit in Boston, Zacha had a breakout season. Playing wing on a line with Patrice Bergeron and Brad Marchand, Zacha racked up 21 goals, his first time reaching the benchmark in the NHL, and 57 points. Before the campaign was over, the Bruins rewarded his efforts by signing him to a four-year, $19 million contract. With the Bruins' forward depth decimated the next year, especially down the middle, after the retirement of Bergeron and David Krejčí, Zacha stepped up his game. Shifting back to centre, he collected 59 points and was critical in the faceoff circle.

JULY 14

BRUINS EXTEND COLIN MILLER, 2016

After getting his first taste of NHL action with the Bruins, blueliner Colin Miller signed a two-year extension with the team on July 14, 2016. Originally taken by the Kings in the fifth round of the 2012 NHL Entry Draft, following his junior days with the Soo Greyhounds, Miller had spent the early part of his pro career in the minors, unable to crack a defensively stacked Los Angeles team. But when he was included as part of the trade for Milan Lucic in 2015, Miller would find more opportunities in Boston.

While he spent some time in Providence for the 2015–16 campaign, his last stint in the minors, he suited up for 42 games for the black and gold. After inking his contract extension, Miller played his first full NHL season, recording 13 points in 61 games. At the end of the campaign, however, Miller was left exposed for the expansion draft and nabbed by the Golden Knights. Miller would have a breakout year in Las Vegas, collecting 41 points and helping the club make a run to the Stanley Cup Final.

JULY 15

MATT BARTKOWSKI SIGNS ONE-YEAR DEAL, 2014

Matt Bartkowski and the Bruins were headed to arbitration, but two weeks before they were set to negotiate they reached a one-year deal worth $1.25 million on July 15, 2014. Drafted 190th overall by the Panthers in 2008, Bartkowski was traded to the Bruins a couple of years later, along with Dennis Seidenberg, for Byron Bitz, Craig Weller, and a second-round pick. Although Bartowski started off his tenure with the Bruins in the minors and the press box, he became a key part of the blue line brigade during the 2013–14 season, his first full campaign in the NHL, when he found himself on the second pairing with Johnny Boychuk.

Following the 2014–15 season, however, Bartkowski left Boston and signed another one-year contract with Vancouver. He'd score his first regular-season goal with the Canucks on October 18, 2015, 137 games into his big-league career. While it may have been his first regular-season tally, Bruins fans may remember that it was actually Bartkowski who opened the scoring in Game 7 against the Maple Leafs in 2013.

JULY 16

MICHAL GROŠEK INKS DEAL WITH BOSTON, 2002

Michal Grošek later said that requesting a trade out of Buffalo was the biggest mistake of his career. Drafted by Winnipeg in 1993, Grošek was traded to the Sabres a few years later. Once in Buffalo, he established himself as an NHL regular and became a bit of a playoff legend with the team in his second post-season appearance. During the opening round of the 1998 playoffs, he scored four goals in a five-game series against Philadelphia.

The next year he had a breakout season, notching 20 goals and 50 points, but not long after that he informed Buffalo's brass that he wanted out. The Sabres ended up trading him to the Blackhawks for Doug Gilmour and J.P. Dumont. After stops in Chicago and New York (with the Rangers), and some time in the minors again, Grošek signed with the Bruins on July 16, 2002. But he was never able to recapture the magic he had in Buffalo. Grošek played two seasons in Boston before finishing out his professional career in Europe.

JULY 17

PETER SCHAEFER TRADED TO BRUINS, 2007

Peter Schaefer was happy to be in Boston, but he wasn't exactly thrilled with how he left Ottawa. Two days before the Senators traded him to the Bruins for Shean Donovan on July 17, 2007, GM Bryan Murray told the left winger that he was looking forward to welcoming him back for another season in Canada's capital. Schaefer later told reporters he had no hard feelings, but he noted that "I'm probably not going to bake cupcakes with him at Christmas, you know?" I'm not sure who bakes cupcakes at Christmas, but evidently not Schaefer with Murray.

Although Schaefer opened the season on the Bruins' top line with Marc Savard and Glen Murray, he ended up pulling fourth-line duty and often found himself watching from the press box as a healthy scratch. The next year, Schaefer was assigned to Boston's American Hockey League affiliate in Providence, his first time in the minors in nearly a decade. He did eventually return to the NHL with the Canucks, playing 16 games in 2010–11, before finishing his pro career in Germany.

JULY 18

BRUINS SIGN CRAIG CUNNINGHAM, 2014

Craig Cunningham had his whole career in front of him. On July 18, 2014, he signed a contract with the Bruins. Cunningham, who was drafted 97th overall by Boston in 2010, spent most of the previous season in Providence but made two appearances with the Bruins. He got more time with the big club the next year, but before the campaign was over, he was placed on waivers and claimed by Phoenix.

When the Coyotes landed an AHL affiliate in Tucson for the 2016–17 season, Cunningham was named inaugural captain. But early into that campaign, tragedy struck. Prior to a game, Cunningham collapsed and went into full cardiac arrest. Had it not been for the medical team that performed CPR for well over an hour, Cunningham would have died on the ice. He survived, but after developing an infection caused by poor circulation, his lower left leg was amputated. Although Cunningham's professional playing days were over, he stayed in the game he loved. In 2023, he won a Stanley Cup with the Golden Knights as a pro scout.

JULY 19

STEVE SHIELDS IS BORN, 1972

Steve Shields quickly endeared himself to the Bruins faithful. When he signed with Boston for the 2002–03 campaign, he sported a mask that paid homage to the stitches mask that Bruins legend Gerry Cheevers made iconic during his tenure. Cheevers started making *X*s on his face protection during the 1967–68 season to record where the puck had struck him; the story goes that during a practice, which Cheevers was always looking for a way out of, he was hit in the mask and retired to the dressing room.

When coach Harry Sinden went to check on him, he discovered he was smoking a cigarette and drinking a beer. After Sinden told him to get his butt back on the ice, assistant trainer John "Frosty" Forristall drew a stitch mark on the mask, drawing laughs from Cheevers's teammates — but not his bench boss. The rest, of course, is history. Even after Shields, who was born July 19, 1972, left the Bruins for the Panthers, he continued wearing the mask as a nod to Cheesie.

JULY 20

BRUINS RE-ACQUIRE FERN FLAMAN, 1954

Gordie Howe said that Fern Flaman was the toughest defenceman he ever played against. That's saying a lot coming from Mr. Hockey, whose elbows and stickwork were some of the most fearsome instruments of his era. Like Howe, Flaman was a rugged farm boy who had grown up in Saskatchewan. After he was signed by the Bruins in 1943, he spent a few years playing in the minors until he made his NHL debut in 1947. He patrolled the Boston blue line for five seasons, terrorizing the opposition with his bone-crunching bodychecks, before being traded to Toronto in 1951, where he won the Stanley Cup.

A few years later, on July 20, 1954, Flaman was traded back to the Bruins for Dave Creighton. In his second tour of duty with the black and gold, Flaman re-established himself as a presence on the back end and in the dressing room. He racked up 150 penalty minutes in the 1954–55 campaign, the most that year. Flaman also served as Bruins captain for six seasons, before finishing his career in the minors.

JULY 21

JEREMY LAUZON TAKEN IN EXPANSION DRAFT, 2021

Jeremy Lauzon is the answer to a trivia question that, until now, probably only Jeff Marek, who has forgotten more about hockey history than most of us will ever know, knew the answer to. In my estimation he is the only player in NHL history to score his first goal against a first-year expansion team and then later be selected first overall by an expansion team in their draft. Lauzon potted his first regular-season tally against the Vegas Golden Knights on November 11, 2018. On July 21, 2021, he was left exposed by the Bruins and selected first by the Kraken in their expansion draft (which hockey insider Frank Seravalli ruined by tweeting out all the picks before they were announced).

Lauzon, who was drafted 52nd overall by the Bruins in 2015, didn't even finish the season in Seattle. Before the trade deadline, he was dealt to the Predators for a second-round draft pick. Although Lauzon didn't find a home in the misty Puget Sound, he did in Nashville. That off-season, he signed a four-year deal to stay in Music City. A couple of years later, he racked up 383 hits in a season, establishing a new NHL record.

JULY 22

LEO THE LION IS BORN, 1931

Leo Labine approached every game like it could be his last. He was a hard-nosed winger from Haileybury, Ontario, a small mining town, and he brought that tough ruggedness to each shift with the Bruins. By his own admission, he often played a little too aggressively, and he once said there were instances in which he was lucky to make it out of the game alive. Born on July 22, 1931, Labine, who was known as "Leo the Lion," made his NHL debut in the 1951–52 campaign for the Bruins.

He quickly made his mark. During the playoffs, in the seventh and deciding series against the Canadiens, Labine hammered Maurice Richard, a hit that should have knocked Montreal's star out of the game. But the fiery Richard returned in the third period, sporting a bandage over a cut above his left eye, and scored the eventual game- and series-winning tally. Had Richard not made it back onto the ice that evening, the Montreal fans might have, in fact, torn Labine apart before his NHL career really even started.

JULY 23

BOBBY ORR MEETS THE GREATEST CANADIAN, 1980

Bobby Orr rolled up one of the pant legs of his suit to compare battle scars. Orr's knees had been battered during his illustrious playing career, but he had nothing on the person sitting next to him. To his right was Terry Fox, arguably the greatest Canadian who ever lived, who had lost his right leg to cancer a few years earlier. The iconic pair had come together in Parry Sound, Ontario, Orr's hometown, on July 23, 1980, when Fox passed through as part of his Marathon of Hope.

A few months earlier, Fox had dipped his artificial leg into the Atlantic Ocean in St. John's, Newfoundland, to begin his incredible quest of running across Canada to raise funds for cancer research. All on one leg. During his visit with Orr, the Bruins legend presented him with a cheque from Planters nuts for $25,000, which represented $10 for every mile he'd run so far. Fox got to meet some of his hockey heroes like Orr and Darryl Sittler throughout his journey, but he was the real hero and remains an inspiration to this day.

JULY 24

BRUINS ACQUIRE PATRICK EAVES, 2009

Patrick Eaves was a bit of a late bloomer. A first-round pick in the star-studded 2003 draft, he started his career in Ottawa and Carolina before he was traded to the Bruins, along with a fourth-round draft pick, on July 24, 2009, for Aaron Ward. Eaves looked like he could have been a fit in black and gold. Before turning pro he spent three years at Boston College, but not long after the deal was announced the Bruins put him on waivers for the purpose of buying him out.

Initially, it appeared as though moving Ward and waiving Eaves was to free up salary cap space to re-sign Phil Kessel, but Boston ended up trading him to the Leafs in a blockbuster deal a few months later. Less than two weeks after his brief stint as a Bruin, Eaves signed a one-year contract with the Red Wings. Nearly a decade later, he enjoyed a career year late in his NHL tenure, scoring 37 points with the Stars, the most points he'd scored at any level since college.

JULY 25

BRUINS SIGN ANDREI KOVALENKO, 2000

When Andrei Kovalenko posted up in front of the net, there was little chance you were moving him away from the crease. That's why he was known as "the Tank." Originally drafted in the eighth round by the Quebec Nordiques in 1990, Kovalenko was listed at 5 foot 10 and 215 pounds, which is pretty much my build these days if I'm lucky, but it certainly doesn't help me much when I'm on the ice. But Kovalenko was more than just an immovable object — he also had some pretty silky mitts. The Russian winger may not have scored in bunches, but he had 157 goals through nearly a decade in the NHL.

The Tank rolled into Boston on July 25, 2000, when he signed a one-year deal. In what would prove to be his final season in the big leagues, he collected 16 goals, which included a three-goal effort against the Penguins, his first hat trick since his rookie season with the Nordiques. Following his stint with the Bruins, Kovalenko returned to Russia, where he finished his playing career and later got into politics.

JULY 26

RYAN SPOONER AND BRUINS AVOID ARBITRATION, 2017

Ryan Spooner didn't want to go through arbitration. I don't blame him. After exchanging briefs you have to sit through a hearing in which your team lays out all the reasons why you are not worth as much as you and your agent think you are. Even after it's all settled, which often leaves neither side completely happy, the memory of that unpleasant process still lingers. You can't take back what you said, and you can't unhear what you heard about yourself. So for all those reasons, Spooner was keen to avoid another round of adjudication.

And so, on July 26, 2017, the very day that he and the Bruins were scheduled to have their hearing, they agreed on a one-year deal worth $2.8 million. The next season, Spooner collected nine goals through his first 39 games, putting him on pace for a career year, but he ended up being part of the package, along with Matt Beleskey, Ryan Lindgren, and a pair of draft picks, going to the Rangers that landed Rick Nash before the trade deadline.

JULY 27

JOHN ADAMS IS BORN, 1946

John Adams had his name engraved on the Stanley Cup before he ever played an NHL game. The goaltender, who was born in Port Arthur (now Thunder Bay) on July 27, 1946, was recalled by the Bruins for the 1970 playoffs, chiefly to serve as a spare for Gerry Cheevers and Eddie Johnston. While Adams won the championship with Boston that year, it would be a couple more years before he made his black-and-gold debut.

During the 1972–73 campaign, Adams was called up from the minors and made 14 appearances in the Bruins' net throughout the year, picking up nine wins in those outings. After spending the next season backstopping the San Diego Gulls in the Western Hockey League, Adams was back in the NHL the next year for the expansion Capitals. But that was a bad year to be a Washington goalie. The club won just eight games in its inaugural season, and Adams collected seven losses in seven starts, letting in no fewer than five goals in each of those appearances.

JULY 28

BRUINS SIGN NICK FOLIGNO, 2021

I so wanted to see Nick Foligno win a Stanley Cup in Boston. I may not be a Bruins fan, but I am definitely a Nick Foligno fan. He's a Sudbury guy and as nice as advertised. So when he signed a two-year deal on July 28, 2021, I was excited. The veteran winger was joining a contender, giving our community its best chance to have Lord Stanley pay a visit. It would have been especially fitting since Sudbury is home to the Beef 'n Bird Tavern, established by the late Jerry Toppazzini, a penalty-killing specialist for Boston in his day. It would have been the perfect stop.

It's best known for hosting porketta bingo, a game in which you gamble to win a pound of delicious Italian pork roast and raise money for minor hockey. When Foligno signed with the Bruins, Jerry's son Anthony, who now runs the Beef 'n Bird with his siblings, said that if Nick brought home the Cup, he would give him porketta for life. Now, to me, that's even better than a championship.

JULY 29

BRUINS ANNOUNCE CAM NEELY'S NO. 8 HEADING TO THE RAFTERS, 2003

It was a long time coming. No Bruin had worn No. 8 since Cam Neely was forced into an early retirement by injuries in 1996, but the club made it official on July 29, 2003, when it announced that his jersey would be raised to the rafters at the FleetCenter (now TD Garden) before Boston took on the Sabres on January 12, 2004. Although Neely brought Bruins fans out of their seats with highlight-reel goals and bone-crunching bodychecks, he never expected his jersey would be among the Boston legends. He later joked that the only time he let his imagination run wild was when he was staring up at the retired numbers from the ice after he had been knocked on his rear end.

Before the ceremony Neely delighted the Bruins crowd one last time by lacing up his skates and taking a lap around the rink. He was later awestruck when reality set in that he would forever be sandwiched between Phil Esposito's No. 7 and Johnny Bucyk's No. 9. Talk about great company.

JULY 30

BRUINS DRAFT MATT LASHOFF, 2005

When Matt Lashoff was being interviewed by teams before he was drafted, one of the questions he was asked was "If you could have dinner with one person, dead or alive, who would it be?" The defenceman didn't have to think about it too much: Stevie Ray Vaughan, the great blues guitarist who died in a helicopter crash a few years after Lashoff was born. It might have been an odd choice for an 18-year-old hockey player, but Lashoff was a musician at heart. When he first left home to pursue his hockey dreams, he took his guitar with him, and it was never too far out of reach.

I can't say for certain whether the Bruins posed that question to him, but he must have given some good answers because Boston drafted him 22nd overall on July 30, 2005. While Lashoff struggled to find a regular spot on the Bruins' blue line and elsewhere around the NHL, he continued to hone his skills on the fretboard. In 2011, he released his debut album, *Living on Heart.*

JULY 31

LINUS ULLMARK'S BIRTHDAY, 1993

Big goalie hugs on this day for Linus Ullmark. Born in Lugnvik, Sweden, on July 31, 1993, Ullmark was only with Boston for a few seasons, but he left a lasting impression. Originally drafted 163rd overall by Buffalo in 2012, Ullmark joined the Bruins via free agency in 2021. He finished his first season in black and gold with 26 victories, but his best was yet to come. The next year, Ullmark racked up 40 victories, scored a goal, earned the Vezina as the league's top netminder, and got a lot of hugs.

After every win, and there were a lot that season — 65 to be exact — he and fellow goalie Jeremy Swayman raised their arms high above their heads and embraced with an emphatic hug. It was a hit with the Bruins faithful, but after one particularly aggressive squeeze, they were warned by the team's medical staff to rein in the jubilation. But the tender tradition ended when Ullmark was traded to the Senators on June 24, 2024. So remember: Hug your goalies while you've got 'em.

AUGUST

AUGUST 1

JEREMY SWAYMAN AWARDED ONE-YEAR DEAL, 2023

Looking back now, this could have easily been a franchise-altering moment. On August 1, 2023, goaltender Jeremy Swayman was awarded a $3.475 million contract by an arbitrator. Swayman continued to share the crease with Linus Ullmark the next season, and together, the dynamic hugging duo earned the William M. Jennings Trophy for the lowest combined goals against. You always sensed that Swayman was the heir apparent, and when the Bruins traded Ullmark to Ottawa the following off-season, it was confirmed.

He just needed a new contract. Although Swayman, a restricted free agent, was once again eligible for arbitration, he elected not to file. It was clear that the process had left a mark that Swayman wouldn't forget. As the 2024–25 season approached and a deal had not been struck, things seemingly became more acrimonious as both sides dug in. For a while, it looked like Swayman might have played his last game in black and gold. But on the morning of October 6, it was announced they had agreed on an eight-year extension. Boston's net was firmly Swayman's.

AUGUST 2

BRUINS LOSE TO FLYERS IN BUBBLE, 2020

The Bruins certainly didn't look like the Presidents' Trophy team from earlier in the season. Sure, they hadn't played in more than four months, but neither had any club that made the NHL's expanded playoffs, which would quickly be known as "bubble hockey" because of the tight restrictions brought on by the Covid-19 pandemic. On August 2, 2020, Boston played its first game of the round-robin seeding for the Eastern Conference bracket. Squaring off against the Flyers, the Bruins appeared listless and sluggish, a far cry from the squad that had 44 victories and 100 points before the world ground to a halt.

Chris Wagner, not exactly known for his goal-scoring prowess, scored Boston's only goal in a 4–1 loss. Jaroslav Halák, who was filling in for the ailing Tuukka Rask, made 25 saves, but he could hardly be blamed since pretty much every goal was preceded by a sloppy turnover. The round robin didn't get any better. Boston lost its next two games but managed to make short work of Carolina in the opening round.

AUGUST 3

THE Bs SIGN BRIAN LEETCH, 2005

Brian Leetch was headed back to New England. On August 3, 2005, the Bruins announced they had signed the future first-ballot Hall of Famer to a one-year deal worth $4 million. Before becoming a defensive cornerstone for the Rangers and earning the Conn Smythe in the team's first championship in more than five decades, Leetch was raised in Cheshire, Connecticut. Drafted ninth overall by the Rangers in 1986, he starred at Boston College for a season before making the jump to the NHL, where he patrolled the Broadway blue line for 17 seasons.

Leetch may have been at the end of his storied career as arguably one of the greatest American-born hockey players, but he could still make a difference on the back end. He picked up 27 assists with Boston and reached the 1,000 career points mark, becoming just the seventh defenceman in league history to reach the milestone. The black and gold, however, would prove to be Leetch's last uniform. He considered returning to New York but decided to retire after sitting out the next campaign.

AUGUST 4

WAYNE CARLETON'S BIRTHDAY, 1946

It may have said Kenneth Wayne Carleton on his birth certificate, but Carleton — born in Sudbury, Ontario, on August 4, 1946 — was better known as "Swoop." I actually had to do some digging to figure out the origins of that nickname. I assumed it was because he had a swooping style, but when I couldn't find a definitive answer, I reached out to someone who would know better: Stan Fischler, one of the most revered hockey historians around. Stan figures it was because Carleton was a very tall guy for his era and his skating had a swoop to it. "When Wayne blew in on goal, he was swooping like an airplane," Fischler wrote to me.

Carleton won the Cup with the Bruins in 1970 and was immortalized in the photograph of Bobby Orr's iconic gravity-defying celebration. Carleton later swooped over to the rival World Hockey Association and was a standout player in that league. Years later, the Bruins had another Swoop: Bob Sweeney, who earned the moniker from Keith Crowder because he said Sweeney reminded him of Carleton.

AUGUST 5

JACK NORRIS'S BIRTHDAY, 1942

Jack Norris couldn't get his hands on goalie pads, but like any good prairie boy, he didn't let that stop him. Like Gordie Howe, who used frozen "road apples," an eloquent Canadian term for horseshit, for pucks, Norris improvised by taping Eaton's catalogues around his legs to protect his shins from pucks and errant sticks while guarding the net. Born in Saskatoon, Saskatchewan, not far from Howe's hometown of Floral, on August 5, 1942, Norris backstopped the Estevan Bruins in junior for four seasons, before eventually making his way to the big-league Bruins.

He played only 23 games for Boston, but Norris is forever linked to an important moment in franchise history. A couple of years later, while plying his trade in the minors, Norris was included as part of the trade to the Black Hawks that sent Phil Esposito to Beantown. After wrapping up his NHL career with appearances in Chicago and Los Angeles, Norris joined the upstart World Hockey Association, tending the twine for the Alberta Oilers in their inaugural season.

AUGUST 6

BRUINS SIGN CHRIS PARADISE, 2002

After leading the University of Denver Pioneers with 22 goals in 40 games, Chris Paradise, who had gone undrafted, signed a two-year deal with Boston on August 6, 2002. Paradise spent most of the next season with the Baby Bruins in Providence but was also sent down to the ECHL, where he played for the Atlantic City Boardwalk Bullies, a name so good I just had to include it in this book. But if you think that's good, wait until you hear where Paradise played a couple of years later.

He spent three games with the Fresno Falcons in the ECHL, but spent most of the 2004–05 season with the Odessa Jackalopes of the Central Hockey League. If you're of my vintage, you might have been introduced to the concept of a jackalope on *America's Funniest People*, but if not, all you need to know is that it's a mythical animal best described as a jackrabbit with antelope antlers. Even if Paradise never played a game for the Bruins, there was no way I was passing up the opportunity to write briefly about jackalopes.

AUGUST 7

MATT GRZELCYK THROWS OUT FIRST PITCH, 2019

It may not have been in the strike zone, but he still managed to get it across the plate. On August 7, 2019, Matt Grzelcyk threw out the first pitch for the Portland Sea Dogs, the Double-A affiliate for the Red Sox, before they took on the Erie SeaWolves at Hadlock Field. Grzelcyk, who grew up in Charlestown and just finished his first full season on the Bruins' blue line, could've used some pointers from Torey Krug, who threw one right down the middle for the Red Sox a few years earlier, but nevertheless he certainly did better than I would have done.

Not like that's saying much and not that it matters, since I would never be invited to throw out a ceremonial first pitch. But if I did, I would probably need to spend hours dialing in my throw, only to blow it once I stepped on the field and had thousands of eyeballs on me. The Sea Dogs, however, weren't able to get a victory for Grzelcyk. After giving up two runs in the first, they got clobbered 10–4.

AUGUST 8

BRUINS SIGN BERGERON AND KREJČÍ, 2022

Christmas had come early for Bruins fans. On August 8, 2022, Boston announced it had signed Patrice Bergeron to a one-year contract. It came as a relief to many who had speculated that perhaps the five-time Selke winner had played his last game in black and gold. After the captain had gone unsigned for most of the off-season, it looked like he might be hanging up his skates.

And if Bergeron's return wasn't enough good news, a few hours later, Boston confirmed it had inked David Krejčí to a bonus-laden deal. The boys were back in town. Krejčí had spent the past year playing in his native Czechia, marking the first time the club had been without both players on the roster since Krejčí broke into the league 15 years earlier. Although the season didn't end with a championship like the two of them might have hoped, it capped off two incredible careers that had already guaranteed that both of their jerseys would one day join the other Bruins legends high above the ice at TD Garden.

AUGUST 9

NHL ENTRY DRAFT, 1979

People often argue that the 2003 draft was the deepest in NHL history, but there's a strong, and perhaps better, case to be made that the 1979 class was the most stacked. Held in the Queen Elizabeth Hotel in Montreal on August 9, the draft would produce seven future Hall of Famers, including Ray Bourque, whom Boston selected eighth overall. The best part about that selection is that it didn't originally belong to the Bruins. Boston obtained the pick when they traded goaltender Ron Grahame to the Kings a year earlier. The club's own pick in the first round was actually 15th overall, which they used to take another defenceman, Brad McCrimmon from the Brandon Wheat Kings.

Following the draft, which also included the Bruins taking Doug Morrison, Keith Crowder, Larry Melnyk, Marco Baron, and Mike Krushelnyski in later rounds, GM Harry Sinden said, "Our defense in the last couple of hours has turned around pretty good." Indeed, Bourque, who was then still better known as Raymond, would turn Boston's blue line around for the next two decades.

AUGUST 10

P.J. AXELSSON SIGNS ONE-YEAR DEAL, 2005

P.J. Axelsson was one of the most underrated players of his era. Over the course of more than a decade in Boston, Axelsson, who answered to "Potatoes" in Boston but "Pebben" in his native Sweden, established himself as one of the league's premier defensive players. Drafted 177th overall by Boston in 1995, he was often tasked with shadowing the league's top players and handled his duties with aplomb, earning the adoration of his coaches, not always an easy task when one of his bench bosses was Pat Burns.

Axelsson never won a Selke, but he consistently earned votes and was the two-way player that every team covets. And so it came as no surprise when, on August 10, 2005, the Bruins announced they had signed him to a one-year extension. Later that year, after winning gold with Sweden at the Winter Olympics, he inked a three-year extension in Boston. When Axelsson's tenure in black and gold came to an end, he had played in 797 games, the 10th most in franchise history at the time.

AUGUST 11

BRUINS RE-SIGN JOE THORNTON, 2005

It looked as though Joe Thornton was staying in Boston. On August 11, 2005, the Bruins announced they had signed the big centre to a three-year, $20 million contract extension. The deal came a few days after Thornton had reportedly rejected a five-year pact. Boston GM Mike O'Connell said the contract underscored how much Thornton meant to the team. Despite the agreement, things were not all rosy between the captain and the Bruins. Most recently, Boston's brass were unimpressed with his performance in the 2004 playoffs.

Meanwhile, Thornton had been critical of the club. He believed they should have signed more players in the off-season following that first-round exit. While the extension may have initially buried that discord, the harmony in Beantown was fleeting. Just a few months later, the Bruins traded Thornton to the Sharks for Brad Stuart, Marco Sturm, and Wayne Primeau. By season's end Thornton would earn both the Art Ross and the Hart Trophies and, over the next 14 seasons in San Jose, would cement his legacy as the greatest player in franchise history.

AUGUST 12

Bs INK SANDY MCCARTHY, 2003

The Bruins were adding some punch to their lineup. On August 12, 2003, they signed Sandy McCarthy, who had a well-earned reputation as one of the league's most fearsome warriors, to a one-year contract. The southpaw heavyweight had some memorable battles over the years against some of the NHL's top enforcers, including Bob Probert, and although he didn't chuck 'em as much as he used to, I sure wouldn't want to tangle with him.

During his time in black and gold, McCarthy almost had more goals than scraps. His final fight was against Tie Domi, with whom he had a history following an allegation that the Toronto pugilist used a racial slur against him a few years earlier in the playoffs. But it wasn't much of a scrap. After some shadowboxing, McCarthy lost his balance and fell over before either of them connected. A couple of months later, the Bruins put McCarthy on waivers. He was claimed by the Rangers, where he had spent the past few seasons, and finished his NHL career on Broadway.

AUGUST 13

BRYAN BERARD INKS ONE-YEAR DEAL, 2002

How could you not root for Bryan Berard? After sustaining a career-threatening eye injury in March 2000 when he was with the Maple Leafs, Berard returned to hockey a year later with the Rangers. In coming back to hockey, Berard had to start paying back the $6.5 million insurance settlement he received, but at the end of the day it was just money. The most important thing was Berard was playing the game he loved once again. While he was glad to be back in the NHL, he wanted to build on his comeback in New York.

Looking for more opportunities, particularly on the power play, Berard signed a one-year deal with the Bruins on August 13, 2002. In Boston he notched 10 goals and 38 points, the most since his sophomore campaign five years earlier. After the Bruins walked away from an arbitrator's award at the end of the season, making Berard a free agent, he signed with Chicago, where he had a near-career year and earned the Masterton Trophy for perseverance and dedication to the sport.

AUGUST 14

DICK REDMOND'S BIRTHDAY, 1949

If Dick Redmond didn't grow up to be a hockey player, he probably could've had a shot at being a golfer. According to the Peterborough and District Sports Hall of Fame, in 1977 Redmond shot a 65 at the Kawartha Golf and Country Club, establishing a new amateur record. I'm lucky if I shoot a 65 on the front nine, and that's on a good day. Redmond, who was born in Kirkland Lake, Ontario, on August 14, 1949, but grew up in Peterborough, was later inducted into that same hall of fame — not for what he did on the links, but on the ice.

After grinding it out with the cellar-dwelling Golden Seals for a few years, Redmond broke out with the Black Hawks and was a key part of the team's run to the Stanley Cup Final in 1973. He later made his way to Boston in 1978 as part of a three-team deal that sent Gregg Sheppard to Pittsburgh and Jean Pronovost to Atlanta. Redmond patrolled the Bruins' blue line for parts of four seasons before hanging up his skates in 1982.

AUGUST 15

BRUINS SIGN PRANKSTER GUY LAPOINTE, 1983

The Bruins were looking to add an experienced defenceman to their back end, but in doing so they retained the services of one of the league's most notorious practical jokers. On August 15, 1983, the Bruins signed Guy Lapointe to a one-year contract, along with an option for the following season. While Lapointe, who answered to "Pointu," was known for his steady play on the blue line for the Canadiens, earning six Stanley Cups, he was also a prankster who spared no one.

When Canadian prime minister Pierre Elliott Trudeau once visited the Montreal dressing room, Lapointe reportedly coated his hand in Vaseline before extending it for a shake. The PM had not expected the slimy grip, but all he could do was laugh it off. Another time, Lapointe snuck a whistle into his glove during practice. After blowing it several times to try to cut some of the drills short, head coach Scotty Bowman angrily scanned the stands for the phantom whistler. It's not clear whether Pointu's hijinks continued in Boston. He played just the one season and then retired.

AUGUST 16

BRUINS TRADE FOR BILL QUACKENBUSH, 1949

Bill Quackenbush finished the 1948–49 season without taking a penalty, an impressive feat for one of the league's top defencemen. It won him the Lady Byng, making him the first blueliner to take home the award, but it also earned him a ticket out of town. On August 16, 1949, the Red Wings traded him and Pete Horeck to Boston for Jimmy Peters, Pete Babando, Clare Martin, and Lloyd Durham. Detroit GM Jack Adams made it no secret he was embarrassed that Quackenbush took home the trophy. In later remarks to the *Montreal Gazette*, he lamented that the game was "substituting the Byng for bang in hockey."

Adams didn't care for Quackenbush's style of play, but it was welcomed on Boston's back end. While he didn't take too many more penalties with the Big Bad Bruins, he provided an offensive boost on the blue line for the next seven seasons, earning him comparisons to Eddie Shore for that aspect of his game. But that is where the comparisons ended. Shore was one of the meanest players in hockey and was pretty much the opposite of gentlemanly conduct on ice.

AUGUST 17

BRUINS TROUNCE HURRICANES IN THIRD-PERIOD COMEBACK, 2020

The Bruins had the Hurricanes on the ropes. After sleepwalking through the round-robin tournament, Boston appeared to be making short work of Carolina. On August 17, 2020, the club picked up a 4–3 victory to take a 3–1 series lead. The Bruins trailed by a pair of goals heading into the third period, but they completely dismantled the 'Canes in the final frame. After getting on the board just before the halfway mark, the black and gold scored three more goals, an offensive flurry in a span of seven minutes, to take the lead.

Following the first tally, Charlie McAvoy absolutely trucked Carolina captain Jordan Staal, knocking him down to the ice and sending him to the locker room, undoubtedly a spark that helped ignite the comeback. Although Boston had allowed a goal late in the period, they had put on a defensive master class, limiting Carolina to just two shots, while firing 16 at goaltender James Reimer. Two nights later, "at home" in the Toronto bubble, the Bruins finished the job, defeating the Hurricanes 2–1 to move on to the second round.

AUGUST 18

FORBES KENNEDY'S BIRTHDAY, 1935

Forbes Kennedy went out swinging. After Pat Quinn knocked out Bobby Orr in Boston's first playoff game against the Leafs in 1969, Kennedy — Toronto's enforcer, who led the league in penalty minutes that year while splitting the season with Philadelphia — got into a few dust-ups with Bruins players, some of whom he played with during his time in black and gold a few years earlier. But at the end of the melee, Kennedy landed a right-hand punch on linesman George Ashley, sending him to the ice.

By all accounts, Ashley was not attempting to restrain Kennedy in any way, so it seemed he struck the official for no reason. Following the infraction, the league suspended him indefinitely but later reduced it to a four-game ban. Kennedy never returned that post-season as Boston swept Toronto, and it would prove to be his final NHL game. He finished out his playing career in the minors. After hanging up his skates, Kennedy, who was born in Dorchester, New Brunswick, on August 18, 1935, returned to the east coast to start coaching.

AUGUST 19

BRUINS SIGN JIM SCHOENFELD, 1983

Jim Schoenfeld was thinking about hanging up his skates. After the Red Wings waived him at the end of the 1982–83 campaign, the hulking defenceman seriously contemplated retirement. He took the off-season to think it over before signing a one-year deal with the Bruins on August 19, 1983; he appeared in 39 games for the Bs and then finished out his NHL career in Buffalo.

Schoenfeld's time in Boston was brief, but he was part of a memorable moment in Bruins history five years later. After the Bruins defeated the Devils 6–1 in the third game of the Wales Conference Final, Schoenfeld, who was then the coach of New Jersey, took issue with referee Don Koharski's officiating. Schoenfeld waited for him in the tunnel after the game and started berating him. Things were getting heated, and that's when Koharski stumbled and fell. Initially, it looked like Schoenfeld shoved him, but he didn't actually make contact. He made that abundantly clear when he told him, "You fell, you fat pig!" followed by a dig that has lived in infamy: "Have another doughnut!"

AUGUST 20

BRUINS GET EDDIE SHORE FROM EDMONTON, 1926

Eddie Shore was as tough as they come. Not long after the Bruins acquired him from the Edmonton Eskimos of the Western Hockey League for cash on August 20, 1926, he got into a skirmish with teammate Billy Coutu. The dust-up damaged one of Shore's ears so badly that a piece of it was dangling. Doctors recommended amputating what they couldn't stitch back together, but the story goes that Shore found his own doc and had his ear sewn back together without any anesthetic.

Shore later said he was just a farm boy "who didn't want his looks messed up." A tough thing to do when you played the game as hard as Shore. Throughout the course of his career, he was said to have broken his nose more than a dozen times. After the first few breaks, most would have found another calling, but it was just an occupational hazard for Shore. But Shore also had the skill to match his toughness. He would win four Hart Trophies patrolling the blue line for the Bruins.

AUGUST 21

BRUINS ACQUIRE KEN HODGE JR., 1990

For the first time in well over a decade, the Bruins would have a Ken Hodge in the lineup again. On August 21, 1990, the team acquired Ken Hodge Jr., the son of the Boston legend, from the North Stars for future considerations. Junior was drafted 46th overall by Minnesota in 1984 but had spent most of his professional career in the minors. Although he started the 1990–91 campaign in the American Hockey League, Hodge was recalled early in the season and stayed with the Bruins.

He racked up 30 goals and 59 points, making him one of the top-scoring rookies that year, and finished as a finalist for the Calder Trophy. Hodge, however, played just 42 more games with Boston before finishing out his playing career in the minors and overseas. Meanwhile, those future considerations turned out to be the pick the North Stars used to draft Jere Lehtinen in 1992. Lehtinen would become a fixture in Dallas for more than a decade, winning three Selke Trophies, and was an integral part of the team's championship in 1999.

AUGUST 22

KEN HAMMOND'S BIRTHDAY, 1963

Ken Hammond told Harry Sinden that he needed the Bruins more than they needed him. Hammond, who was born in Port Credit, Ontario, on August 22, 1963, played parts of four seasons for the Kings after starring as an all-American defenceman at Rensselaer Polytechnic Institute, where he earned a degree in civil engineering. But after his time in Los Angeles, Hammond couldn't stick in an NHL lineup, bouncing between Edmonton, New York, and Toronto, along with spending some time in the minors.

So during the 1990 off-season, he approached the Boston GM, hat in hand, looking for a chance to prove himself. Hammond only managed to suit up for one game with the team, but he made it count. In a game against the Hartford Whalers on March 31, 1991, he scored his first NHL goal in more than three years. Although Hammond didn't find many opportunities in black and gold, he found more steady work with expansion teams, patrolling the blue line for the Sharks and Senators in their inaugural seasons, respectively.

AUGUST 23

BRUINS DEFEAT LIGHTNING, 2020

The Bruins struck first before the Lightning. After making short work of the Hurricanes, Boston opened its second-round playoff series in "the bubble" at Scotiabank Arena against Tampa Bay on August 23, 2020. Late in the first period, Charlie Coyle scored to put the Bruins on the board. David Pastrňák added to the lead early in the middle session, and just over a minute into the third, Brad Marchand potted his fourth of the post-season to make it 3–0.

Jaroslav Halak, who took over the starting duties after Tuukka Rask left the bubble to be with his family — a decision that should never have been questioned, because hockey is just a game and family comes first — was working on a shutout until the Lightning's Victor Hedman broke the bid just before the halfway mark of the final frame. Hedman would add another with just over a minute remaining, but it was too little, too late; Boston won 3–2. Although Bruins fans hoped it was a sign of things to come, it would prove to be their only victory that series.

AUGUST 24

MURRAY BALFOUR BORN IN REGINA, 1936

Murray Balfour should have had many more birthdays ahead of him. Born in Regina, Saskatchewan, on August 24, 1936, Balfour got his start with the Canadiens organization but made a name for himself in Chicago. Playing with Bobby Hull and Bill Hay, the trio formed the legendary Million Dollar Line. Balfour was an integral part of the Black Hawks' Stanley Cup championship in 1961, but he broke his arm in the penultimate game of the Final. A few years later, Chicago sent him, along with Mike Draper, to Boston for Jerry Toppazzini and Matt Ravlich.

Balfour, who was never the same player after his injury, played just 15 games for the Bruins and spent most of the 1964–65 campaign in the AHL. During his time in the minors, Balfour complained of shortness of breath, and after a series of tests, it was discovered he had a tumour on his lung. Although doctors removed a lesion reportedly the size of a baseball, Balfour succumbed to the illness two months later at home in Regina, just shy of his 29th birthday.

AUGUST 25

BRUINS ACQUIRE NICK MICKOSKI, 1959

By the time Nick Mickoski arrived in Boston, he had already been in the NHL for more than a decade, but he had plenty of hockey still left in him. On August 25, 1959, the Bruins acquired the veteran winger from Detroit for defenceman Jim Morrison. While Mickoski still wanted to stay in the game, his time in the big leagues was winding down. After suiting up for 18 games for the Bruins, he was sent down to the minors, where he played out the rest of the season, recording 51 points in 48 games for the Providence Reds.

The next year, he went to the Western Hockey League, where he later starred for the San Francisco Seals as a player-coach, winning back-to-back championships with the team in 1964. Even when his production started to drop off in the WHL, Mickoski still wasn't ready to hang his skates up. He moved east to the Newfoundland Senior Hockey League and played for the Grand Falls-Windsor Cataracts for a few more seasons, before finally calling it a career at the age of 41.

AUGUST 26

BOBBY ORR SIGNS MILLION-DOLLAR CONTRACT, 1971

Bobby Orr became the highest-paid player in NHL history, and yet he was still probably underpaid. On August 26, 1971, he signed a five-year deal worth $1 million, another league first, with the Bruins. While Orr was smiling from ear to ear at the press conference, there still might have been a snag. U.S. president Richard Nixon, through the Cost of Living Council, had recently announced a 90-day wage and price freeze that prevented new contracts from being negotiated and signed during the moratorium, which was expected to last until at least mid-November.

And since professional athletes were not exempt, it was unclear whether Orr would be able to play under the deal when the season started. Orr's agent, Alan Eagleson, said that if the government took issue with the agreement, his client would continue playing under his old salary. Luckily for Orr, in case Uncle Sam came calling, GM Harry Sinden stated the contract had actually been signed back in February, but a few minor points had to be resolved before it could be announced.

AUGUST 27

MANNY FERNANDEZ'S BIRTHDAY, 1974

Things might have been a little awkward at the next Fernandez family reunion. Manny Fernandez, who was born in Etobicoke, Ontario, on August 27, 1974, but grew up in Kirkland Lake, wanted the Wild to trade him because he was not feeling the love from his teammates and coaches. His bench boss, Jacques Lemaire, however, was also his uncle. But Lemaire just shrugged it off and said, "It's just Manny being Manny," and he didn't take it personally. One of the original members of the Wild, Fernandez did eventually get his wish when he was traded to the Bruins on July 1, 2007, for Petr Kalus and a fourth-round draft pick.

Although injuries limited Fernandez to just four appearances in his first season in Boston, the next year, for the 2008–09 campaign, in what would prove to be his last in the NHL, he and Tim Thomas earned the William M. Jennings Trophy for having the lowest combined goals against. It was Fernandez's second Jennings win; he'd earned it a couple of years earlier in Minnesota with Nicklas Bäckström.

AUGUST 28

GAMBLING BANS LIFTED, 1970

Better late than never. On August 28, 1970, NHL president Colin Campbell rescinded the lifetime bans he handed down to a pair of former Bruins, Billy Taylor and Don Gallinger, more than two decades earlier. During their time in Boston, the pair started gambling on games, including some against their own team. They got away with it until their activities were uncovered in a police-surveillance sting operation against their bookie, Detroit gangster James Tamer. With the notorious Black Sox Scandal, in which eight players of the Chicago White Sox were accused of throwing the 1919 World Series, still in the public consciousness, Campbell threw the book at Taylor and Gallinger.

Although both players were well past their playing time when their suspensions were lifted, Taylor found work in the NHL again, serving as a scout for the Penguins, but Gallinger never returned to the league. More than a half-century later, Shane Pinto became the first player since the duo to be suspended for gambling activities, a decision that was not without controversy considering the league's newfound ties with sports betting.

AUGUST 29

BABE SIEBERT INDUCTED POSTHUMOUSLY, 1964

They don't make 'em like Babe Siebert anymore. A versatile player, Siebert started his NHL career as a winger but switched to defence during his second of three campaigns in Boston. The move paid off. He later earned the Hart Trophy patrolling the blue line for the Canadiens. But what really made Siebert a cut above was what he did off the ice. A devoted husband and doting father, after his wife, Bernice, was paralyzed from the waist down following the birth of their second daughter, Siebert took on the lion's share of the duties at home.

When Bernice watched his games at the Forum, he always carried her to her seat. He never won the Lady Byng, but that's gentlemanly conduct. Siebert was slated to become Montreal's coach after retiring in 1939, but over that summer he drowned while swimming with his daughters. As a father of two girls myself, that detail crushed me. Siebert was inducted posthumously into the Hockey Hall of Fame on August 29, 1964, with his nine-year-old grandson, whom he never got the chance to meet, accepting the honours.

AUGUST 30

DOMINIC MOORE SIGNS WITH BRUINS, 2016

Every NHL dressing room was better when Dominic Moore was in it. You would be hard-pressed to find a more beloved and respected player. After getting his start with the Rangers, Moore went on to play with eight different teams before sitting out the 2012–13 season to care for his wife, Katie, who had been diagnosed with a rare liver cancer. After Katie tragically passed away in January 2013, Moore established a foundation in her memory to raise funds for cancer research.

Although hockey was still the furthest thing from his mind, he returned to the game the next year, playing a key part in New York's Stanley Cup run. The Blueshirts came up short, but Moore earned the Bill Masterton Memorial Trophy for his perseverance and dedication to the game. Nobody embodied those characteristics more that year than Moore. Following a couple more seasons on Broadway, he made his way to Boston, signing a one-year contract on August 30, 2016. Moore played out the campaign with the Bruins before finishing his NHL career in Toronto.

AUGUST 31

JOHN GRAHAME IS BORN, 1975

Ron Grahame contributed to one of the greatest gifts the Bruins had ever received when they traded him to Los Angeles for a draft pick they would later use to select Ray Bourque eighth overall. One of Grahame's greatest gifts, however, was arguably the birth of his son, John, on August 31, 1975. Like his father, John also tended the twine and had the opportunity to protect the Boston net.

The Bruins drafted him in the ninth round, 229th overall, in 1994. John played parts of four seasons for the black and gold before he was traded to the Lightning for a fourth-round pick. He backed up Nikolai Khabibulin for the 2003–04 campaign and won the Stanley Cup that year. Following the lockout, Grahame picked up the lion's share of Tampa Bay's goaltending duties but later drew the ire of head coach John Tortorella — but then again, who hasn't — for his poor performance in the playoffs. Grahame signed with Carolina in the off-season, where he'd make his final NHL appearances before rounding out his career in the minors and a stint in Russia.

SEPTEMBER

SEPTEMBER 1

TOMÁŠ NOSEK'S BIRTHDAY, 1992

Tomáš Nosek was one of the original Golden Misfits. Born in Pardubice, Czech Republic, on September 1, 1992, he was nabbed by Vegas from the Red Wings in the 2017 expansion draft. He would score the Knights' first-ever regular-season home goal and was part of the team's historic and improbable run to the Stanley Cup Final in its inaugural year. But after four seasons in Sin City, Nosek packed his bags and signed a two-year contract with the Bruins. Known for his skill on both sides of the puck, he brought depth and strong defensive play to the lineup, particularly on the penalty kill.

Following Boston's stunning loss to the Panthers in the first round of the 2023 Stanley Cup Playoffs, which included a controversial moment in which Matthew Tkachuk said some nasty things about Nosek's wife that you should never say about any woman, regardless of how you feel about playing against their partner, Nosek inked a deal with Florida just over a year later. Nosek said there were no hard feelings when he joined the Panthers, but hopefully Tkachuk welcomed him with a sincere apology.

SEPTEMBER 2

BRUINS SIGN MATTIAS TIMANDER, 1999

Mattias Timander was not being signed for his lamp-lighting abilities. Drafted 208th overall by the Bruins in 1992, Timander, a hulking Swedish blueliner, could contribute offensively from the back end but rarely bulged the twine. In parts of his first two seasons with Boston, he scored two goals. During the 1998–99 campaign, in which he made 22 appearances in black and gold, he picked up six assists but no goals.

Just before the start of the next season, on September 2, 1999, the Bruins re-signed him to a two-year deal. Timander suited up for 60 games that year, a career high, but once again couldn't find the back of the net. Among the 404 players — trust me, I counted them — who played 60 games or more in the NHL that season, Timander was among the handful who went without a goal. At the end of the season, he was taken by the Blue Jackets in the 2000 expansion draft. In his first campaign in Columbus, he scored two goals, the same number he scored across parts of four seasons in Boston.

SEPTEMBER 3

BRUINS SIGN BOBBY ORR, 1966

Along the shores of Barrie, Ontario, Bobby Orr put pen to paper and officially became a Boston Bruin when he signed his first NHL contract on September 3, 1966. Aboard the boat of GM Hap Emms, along with his father, Douglas, and his adviser — now agent — Alan Eagleson, Orr took the next step in his hockey career.

The Bruins' brass had been captivated by Orr ever since long-time coach Milt Schmidt and scout Wren Blair had spotted him playing in Gananoque, Ontario, as a 13-year-old. Blair spent the next year convincing Orr's parents that their son should play for the Oshawa Generals, a junior club sponsored by the Bruins. They eventually agreed. Orr would develop in the Bruins' farm system, and in exchange, the family received a cash bonus, a new car, and an assurance that the team would pay to stucco the family home. Orr now had plenty of money in his bank account to help pay for home renovations; the contract was reportedly the most lucrative deal ever offered to a player coming out of junior hockey.

SEPTEMBER 4

BRUINS INK DAVID KREJČÍ TO EXTENSION, 2014

David Krejčí may have been coming off a disappointing playoff run by his standards, recording four assists in 12 games, but there was no doubting his value to the franchise. Just a year earlier, he led the Bruins in playoff scoring, with 26 points in 22 games, and all the way to the Cup Final. And two years before that, he led the team in post-season scoring en route to the Stanley Cup — and you could make a case that had Tim Thomas not played otherworldly and the Bruins still found a way to win, Krejčí would've been next in line for the Conn Smythe.

Despite the recent blip, Krejčí had already proved he was worth every penny and then some. So on September 4, 2014, it was announced that Boston had inked him to a six-year, $43.5 million extension that would kick in at the end of the 2014–15 campaign. Krejčí's season, however, was limited by a knee injury; he suited up for only 47 games. The following year, the first in his new deal, Krejčí returned to form, collecting 63 points in 72 games.

SEPTEMBER 5

MATT FRASER SIGNS ONE-YEAR DEAL, 2014

Matt Fraser had a good reason for being late to Bruins training camp, and yet he still made it on time. The undrafted forward was still recovering from a broken foot he sustained in the playoffs. The injury actually happened while he was playing for Providence in the post-season, but then he was called up to Boston. Despite skating on only one good foot, Fraser scored the overtime winner, the lone goal that match, in the fourth game against the Canadiens in the second round. He continued playing the rest of the series, until the Bruins were eliminated in Game 7.

Following the playoffs, Fraser had a plate and six screws inserted into his foot. Amalie Benjamin of the *Boston Globe* reported he planned to leave it in unless it started bothering him, but I think the bigger issue would be how much longer it would take him to get through airport security. Nevertheless, in addition to arriving in Boston with new hardware, Fraser also had a new one-year two-way contract that he signed on September 5, 2014.

SEPTEMBER 6

BRUINS SIGN MALCOLM SUBBAN, 2012

As Canadiens fans eagerly awaited for P.K. Subban to sign a new contract, they almost fainted when they saw that a Subban had been signed. But it wasn't P.K. — it was his younger brother, Malcolm, who had just inked his first NHL deal with the Bruins. On September 6, 2012, Boston signed the netminder, whom they drafted 24th overall a few months earlier, to a three-year entry-level contract. But with the Bruins' goaltending battery set, Subban went back to junior for the Belleville Bulls. He attended his first training camp the following year and then turned pro in Providence.

The younger Subban remained in the minors for the next four seasons but made two appearances for the Bruins, although he was yanked in both outings. Not long into the 2017–18 campaign, he was claimed off waivers by Vegas, in what would prove to be a shrewd move. As luck would have it, Subban's first start for the Golden Knights would be against his former team. He stopped all but one shot Boston threw at him to record his first NHL victory.

SEPTEMBER 7

BRUINS RE-UP BRAD MARCHAND, 2012

With the NHL lockout looming, the Bruins signed Brad Marchand to a four-year extension on September 7, 2012, that was set to kick in the following season. Less than two weeks later, after negotiations failed and the collective bargaining agreement expired, the league closed its doors. With the season in jeopardy, players started signing contracts to suit up overseas. Marchand, however, stayed put. He later acknowledged that he wanted to give it one more week, but when one more week turned into one more week, he started to worry that when the NHL resumed its operations he'd be out of shape.

After all, his linemates (Patrice Bergeron and Tyler Seguin) were both playing in the Swiss League. When the NHL managed to salvage half the campaign and start in January, Marchand may have been a little rusty, but he hadn't really lost a step, a testament to his skill and determination. He finished the season with a team-leading 36 points, not bad for a guy who initially hadn't played an NHL game in nearly nine months.

SEPTEMBER 8

PHIL ESPOSITO MAKES IMPASSIONED SPEECH, 1972

Phil Esposito didn't mince words. Following another dispiriting loss to the Russians on home soil, on September 8, 1972, a sweaty, winded Esposito made an impassioned speech to Canadians, taking aim at the fans who booed the team off the ice, in an interview with CTV's Johnny Esaw. "For the people who booed us, geez … all of us guys are really disheartened and we're disillusioned and we're disappointed in some of the people. We cannot believe the bad press we've got, the booing we've got in our own buildings. Every one of us guys, thirty-five guys who came out to play for Team Canada, we did it because we love our country."

He could've said much worse, and he probably should have. Esposito knew what was at stake. The Summit Series was as much a battle of political ideologies as it was for hockey supremacy, so it was not exactly the send-off Team Canada had hoped for as the tournament shifted to the Soviet Union for the final four games, which Canada needed to win. It's hard not to look back and think Esposito's pointed words didn't somehow have a galvanizing impact.

SEPTEMBER 9

RAY BOURQUE RE-SIGNS WITH BOSTON, 1998

There were no active players in all of professional sports who had been around longer than Ray Bourque. After signing a two-year contract with the Bruins on September 9, 1998, he was set to enter his 20th season. Joe Thornton, who was heading into his sophomore campaign, was born just a few months before Bourque made his NHL debut, and now they were teammates once again. For Boston's brass, they hoped the extension would keep Bourque in a Bruins uniform for the rest of his career.

GM Harry Sinden said he hoped to sit down with Bourque in a year and look to extend the contract even further. Although Bourque bled black and gold, he knew his time was running out and he wanted a final crack at the Stanley Cup. Early into the 1999–2000 season, the Bruins attempted to get him to put pen to paper again, but Bourque wouldn't commit. Instead, looking to chase his championship dream, he requested a trade to a contender. He was later dealt to Colorado, where he would finally hoist Lord Stanley's mug.

SEPTEMBER 10

DENNIS VASKE SIGNS WITH BOSTON, 1998

Dennis Vaske knew he was taking a risk every time he stepped on the ice. After suffering a concussion in November in each of the past three seasons — he played a combined 55 games over that span — he was worried that the next one could end his career … or worse. The Islanders' physician even went as far as suggesting he should never play again. But Vaske wasn't ready to hang up his skates, and after he received medical clearance from the Mayo Clinic in Rochester, Minnesota, he was ready to get back to the rink.

On September 10, 1998, he signed a one-year deal, with the option for a second, with Boston. Vaske managed to avoid another November concussion while he was with the Bruins, but back spasms kept him from playing in consecutive games, and he appeared in only a few matches that season. While Vaske would have preferred to be in an NHL lineup, he suited up for 43 games in the American Hockey League, the most at the pro level in five years.

SEPTEMBER 11

BRUINS DEBUT NEW SWEATER, 1995

There was a new bear in town. When Boston opened training camp on September 12, 1995, it included a new look. Rookie Bill McCauley was sporting a gold alternate jersey with a bear head that would be debuted later in the season following the All-Star Game. It has become known as the "Pooh Bear" sweater, either affectionately or infamously, depending on how you feel about it. Cam Neely was in the latter camp. Following the reveal, he told reporters that he questioned its ferocity because it wasn't baring any teeth.

Bruins president and GM Harry Sinden, however, reportedly had an encounter with a growling grizzly over the summer while on a fishing trip with former president George H.W. Bush, so he was quite all right with the more relaxed demeanour, which was inspired by a painting he had hanging in his office. Pooh stuck around as an alternate until 2006, but the club brought it back in white as part of the Adidas Reverse Retro campaign for the 2022–23 season.

SEPTEMBER 12

BOBBY ORR INDUCTED INTO HOCKEY HALL OF FAME, 1979

Bobby Orr should have been at the rink getting ready for the next season. Instead, he was in a suit being inducted into the Hockey Hall of Fame. On September 12, 1979, Orr joined the pantheon of hockey's greatest players, but he should have been enshrined long before. At the age of 31, he was the youngest player to ever be inducted. To put things in perspective, Harry Howell was also inducted that day. Howell played his last NHL game six years before and was a few months away from turning 47. He famously won his first Norris Trophy as a greybeard right before Orr went on his run, winning it in eight consecutive seasons.

Although Orr would have given up all his hardware for a set of knees that would've allowed him to keep playing, it wasn't meant to be. He left the game as the most decorated defenceman in NHL history, and one can only imagine where he would've ended up in the record books if he'd had even just a few more seasons.

SEPTEMBER 13

STEVE HEINZE RE-SIGNS WITH BRUINS, 1998

Steve Heinze felt the Bruins needed to ketchup with the times. During his tenure in Boston, he always wanted to wear No. 57, a nod to the condiment giant Heinz that was famous for its marketing slogan of "57 varieties" along with a steak sauce that bore its name. But when Heinze was in Beantown, players weren't permitted to wear high numbers. The only exception was franchise cornerstone Ray Bourque, who had donned No. 77 when the Bruins sent his No. 7 to the rafters to honour Phil Esposito, who made that single digit legendary in black and gold.

It may have just been a number, but it meant something to Heinze. After signing what would be his last contract with Boston, on September 13, 1998, he later left via free agency, citing that he needed a change of scenery after being in the club's stuffy atmosphere for nearly a decade. He signed with Columbus and immediately switched to No. 57 and wore it for the rest of his career.

SEPTEMBER 14

BRUINS SIGN DAVID PASTRŇÁK TO SIX-YEAR EXTENSION, 2017

It was good to see that the new, big contract hadn't changed David Pastrňák. After inking a six-year, $40 million deal with the team on September 14, 2017, Pastrňák, who was coming off career highs with 34 goals and 70 points, divulged that his first purchase wasn't an extravagant meal at a Michelin-starred restaurant. Rather, he told reporters that he grabbed dinner for $8, drawing some hearty laughs as he explained that the modest meal of rice and chicken teriyaki was the first thing he bought. While the contract didn't necessarily change the way he lived his life — finding pleasure in the little things — it still kept him hungry on the ice.

In his first season under the new deal, he once again set benchmarks in goals and points, milestones he later shattered in the 2022–23 campaign when he racked up 61 goals and 113 points. But before that season came to a close, with his agreement set to expire in the off-season, Boston signed him to an eight-year, $90 million extension, making him the highest-paid Bruin.

SEPTEMBER 15

BRUINS PLAY IN CHINA, 2018

Not long after arriving for training camp in 2018, the Bruins were once again packing their bags. They were off to China for the second-ever NHL China Games, a name so uninspiring that it could have only been dreamed up by a league not known for thinking outside the box. Nevertheless, with the NHL looking to continue making inroads into one of the globe's largest markets, it sent Boston and Calgary over for a pair of exhibition games.

The series kicked off on September 15, 2018, in Shenzhen at the Universiade Sports Center. After the game went to overtime and the extra session solved nothing, the Bruins and Flames went to a shootout. When Brad Marchand stepped onto the ice, he needed to score to keep things alive. He didn't disappoint. After Calgary missed on its next attempt, Jake DeBrusk had the game on his stick. He scored to earn a 4–3 win. Before their next game in Beijing, the Bruins visited the Great Wall, crossing off a bucket-list item for many on the team, particularly the shootout hero, DeBrusk.

SEPTEMBER 16

BOBBY BAUER CALLED TO THE HALL, 1996

It took them long enough, but the Kraut Line was finally reunited in the Hockey Hall of Fame. The family of the late Bobby Bauer learned on September 16, 1996, that he would be inducted posthumously in a ceremony a couple of months later. In addition to joining his former linemates in hockey's pantheon of greatness, Bauer was also reunited with his late brother, Father David Bauer, a true Canadian hockey pioneer.

More than three decades earlier, Milt Schmidt was the first of the trio to get the nod. Woody Dumart got his call in 1992 in the veteran player category, a mechanism the Hall used to help recognize players who had been overlooked in past years. Bauer, who passed away far too soon at the age of 49 in 1964, was actually one of the last players to be inducted in this category. The Hall scrapped the veteran category a few years later, but I say it's high time to bring it back to include players who have been passed over for far too long.

SEPTEMBER 17

SCOTT ARNIEL'S BIRTHDAY, 1962

Scott Arniel played for three teams in the 1991–92 campaign but somehow avoided a lot of travel. He started the season in the AHL in New Haven, Connecticut, on loan from Winnipeg, but was then traded to Boston for future considerations on November 22. He made his Bruins debut the next day. After playing some games and spending time in the press box, Arniel missed some time with a thumb injury before he was sent down to Boston's minor-league team in Portland, Maine, less than two hours north.

At this point, I should probably note that Arniel was born in Kingston, Ontario, on September 17, 1962. Now that we've got that included and out of the way, Arniel eventually made his way back to Boston, where he would play his final stretch of NHL games. While he managed to keep his travelling down that season by staying in New England for all his home games, he logged plenty of miles over the next seven seasons in the International Hockey League, playing in San Diego, Houston, Salt Lake City, and Winnipeg.

SEPTEMBER 18

BRUINS TRADE PHIL KESSEL TO TORONTO, 2009

I loved when Phil Kessel was on the Leafs. As his Twitter bio once said, he's a nice guy who tries hard and loves the game. From his speed and goal-scoring ability to his seemingly carefree attitude and the fact he battled back from testicular cancer, it was hard not to root for the guy. All that being said, the Bruins made out like bandits when they traded him. On September 18, 2009, they sent Kessel to Toronto for first-round draft picks in 2010 and 2011 and a second-rounder in 2010.

The first-round pick in 2010 would turn out to be second overall, which the Bruins would use on Tyler Seguin, who would play an important role as a rookie in their 2011 Stanley Cup win. They'd use the second-round pick that year on Jared Knight, and the following year, they would take defenceman Dougie Hamilton ninth overall. Kessel, who was in need of a new contract, would continue to be a perennial 30-goal scorer for the next decade, but it was hard to argue with that return.

SEPTEMBER 19

BOSTON SIGNS COLTON ORR, 2001

For the first time in nearly four decades, the Bruins had an Orr in the lineup. The significance of the nameplate was certainly not lost on 19-year-old Colton Orr, a Winnipeg native, who was not related to the Boston legend. "Everyone's pointing at the Orr on the back of the jersey, obviously," he said after signing a three-year contract with the Bruins on September 19, 2001. After turning pro in Providence, Orr eventually made his black-and-gold debut a couple of years later. Despite sharing the same surname, the two players couldn't have been more different. Bobby was known for his finesse and skill, while Colton was known for his truculence.

After getting into his first NHL bout on October 13, 2005, he made a name for himself when he pummelled Leafs tough guy Wade Belak, no small feat, a couple of weeks later. Orr played 20 games that season for Boston but then was claimed by the Rangers, where, in New York and later Toronto, he would establish himself as one of the league's top enforcers.

SEPTEMBER 20

BRAD MARCHAND NAMED CAPTAIN, 2023

There would be no replacing Patrice Bergeron or Zdeno Chara, but if anyone had learned what it took to be a leader in Boston, it was Brad Marchand. Both had been his captains throughout his career with the Bruins, so when it came time to appoint a new leader, there was no better fit than Marchand. On September 20, 2023, a few months after Bergeron retired, the Bruins named Marchand captain, the 27th in franchise history. The significance of seeing the *C* on his jersey for the first time was not lost on Marchand. "I am extremely proud and honoured," he said. "It means more to me than I think anyone will ever know."

Although Marchand knew he could never fill Bergeron's and Chara's skates, especially Chara's, which are probably six sizes bigger, there was plenty he could draw from their tutelage. And while Marchand will go down as one of the greatest players in franchise history, his tenure as captain was rather forgettable. Just two years into his captaincy, he was traded to the Florida Panthers amid a disastrous, and at times controversial, 2024–25 season.

SEPTEMBER 21

WOODY DUMART INDUCTED INTO HOCKEY HALL OF FAME, 1992

For Woody Dumart, it was worth the wait. Nearly four decades after he hung up his skates, Dumart was inducted into the Hockey Hall of Fame on September 21, 1992, joining former Bruins teammates such as Milt Schimdt, whom he skated with as part of Boston's famed Kraut Line. But before they ever got to Beantown, the trio of Dumart, Schmidt, and Bobby Bauer, who was still waiting for his call to the hall, was called "the Kitchener Kids."

During their brief stint in Providence, they earned the nickname because they all hailed from the Kitchener-Waterloo region. But because Kitchener — which was once actually called Berlin — was known for its German heritage, they became known as "the Kraut Line." While the Kraut Line had longer staying power, especially when the line came to dominance in the Second World War, they were still Kitchener Kids, and it would always have a nicer ring to it. Four years after Dumart got his call, Bauer, who had passed away unexpectedly three decades earlier while golfing, was inducted posthumously, bringing all the Kitchener Kids in the hall.

SEPTEMBER 22

HARRY SINDEN INDUCTED INTO HALL OF FAME, 1983

Just days after leading the Bruins to their first Stanley Cup in nearly three decades, head coach Harry Sinden announced his retirement. He stepped away because of a contract dispute and got a job in home construction. Sinden received offers to coach other teams, including the Leafs and Islanders, but took the job as bench boss for Canada in the 1972 Summit Series. Not long after guiding Canada to the championship, he returned to Boston as general manager. Over the next decade, the team would advance to the Stanley Cup Final three times.

For his efforts as the Bruins' chief architect and his contributions to the game on the international stage, Sinden was inducted into the Hockey Hall of Fame in the builder category on September 22, 1983. He went in alongside Ken Dryden, who was his goaltender in the Summit Series, Stan Mikita, and Bobby Hull. Following his induction, Sinden would go on to preside over the Bruins for nearly another two decades, which included a Presidents' Trophy and two more trips to the Cup Final.

SEPTEMBER 23

DIXON WARD IS BORN, 1968

Dixon Ward is the only player in the history of the University of North Dakota's men's hockey program to rack up 100 career goals and 100 career assists. Following his collegiate career, Ward — born in Leduc, Alberta, on September 23, 1968 — turned pro with the Vancouver Canucks, who had drafted him in the seventh round following his 60-goal junior campaign with the Red Deer Rustlers. Despite a strong rookie season in which he collected 22 goals and 52 points, Ward couldn't maintain his production at the NHL level and bounced around between Los Angeles and Toronto before winding up in the minors.

But after guiding the Rochester Americans to a Calder Cup championship and earning the Jack A. Butterfield Trophy as playoff MVP, Ward got another shot with the Sabres. He returned to form in Buffalo, and after four seasons of consistent play he signed with the Bruins on November 3, 2000, and made his debut for the black and gold the next day. Ward recorded five goals and 18 points in 63 games, his last full NHL campaign.

SEPTEMBER 24

BRUINS TRADE MARK MOWERS, 2007

Mark Mowers was coming off his best NHL campaign to date. In the 2006–07 season with the Bruins, he had appeared in 78 games, scored five goals, and recorded 17 points, all career milestones. Mowers, who had been a standout at the University of New Hampshire, where he was a Hobey Baker Award finalist, had been a prolific scorer in the minors, once racking up 81 points in 78 games with Grand Rapids, but he couldn't find the same production in the big leagues. Instead, Mowers adapted his game and took on a checking role.

Following his season in Boston, Mowers was traded to Anaheim on September 24, 2007, for a pair of minor-league defensemen, Nathan Saunders and Brett Skinner. After the deal Mowers hopped a flight to London, England, to join his new team for a two-game series against the Kings, marking the first time the NHL had opened its regular season in Europe. Mowers would play just 16 games for the Ducks before going back across the pond to finish his career in Switzerland.

SEPTEMBER 25

BRUINS SIGN BRANDON CARLO, 2015

A few months after the Bruins drafted him 37th overall, Brandon Carlo took the next step in his NHL career when he signed a three-year entry-level contract with Boston on September 25, 2015. Carlo had attended the team's rookie camp and impressed enough that he was invited to stick around for the main camp. The towering blueliner, who stood at six foot five without skates, was one of the few Bruins who could almost stand eye-to-eye with Zdeno Chara, who had been drafted five months before Carlo was born, and was fittingly paired with the gigantic captain in a pair of pre-season games.

Although Carlo was sent back to junior, he turned pro with Providence at the end of the season and then made Boston's opening night roster for the 2016–17 campaign. His defence partner to start the year was Chara, forming a monstrous pair that undoubtedly terrified oncoming opponents. Carlo may have been overshadowed by fellow rookie blueliner and teammate Charlie McAvoy, but he had a solid first-year campaign, playing in every game and averaging more than 20 minutes of ice time.

SEPTEMBER 26

BRUINS PLAY FINAL GAME AT THE GARDEN, 1995

Normand Léveillé stole the show. After the Bruins played their final game at Boston Garden on September 26, 1995, a 3–0 shutout against the Canadiens in the pre-season, the team said one final goodbye to the building by honouring some of the franchise's legends. Among the invitees was Léveillé. Drafted 14th overall by the Bruins in 1981, Léveillé had a promising career ahead of him, but following a game against the Canucks, he was rushed to the hospital. It turned out the young winger was suffering from an acute intracerebral hemorrhage as a result of an undiagnosed congenital condition.

He underwent emergency surgery that left him in critical condition. Léveillé spent the next month in a coma before he was transferred home to Montreal, where he began his lengthy recovery process. Although he eventually learned to walk again and regained some of his speech, the right side of his body remained paralyzed. He was never able to play hockey again, but with some help from captain Ray Bourque and the support of the Bruins faithful, Léveillé went for one last skate at the Garden.

SEPTEMBER 27

CALLUM BOOTH SIGNS WITH COACHELLA, 2022

Callum Booth had built up quite a collection of jerseys. After the goaltender was drafted 93rd overall by the Hurricanes in 2015, he turned pro with the Florida Everblades a few years later in the ECHL. He played some games with Carolina's AHL club but spent most of the next few seasons in "the Coast," protecting the twine for Florida, the Reading Royals, the Greenville Swamp Rabbits — which has got to be one of the best team names of all time — and the Atlanta Gladiators.

In October 2020, Booth signed with Boston. He played a pair of games for Providence but remained a couple of rungs below the NHL, backstopping ECHL clubs in Jacksonville and later Maine. Just before the 2022–23 campaign was set to begin, Booth left the Bruins organization and signed with the Coachella Valley Firebirds, Seattle's AHL affiliate on, September 27. He made two appearances for Coachella but spent most of the season back in the ECHL with the Kansas City Mavericks. Booth continued stockpiling jerseys in Europe, playing in Germany and Wales.

SEPTEMBER 28

BRUINS TAKE ROBERT LANG IN WAIVER DRAFT, 1997

Some of you may not be old enough to remember this, but once upon a time, the NHL used to hold an annual waiver draft. From 1977 until it was scrapped in 2003, teams could exercise an option to select unprotected players for cash or other compensation in an annual draft that was held a week before the regular season commenced. The Bruins didn't take advantage of the waiver draft until 1987, when they used it to take Willi Plett from the Rangers, and only a few more times after that before they snagged Robert Lang from the Penguins on September 28, 1997.

The Bruins reportedly looked into signing Lang in the off-season, but the Czech centre ended up signing with Pittsburgh. But Lang wasn't in Boston for very long. After just three games, he was placed on waivers and the Penguins claimed him back. It all worked out for Lang. A few years later, he had a career year with Pittsburgh, scoring 32 goals and 80 points, the fourth most on the team that year behind Alex Kovalev and fellow countrymen Jaromír Jágr and Martin Straka.

SEPTEMBER 29

PATRICE BERGERON WINS WORLD CUP OF HOCKEY, 2016

Patrice Bergeron was once again on top of the hockey world. On September 29, 2016, Canada defeated Team Europe 2–1 in the second game of the World Cup of Hockey final to take the championship. For the Bruins centre, it was another addition to his growing trophy case that included a world junior title, a world championship, the Stanley Cup, the Spengler Cup, two Olympic gold medals, and now the World Cup.

I was actually hoping to watch the game that night, but I was at the hospital as we welcomed our first daughter, Zoe, into the world. There was a room not far from ours that had the game on, and I thought about bringing Zoe in there in my arms, so we could experience our first game together. It was a good thing I didn't do that. I found out the next day that had I taken her out of the room before we received our formal discharge, an alarm would have gone off. Not the kind of red light I was looking for.

SEPTEMBER 30

BRUINS ACQUIRE ROB DIMAIO, 1996

The Bruins saved Rob DiMaio some significant travel. After the Sharks nabbed him from the Flyers in the NHL's annual waiver draft, on September 30, 1996, they traded him to Boston in exchange for a fifth-round draft pick. Bruins bench boss Steve Kasper called DiMaio to tell him that he wasn't heading to San Jose, but was instead just going northeast. Kasper knew exactly what type of player he was getting in DiMaio. The two had played together in Tampa Bay a few years earlier in what was Kasper's final big-league campaign.

DiMaio was the kind of lunch-bucket player that would fit well in Boston. He competed for every inch of ice and could contribute offensively. In his first season in Beantown, he scored 13 goals and 28 points, both career highs. DiMaio hit double digits again in goals the next season and consistently provided 20 points for the black and gold, while being reliable on both sides of the puck, until he was traded to the Rangers at the tail end of the 1999–2000 season.

OCTOBER

OCTOBER 1

HAPPY BIRTHDAY TO ALEXEI ZHAMNOV, 1970

Alexei Zhamnov is probably one of the most underrated players in NHL history. Over the course of 14 seasons in the league, he racked up 719 points in 807 games. Born in Moscow on October 1, 1970, Zhamnov played for his hometown team, Dynamo, before joining the Jets in 1992. In Winnipeg, he would form a formidable line with Teemu Selanne and Keith Tkachuk, dubbed "the Olympic Line," because they had each represented their respective countries at the Winter Games, with Zhamnov bagging gold with the Unified Team in 1992.

Before the Jets moved to Arizona, Zhamnov was dealt to the Blackhawks, where he would serve as captain, becoming just the fourth Russian player in NHL history to wear the *C*. After nearly a decade in the Windy City, Zhamnov made a brief stop in Philadelphia before finishing his NHL career with the Bruins in the 2005–06 campaign. He scored his first goal for the black and gold against the Leafs on December 22, 2005, but then a few weeks later he broke his ankle and was done for the season.

OCTOBER 2

RAY BOURQUE TAKES GOAL-SCORING RECORD, 1999

You could make a case that no one enjoyed season-opening games more than Ray Bourque. In 19 season openers, Bourque, who had missed only one in his two decades with the Bruins, had collected eight goals and 21 assists, an NHL record for the most points in that category. On October 2, 1999, he hit the ice for his 20th season opener, and while he looked to add to his impressive tally, he was chasing some other history that night. Heading into that contest against Carolina, Bourque was tied with Paul Coffey, who just so happened to be on the opposing team, but wasn't on the ice that night, for the most career goals by a defenceman.

Following a scoreless first period, Bourque opened the scoring early in the second frame, notching his 386th career marker to take sole possession of the benchmark. He finished the campaign, split between Boston and Colorado, with 403 goals. Coffey, who joined the Bruins in 2000, trailed him by seven goals, but he never found the back of the net in Boston and retired before the next season. Bourque hung up his skates with 410 goals, a milestone that could stand the test of time.

OCTOBER 3

BOBBY CARPENTER HITS 250, 1991

When the Capitals drafted Bobby Carpenter third overall at the 1981 NHL Entry Draft, he made the cover of *Sports Illustrated* and was billed as "the Can't-Miss Kid." And for a while he couldn't. He made the NHL a few months later, becoming the first player to go from high school hockey directly to the big leagues. He finished his rookie campaign with 32 goals and consistently lit the lamp for Washington over the next four seasons, including a 53-goal effort in 1984–85 that made him the first American-born player to reach the milestone.

But after his production slowed down, Carpenter was shipped out to New York and later Los Angeles. He was traded to the Bruins in 1989 for Steve Kasper to complete an earlier deal that sent Jay Miller to the Kings. But in Boston, Carpenter proved he still couldn't miss. He put together two 25-goal campaigns, his best goal-scoring totals since his last full season in Washington, and on October 3, 1991, he notched his 250th career goal, another first for an American-born player.

OCTOBER 4

BRUINS RETIRE BOURQUE'S NUMBER, 2001

Ray Bourque was back where he belonged: in Boston. On October 4, 2001, the Bruins honoured their longest-serving captain by raising his No. 77 to the rafters. Bourque, who retired a few months earlier after capping his illustrious career with a Stanley Cup in Colorado, divulged he was a little nervous about coming back but immediately felt at home.

When he stepped out onto the ice at the FleetCenter, he received a standing ovation from the Bruins faithful that lasted more than three minutes. In a touching full-circle moment, Phil Esposito handed Bourque his jersey for the ceremony. Nearly two decades earlier, when Esposito's No. 7 was retired, Bourque gave up his jersey, a surprise twist that visibly touched Esposito, and switched to 77, wearing it for the rest of his career, making him one of the few athletes in any sport to have worn two numbers that were retired by the same franchise. Bourque was showered with gifts as part of the ceremony, but the coolest one had to be a custom black-and-gold snowmobile.

OCTOBER 5

HAT TRICK OF MILESTONES, 2017

It was a hat trick of milestones for a trio of Bruins rookies. On October 5, 2017, Jake DeBrusk, Charlie McAvoy, and Anders Bjork all appeared in their first NHL regular-season game, and each collected points. McAvoy, who had suited up for six contests in the previous playoffs, assisted on David Pastrňák's opening goal and added a tally of his own late in the second period. DeBrusk gave the Bruins a 2–1 lead early in middle frame with some help from Bjork, who recorded his first assist. DeBrusk later added a helper on McAvoy's goal.

Following the game, a 4–3 victory at home over Nashville, McAvoy told reporters, "It's awesome for the three of us [rookies] to kind of get that out of the way and now you can roll." McAvoy finished the season with 32 points, the sixth most by a first-year Bruins blueliner, and finished fifth in Calder Trophy voting as the league's top rookie. DeBrusk, who picked up a respectable 43 points that year, earned a fifth-place vote for his efforts.

OCTOBER 6

GEORGE PLIMPTON TENDS GOAL, 1977

There wasn't anything George Plimpton wouldn't do to get a story. To get a first-hand account, Plimpton had thrown himself into all sorts of situations that most writers could only dream of. He quarterbacked the Detroit Lions, he played hoops for the Boston Celtics, he pitched at Yankee Stadium, and on October 6, 1977, he tended the twine for the Bruins. To prepare for a five-minute exhibition game against the Flyers, Plimpton practised with the team daily for two weeks.

For a 50-year-old rookie, he handled himself pretty well. Plimpton allowed only one goal from Orest Kindrachuk and may have cheated certain injury when Reggie Leach, who was known as "the Riverton Rifle" for his cannonading shot, missed on a penalty shot. His only real mishap occurred when he slipped skating off the ice, drawing a chorus of cheers. Plimpton later wrote about the experience for his book *Open Net*. I tried to get the Bruins to let me on the ice for *Bruins 365*, but they didn't return my calls.

OCTOBER 7

CAM NEELY RECORDS SEASON-OPENING HAT TRICK, 1995

For Cam Neely, an afternoon delight might have been about a different kind of scoring. Despite notching a hat trick on October 7, 1995, his 14th career three-goal performance — as well as the first in Boston's new home, the FleetCenter, and the second straight season opener in which Neely recorded a hat trick — he told reporters after the game that he preferred matinee games.

For Neely, it was simple: You didn't need to spend the entire day thinking about the game. Rather, he just showed up at the rink once and was ready to play. "Night games, the waiting can wear on you and drain you," he explained. And then, of course, once an afternoon game was over, the evening was open for all sorts of other delights. He might have been onto something. A couple days later, in Boston's first matinee of the season against the Sabres, Neely opened the scoring. He tickled the twine in two more afternoon games that season and added an assist in another, before a recurring hip injury ultimately ended his career.

OCTOBER 8

BYRON DAFOE NETS 100TH VICTORY, 2001

Coming off a pair of disappointing seasons for himself and the Bruins, who missed the playoffs in consecutive years for the first time in more than three decades, goaltender Byron Dafoe was ready to turn the page. After opening the 2001–02 campaign with a pair of victories, Dafoe continued his winning ways on October 8, when he stopped all 22 shots he faced from the Capitals to record his 23rd career shutout — one more save and that would have been too perfect — and backstop Boston to a 4–0 triumph.

It was also his 100th victory with the Bruins, joining just a handful of goaltenders at the time (Tiny Thompson, Frank Brimsek, Gerry Cheevers, Eddie Johnston, Gilles Gilbert, Andy Moog) to accomplish the feat in black and gold. Dafoe finished the season with 35 wins, a career best. The only goalies with more victories that regular season were Dominik Hašek, Martin Brodeur, and Evgeni Nabokov. But after Boston was upset by the Canadiens in the playoffs, the team didn't bring Dafoe back and he ended up signing with the Atlanta Thrashers.

OCTOBER 9

PETER MCNAB SCORES 300TH GOAL, 1983

Peter McNab made an immediate impact in Boston. After the Bruins acquired his rights from the Sabres in 1976 in exchange for the rights to Andre Savard, the first-ever deal between the two teams, McNab scored 38 goals in his first campaign with the black and gold. It would actually be the start of six straight 30-goal seasons, including two in which he reached the 40-goal mark. McNab's production eventually dropped off, but he still had a penchant for finding the back of the net.

On October 9, 1983, just after the halfway mark of the first period in a game against the Hartford Whalers, McNab scored his 300th career goal, and his 251st with the franchise. He scored 12 more goals for the Bruins that year before he was traded to the Canucks. At the time of the deal, he had 263 goals with Boston, the seventh most in franchise history. Following his playing career, McNab served as the inaugural colour commentator for the Avalanche for more than two decades until he passed away in 2022 following a battle with cancer.

OCTOBER 10

DON CHERRY'S FIRST GAME AS COACH, 1974

It was not how Don Cherry drew it up. In his first game as Bruins coach on October 10, 1974, the team was trounced 9–5 by the Sabres and were reportedly outshot 40–18. Bobby Orr, who was on the wrong side of four Buffalo goals, felt personally responsible. "Here it was his first game as a coach and we let the poor bugger down," he told reporters after the shellacking. "It may not have looked like it on the ice but the guys really feel bad about what happened. We stunk and I was the worst offender."

The team wanted to make it up for their skipper, but it took a little while longer than they would have hoped. After tying the next game against Toronto and then getting shut out by the Black Hawks, Cherry finally got his first victory behind the Boston bench on October 17 against the Flyers. Despite getting off to an inauspicious start, Cherry and the Bruins finished with 40 wins, the second most in the Adams Division, but lost in the preliminary round of the playoffs to Chicago.

OCTOBER 11

RAY BOURQUE VS. MARIO LEMIEUX, 1984

Everybody remembers Mario Lemieux's first NHL goal. You know the refrain: first game, first shift, first shot, first goal. There's also the pesky little detail that, before lighting the lamp, Lemieux managed to snag the puck from Ray Bourque, giving himself a clear breakaway. Bourque will always be remembered for being on the other side of that history, but what people often forget is that, after Lemieux's goal on October 11, 1984, Bourque redeemed himself.

Following a sloppy first period, in which the Penguins scored a pair of goals, the Bruins mounted a comeback late in the middle frame after trailing 3–1. Bourque assisted on Ken Linseman's power-play marker with just over a minute remaining to bring the Bs within one. In the final session, after Mike O'Connell tied it up just 38 seconds after puck drop, Bourque ripped a slapshot from 40 feet out, beating goaltender Denis Herron, to give Boston its first lead of the match. It held up as the game-winner — but most Penguins fans always seem to leave out that detail.

OCTOBER 12

MILAN LUCIC SCORES FIRST NHL GOAL, 2007

Milan Lucic was the perfect Big Bad Bruin. He was a fearsome power forward who could level opponents with bone-crunching hits and also fill the back of the net. After the Bruins drafted him 50th overall in 2006, he made the club the following year as a 19-year-old. In his fourth game as a rookie, on October 12, 2007, Lucic scored his first NHL goal in a barnburner against the Kings. Late in the third period, he and David Krejčí had a clear-cut two-on-one.

With Lucic driving to the net on the left side, Krejčí dished the puck over to him and he popped it in on the doorstep to make it 7–5 for the Bruins. Chuck Kobasew added another one a few minutes later, and Boston ended up taking the game with an 8–6 victory, buttressed by Phil Kessel's first career hat trick. Lucic, who also picked up an assist early in the second period, collected seven more goals that season, but within a few years he would establish himself as a consistent 20-goal scorer.

OCTOBER 13

DICK REDMOND PICKS UP FOUR ASSISTS, 1979

Dick Redmond was all smiles following a 5–2 victory over the Capitals on October 13, 1979. The defenceman had factored in all but one of Boston's goals, picking up four assists, a career high. But Redmond wasn't just happy about picking up those helpers in the second game of the year. After being sidelined for 16 games the previous season with back spasms, he was healthy again and feeling good. And while Redmond may not have cared about the stats, Terry O'Reilly sure did. O'Reilly — who found the back of the net twice, with some help from Redmond — told reporters that if the defenceman keeps playing like that, "I'm going to score a lot of goals this season."

It was certainly Redmond's best campaign in Boston. With his back holding up and his increased responsibility on the ice with Brad Park sidelined to start the season, Redmond pulled more duties on special teams. He finished with 14 goals and 47 points, his best offensive output since his final outing with the Black Hawks a few years earlier.

OCTOBER 14

DAVID PASTRŇÁK SCORES FOUR, 2019

When David Pastrňák strolled into TD Garden for a matinee game in a salmon suit with a white shirt and black tie, topped off with a black fedora, you knew the opposing team was going to have a rough afternoon. On October 14, 2019, the Ducks found themselves at Pastrňák's mercy. He scored all four of Boston's goals, his fifth career hat trick, in a 4–2 victory against Anaheim. His line with Brad Marchand and Patrice Bergeron had been cranking out points to start the season, but Pastrňák just kind of shrugged it off. He told reporters it was a nice performance, but reminded them that's what he was paid to do.

That's the kind of dutiful confidence you want from your star players. A few nights later, Pastrňák picked up another pair of goals and was quickly off to his best goal-scoring pace in Boston. Had the world, and the league, not been upended by the Covid-19 pandemic later that season, he most certainly would've reached the 50-goal mark, and there's a case to be made he would've flirted with 60.

OCTOBER 15

ANDREW RAYCROFT GETS FIRST CAREER SHUTOUT, 2003

As the old saying goes, sometimes the post is a goaltender's best friend. Even if you're flawless, you still might need some help from some tubular, powder-coated steel. And as a rookie, Andrew Raycroft had no trouble admitting that. On October 15, 2003, he turned aside everything that Dallas threw his way, 27 shots in all, to record his first career NHL shutout in a 2–0 victory. Of course, Raycroft got a little help from his posts.

The Stars wrung the iron four times, including a pair by Jason Arnott, and it also didn't hurt that Dallas failed to capitalize on six power plays. But even with some puck luck, it was all Raycroft that game. The Bruins were outshot 27–13; in the second period alone the Stars threw 15 shots at him, and without his performance between the pipes, it could have gone a whole lot differently. Raycroft picked up two more shutouts that season to go along with his 29 victories, enough to earn him the Calder Memorial Trophy as the league's top rookie.

OCTOBER 16

TOPPER FILLS IN IN NET, 1960

If there was ever a hockey player who didn't need to wear goalie equipment to tend the twine, it was Jerry Toppazzini. Hailing from Copper Cliff, Ontario, Toppazzini was as tough as the hardscrabble landscape he grew up in. Had he not made it to the big leagues, he would have made one hell of a production miner. With the Bruins, he established himself as a hard-nosed checking player who could also do some damage on the penalty kill. But on October 16, 1960, he found himself in a new spot.

After Boston goaltender Don Simmons took a shot to the face and sustained a deep gash in the final minute of play in a matchup against the Black Hawks, the team needed someone to fill in between the pipes. Toppazzini dutifully obliged and didn't bother putting on any protective equipment. Chicago coach Rudy Pilous dispatched his top scorers, including bourgeoning sniper Bobby Hull, for one last onslaught, but luckily Toppazzini faced no shots and came away unscathed, becoming the last position player to replace a goaltender during an NHL game.

OCTOBER 17

TUUKKA FOR TWO POINTS, 2016

Tuukka Rask went above and beyond in Winnipeg. Not only did he turn away all but one of the 35 shots Winnipeg threw his way in a 4–1 victory on October 17, 2016, but he also set up two of the goals. After assisting on David Pastrňák's goal late in the second period, which held up as the game-winner, Rask got another assist on Zdeno Chara's empty-net goal in the final 50 seconds. Following the game, Rask was told by a reporter that he was the first Bruins goalie to earn two assists in a game. The Finnish netminder chuckled and said he was happy to take that record and that he'd have to get three next game.

It was a lofty goal, but that game would prove to be Rask's first and only multi-assist performance. The outburst in Winnipeg, however, brought him up to nine career helpers, just a couple behind Gerry Cheevers for the franchise record. By the time Rask hung up his pads, he had 17, a benchmark that could hold up for a long time.

OCTOBER 18

PATRICE BERGERON SCORES FIRST NHL GOAL, 2003

Patrice Bergeron was the youngest player in the NHL. Just a few months after the Bruins drafted him in the second round, which will go down as one of the biggest bargain picks in league history, the freshly minted 18-year-old from L'Ancienne-Lorette, Quebec, was playing in the big leagues. Bergeron was born only a month before me, but I can honestly tell you that at age 18, I wasn't doing half as much with my life. I was in university, but just barely. I eventually figured it out, and here I am, writing about Patrice Bergeron.

After making his Boston debut a couple of weeks earlier, on October 18, 2003, Bergeron notched his first NHL goal with less than three minutes remaining in the third period against the Kings to tie the game 3–3. Mike Knuble gave the Bruins the game-winning goal just 44 seconds later. Bergeron finished the campaign with 16 goals and 39 points. He earned some Calder Trophy votes, but the trophy ended up in Boston anyway when goaltender Andrew Raycroft took it home in a landslide.

OCTOBER 19

BOBBY ORR GETS FIRST AND LAST ASSIST, 1966, 1978

It was the first of many assists. Early in the second period in a game against the Red Wings on October 19, 1966, Bobby Orr, who was making his NHL debut, assisted on Wayne Connelly's goal to notch his first big-league point and assist. Exactly twelve years later, in what he hoped would be a comeback season with the Black Hawks, Orr picked up an assist, his 645th, on John Marks's first-period tally. It would prove to be his final helper.

After sitting out the entire 1977–78 campaign following another procedure on his battered knees, Orr hoped his joints would hold up for at least one last season. But after just a few more games, Orr made the difficult decision that, at the age of 30, he had no choice but to hang up his skates. At the time of his retirement, no other blueliner in league history had collected more assists. Had his knees not given out so early into his career, who knows how many more assists he might have racked up.

OCTOBER 20

BRUINS ACQUIRE DANIEL PAILLE, 2009

This trade would age like a fine wine. On October 20, 2009, the Bruins acquired Daniel Paille from the Sabres for a third-round draft pick in 2010. Drafted 20th overall by Buffalo in 2002, Paille had scored 19 goals and 35 points in his first full season with the Sabres, but he would bring scoring depth and strong play on both sides of the puck to the Bruins lineup. Once in Boston, Paille clicked with Shawn Thornton and Gregory Campbell, forming one of the most effective fourth lines in NHL history. Known as "the Merlot Line" because of the burgundy-coloured jerseys they wore in practice, the trio became a formidable shutdown unit.

During the team's Stanley Cup run in 2011, Paille and company played an integral part in limiting Vancouver to just four goals in the final five games of the Final, with Paille chipping in a short-handed tally in Boston's first victory in the series, an 8–1 drubbing. Paille played four more seasons with the Bruins before finishing his NHL career with the Rangers on Broadway.

OCTOBER 21

BRAD MARCHAND PLAYS FIRST GAME, 2009

Long before Brad Marchand became a Bruins legend, he was already a legend in the eyes of one of my friends. Before suiting up for his first game with Boston on October 21, 2009, Marchand represented Canada for a second time a couple of years earlier at the World Juniors. His biggest moment of that tournament arguably came when he opened the scoring for Canada in the gold medal game against Sweden. Canada ended up taking it 3–2 in overtime to secure its fourth straight title.

A few years later, during Marchand's first full big-league campaign, for at least one of my pals who will remain nameless, he was still larger than life. Following a Boston road game against the Leafs, two of my friends ran into Tyler Seguin and Marchand on the streets of Toronto. When my more level-headed pal, at least that evening, tried to introduce my other highly inebriated friend to Seguin, he basically blew off the second overall pick to make a beeline over to Marchand. That's how much the World Juniors mean to some of us in Canada.

OCTOBER 22

REGGIE FLEMING SCORES TWO SHORTIES, 1964

Reggie Fleming was one tough customer. To many around the league, he was known as "Reggie, the Ruffian" for his imposing style of play. He came by it honestly, with a well-earned reputation as one of the game's most fearsome players. But Fleming was known for more than just his physical presence. He was a proficient penalty killer and was often tasked with shadowing the opposing team's star players.

During his first season in Boston, on October 22, 1964, Fleming scored two short-handed goals, the Bruins' only tallies that evening, matching a franchise record. He ended the campaign with 18 goals, a career high, while still finishing with the ninth-most penalty minutes. Fleming's hard-nosed style of play certainly endeared him to his teammates, but it came with a price. Following his death in 2009, researchers at Boston University determined he had been suffering from chronic traumatic encephalopathy (CTE), a degenerative brain disorder caused by repeated head injuries. Fleming was the first NHL player to be diagnosed posthumously with CTE, but sadly, he wouldn't be the last.

OCTOBER 23

MILAN LUCIC SENDS MIKE VAN RYN THROUGH THE GLASS, 2008

As someone who grew up in the heyday of Don Cherry's Rock'em Sock'em series, this was the kind of hit that would have sent eight-year-old Mike into a frenzy. Early in the second period of a game against the Leafs on October 23, 2008, Milan Lucic nailed Mike Van Ryn so hard into the glass along the side boards that one pane shattered. Actually, it's more like it exploded. Even after Van Ryn dusted himself off, he was still pulling pieces of glass out of his jersey. Following the game, he told reporters his neck still felt itchy.

And while it could have been a lot worse for Van Ryn, some fans who had front-row seats weren't as lucky. A couple of spectators sustained cuts to their faces from the flying shards and had to leave the game to receive treatment at the hospital. The thundering hit put Van Ryn on the wrong end of highlight reels for years to come, but just six minutes later he got Toronto on the board. The Leafs ended up winning 4–2.

OCTOBER 24

JAROME IGINLA SCORES FIRST GOAL AS A BRUIN, 2013

In his first eight games as a Bruin, Jarome Iginla hadn't managed to find the back of the net. But it was only a matter of time. The power forward hadn't had too many stretches in his career like that in which he didn't light the lamp. In fact, the night before Boston hosted San Jose on October 24, 2013, it looked like Iginla had indeed notched his first in black and gold, but it deflected off Milan Lucic before bulging the twine.

But late in the second period of that matchup against the Sharks, after Dennis Seidenberg fired the puck from the blue line, it caromed off the end boards and popped out to Iginla. The 36-year-old winger managed to slip the disc between the pads of San Jose netminder Antti Niemi and it slid past the goal line. It might not have been how he'd imagined it, but Iginla officially had his first as a Bruin. He finished the season with 30 goals, tied with Patrice Bergeron for the team lead, his 12th 30-goal campaign.

OCTOBER 25

BRUINS HIRE MIKE KEENAN, 2000

It wasn't going be any easier on the Bruins' bench. On October 25, 2000, the team fired Pat Burns early in the season after the team was mired in a four-game losing streak and replaced him with Mike Keenan, who was known as "Iron Mike" for his no-nonsense approach. Keenan was the type of coach you'd bring in to get your players in line, but it's not like Boston didn't already have that. Burns, a former Quebec police officer, was not exactly a pushover and was known for his fiery temper.

He was also one of the league's top coaches and won his third Jack Adams in his first campaign in Boston. But the Bruins had been eyeing Keenan for some time. He had been considered for the job a few years earlier when they sent Steve Kasper packing, but they ended up hiring Burns and Keenan wound up in Vancouver. While the Bruins hoped Keenan would be the wake-up call the team needed, they continued to sputter and missed the playoffs in his only stint as Boston's coach.

OCTOBER 26

BILL RANFORD GETS FIRST SHUTOUT, 1986

It was a big night for Bill Ranford. Both of them. On October 26, 1986, Ranford stopped all 43 shots from the Flames in a 6–0 Bruins victory at the Olympic Saddledome in Calgary to record his first big-league shutout. It was a big moment for the young goaltender, but it was just as big for his father, Bill Ranford Sr., who was in the stands to see his son play in the NHL for the first time.

Ranford, who was turning 20 in December, became the youngest Bruin to ever turn in a shutout, but he was also the first goaltender to shut out the Flames at home for nearly five years. Ranford picked up two more shutouts for the black and gold that season, but after starting the next year in the minors with the Maine Mariners, he was later dealt to Edmonton, along with Geoff Courtnall and a second-round draft pick, for Andy Moog. Ranford would win two Stanley Cups with the Oilers, along with a Conn Smythe, before returning to Boston for a pair of seasons.

OCTOBER 27

PASTA GETS FIVE HELPERS, 2019

I feel like I've been writing about David Pastrňák a lot this chapter, but how could I not? After starting off the 2019–20 campaign with 11 goals, including a four-goal performance against Anaheim, through the first 10 games of the season, on October 27, Pastrňák proved he could do it all. In a 7–4 victory over the Rangers, he picked up five assists, including three primary helpers, becoming just the 10th Bruin to record five assists in a game and the first to do it in more than a decade.

The last player in black and gold to accomplish the feat was Pastrňák's linemate Patrice Bergeron. In a full-circle moment, Pastrňák reached the milestone by picking up an assist on Bergeron's third goal of the game, a rare hat trick for the perennial Selke candidate. Following the game, Pastrňák's other linemate, Brad Marchand, who also picked up five points that night, gushed to reporters that the Czech winger was just so fun to watch. A seemingly evergreen statement that Bruins fans everywhere would co-sign heartily.

OCTOBER 28

FELIX POTVIN GETS FIRST BRUINS SHUTOUT, 2003

Dear reader: I'm not going to lie to you; Felix Potvin never looked right in a Bruins uniform. At least to me. He was my favourite Leaf growing up and I wasn't even a goaltender — well, truthfully, I'm not much of a hockey player at any position, but I try. And as much as I would argue that Potvin only looked good in blue and white, a case that's probably not winning me any points with you as you read this, I can concede that it would be pretty difficult for his iconic "Cat" mask to look bad in any combination of colours.

So when Potvin signed with Boston a month before the 2003–04 campaign began, the mask that every '90s kid wanted got the black-and-gold treatment. Potvin may have been more than a decade removed from his incredible rookie campaign with the Leafs, but he still had it. On October 28, on the road against Montreal, he stopped all 23 shots he faced to record his first shutout for the Bruins and his first in nearly a year.

OCTOBER 29

GREGG SHEPPARD COLLECTS FIRST HATTY, 1972

On a night when Johnny Bucyk, one of Boston's elder statesmen, scored his 400th career goal, it was a rookie who stole the show. On October 29, 1972, Gregg Sheppard, playing in just his second NHL game, notched three goals, his first hat trick, as the Bruins handily cruised to a 9–1 victory over the Islanders. The three-goal outburst wasn't just beginners' luck; it was a sign of things to come for the undrafted and undersized native of North Battleford, Saskatchewan.

Sheppard finished the campaign with 24 goals and 50 points and earned some consideration for the Calder Trophy, awarded annually to the league's top rookie. A couple of years later, he established himself as a key offensive contributor in Boston, beginning what would be a run of three straight 30-goal seasons. He would've hit four had injuries not limited him to just 54 games in the 1977–78 campaign, his last with the Bruins. But Sheppard wasn't just a goal scorer — he was reliable on both sides of the puck and a trusted penalty killer.

OCTOBER 30

JOHNNY BUCYK HITS 500, 1975

Gregg Sheppard may have taken some of the spotlight from Johnny Bucyk, but almost exactly three years later, the Bruins faithful were only hailing to the Chief. On October 30, 1975, Bucyk, who was now 40 years old and the oldest player in the league, picked up his 500th career goal, joining Maurice Richard, Gordie Howe, Bobby Hull, Frank Mahovlich, Phil Esposito, and Jean Béliveau as the only players in NHL history to accomplish the feat.

Just over the halfway mark of the first period in a game against the Blues, Bucyk caught a pass from Ken Hodge and wired it from 20 feet out, beating St. Louis netminder Yves Bélanger to notch his milestone goal. The crowd at Boston Garden erupted into a chorus of cheers, and his teammates hopped over the boards to congratulate him. Following the game, crowding around his stall, reporters asked Bucyk if he would go for 600 next. He smiled and said he would definitely aim for 501. By the time he hung up his skates, he had gotten more than halfway there, finishing with 556 tallies.

OCTOBER 31

HALLOWEEN TRIUMPH OVER NEW YORK, 1970

It was all treats for the Bruins on Halloween 1970. Somehow, they had tricked Eddie Giacomin, who had the lowest goals-against average among starting netminders to start the season, to give up six goals. Through his first six games, the Rangers netminder had already posted two shutouts and had not given up more than two goals in his other outings. But after Johnny Bucyk got the Bruins on the board early in the second period, they quickly upended Giacomin's stats.

Much to the delight of the Boston Garden crowd, who had given up trick-or-treating that evening to cheer on the black and gold, the Bruins scored five more unanswered goals to cruise to a 6–0 victory. Among the offensive onslaught, Bobby Orr collected four points, while Phil Esposito picked up three assists, one of them his 500th career point, becoming the 45th player in NHL history to reach the milestone. At the other end of the ice, Eddie Johnston, who was making just his second appearance that season, stopped all 35 shots he faced to notch his 17th career shutout.

NOVEMBER

NOVEMBER 1

BOSTON RECEIVES NHL FRANCHISE, 1924

The NHL was coming to Boston. On November 1, 1924, Charles Adams, a business magnate, reportedly paid the league $15,000 to bring a team to Beantown. The team would start playing the next month, so Adams had to get to work. He hired Art Ross to serve as manager and bench boss. At the time of the appointment, Ross was managing a sporting goods store in Montreal, but he was one of the most innovative minds in hockey. He had redesigned a puck with bevelled edges that the NHL adopted in its second season.

And while naming Ross to run the team was a shrewd move, Adams still needed a name. He held a contest but wasn't taken by any of the suggestions. It was only after his secretary, Bessie Moss, suggested "Bruins" that Ross knew he had a winner. The name inspired the type of ferocity he was looking for on the ice, and it was the perfect fit to match the brown and gold colour scheme of the Brookside stores in his growing grocery empire.

NOVEMBER 2

MIKE KEENAN HITS 1K, 2000

There was a time when Mike Keenan thought he might never coach again. After he was fired by the Canucks a little over halfway through the 1998–99 campaign, he spent the next season working as a television analyst. So when Keenan reached the 1,000-game benchmark behind the Bruins' bench on November 2, 2000, it made the milestone even more special. Keenan became just the fifth coach in NHL history to accomplish the feat, and he just so happened to do it against one of his former teams, the Blackhawks, with Boston picking up a 5–4 victory.

Although Keenan didn't always stay with clubs very long — his authoritarian style usually wore thin on his players — he had been in the league for the better part of 16 years since breaking in with the Flyers and winning the Jack Adams in his rookie season behind the bench. His longevity continued following his stint with the Bruins. Keenan made stops in Florida and Calgary before taking positions in the KHL. When he left the NHL, only three head coaches had appeared in more games than him.

NOVEMBER 3

CHRIS NILAN SCORES FIRST GOAL FOR BOSTON, 1990

It was the goal Chris Nilan had always dreamed of scoring. Growing up in Boston, the scrappy winger had always wanted to light the lamp for the Bruins. And while he had scored a couple of goals in Beantown as a member of the Canadiens, it just wasn't the same. But after the Rangers traded him to his hometown team in the 1990 off-season, Nilan would get his chance to make his dream come true. On November 3, he found the back of the net at Boston Garden, his first in black and gold.

Nilan would add five more tallies that season, along with 15 points, his best offensive output since the 1986–87 campaign in Montreal. He actually got some time on the penalty kill early in that first year in Boston, but when you're in the penalty box as much as Knuckles was, those opportunities were fleeting. Later that season in a game against the Whalers, Nilan managed to earn 10 penalties: six minors, two majors, one misconduct, and one game misconduct, an NHL record that still stands.

NOVEMBER 4

MARC SAVARD SCORES FIVE POINTS, 2006

Marc Savard taught me how to tape my stick. No, he didn't teach me personally, but years after he hung up his skates, he started doing a series of YouTube videos called "Taping Twigs with Savvy" in which he would showcase the different tape jobs of players around the league, including his own in his playing days. I didn't necessarily play any better, but my twig sure looked nice. But what I appreciated about the videos were those little details Savard shared and why they made a difference on the ice. It was clear that, in addition to his silky mitts, he had a shrewd hockey mind.

This was why the Bruins signed Savard to a big ticket in 2006, and early into his tenure in Boston, he proved he was worth every penny. On November 4, he picked up two goals and three assists in a 6–5 overtime victory over Tampa Bay. Savard would go on to lead the black and gold in scoring with 96 points that season, and the only players in the league with more assists than his 74 were Sidney Crosby and Joe Thornton.

NOVEMBER 5

HARVEY BENNETT GETS FIRST BRUINS VICTORY, 1944

Harvey Bennett earned his first NHL win the hard way. After dropping his first game with the Bruins, the Saskatchewan goaltender then gave up seven goals in each of his next two games. But on November 5, 1944, a day after the Leafs lit the lamp behind him seven times, Bennett managed to record his first victory with Boston. He would pick up nine more wins that season, and while some would suggest he was best known for being the goaltender of record when Maurice Richard potted his 50th goal later that year, Bennett should be remembered for being one of the finest American Hockey League netminders.

Following his one and only campaign with the Bruins, Bennett started out his tenure in the AHL, first with Hershey and then Providence, by leading the league in wins for three straight years. He backstopped the Reds to a Calder Cup in 1949 and stayed between the pipes for the next decade. When Bennett hung up his pads, only two goaltenders, Johnny Bower and Gil Mayer, had more AHL victories than him.

NOVEMBER 6

BRIAN ROLSTON SCORES IN OVERTIME, 2001

Bruins fans were certainly getting their money's worth. Fifteen games into the 2001–02 campaign, more than half of their contests had gone into overtime, giving ticket holders the second-best thing to free beer in an arena: bonus hockey. When Boston hosted the Oilers on November 6, 2001, neither team had scored in regulation, sending the Bruins to their eighth extra session. Fifty-nine seconds into sudden death, Brian Rolston, who had a great opportunity early in the third period, caught a pass from Sergei Samsonov and beat Edmonton goaltender Tommy Salo with a wrist shot.

Although Bruins goaltender Byron Dafoe was happy to earn his 24th career shutout after stopping all 20 shots he faced, he lamented that it would be nice to have a four-goal win every once and a while. The victory also gave the Bruins their fourth straight overtime at home, a franchise record. The streak came to an end two nights later when they were defeated 5–3 by the Wild at the FleetCenter. Dafoe wasn't in net that night, but at least his goaltending partner, John Grahame, got some additional run support.

NOVEMBER 7

ESPO TRADED TO NEW YORK, 1975

Phil Esposito heard a knock on his hotel room door. It was November 7, 1975, and he and his Boston teammates were in Vancouver to face the Canucks the following evening. Esposito opened the door and standing there was his coach, Don Cherry. The bench boss wasn't delivering room service. He had urgent news. Esposito was being traded. A stunned Esposito, who was just coming off his fifth straight 50-goal season with the Bruins, was distraught. "Please don't tell me it's New York, because if you do, I'm going to jump out the window," he said.

In one version of the story, Cherry looked over at Bobby Orr, who was hanging out in the room with Esposito, and said simply, "Close the window." Although Esposito never made a mad dash for the window, he was indeed on his way to Broadway, along with Carol Vadnais, in exchange for Brad Park, Jean Ratelle, and Joe Zanussi. Esposito made his Blueshirts debut later that evening, scoring two goals and picking up an assist in a 7–5 loss to the California Golden Seals.

NOVEMBER 8

BOBBY ORR RETIRES, 1978

Bobby Orr retired far too early. His knees, scarred by multiple procedures, finally gave out on him, forcing him to hang up his skates on November 8, 1978, a few months before he turned 31 years old. Orr played his final NHL game as a member of the Chicago Black Hawks, but he should've gone out as a Bruin. Two years earlier, however, his longtime agent, Alan Eagleson, convinced him there was a better deal to be had with the Hawks, a team owned by his pal Bill Wirtz, who was known as "Dollar Bill" for his frugality.

Orr, who had been represented by Eagleson his entire career, trusted him implicitly and took him at his word. It was only years later, when Eagleson was exposed as the fraud and swindler he was, that the public learned Boston had offered Orr a multi-year extension and a lucrative ownership stake in the team. Eagleson committed serious crimes against Orr and his other clients, but perhaps the greatest injustice was depriving Orr the opportunity to finish out his career in black and gold.

NOVEMBER 9

JOHNNY BUCYK HITS 1K, 1972

Johnny Bucyk may have been overshadowed by Phil Esposito and Bobby Orr, but for a week, just as the calendar flipped from October to November in 1972, all eyes were on the Chief. After scoring his 400th career goal with the Bruins, the first member of the team to reach the benchmark, just over a week later, on November 9, 1972, Bucyk recorded his 1,000th career point, becoming the seventh player in league history to accomplish the feat. What made both milestones so special was that he did it on home ice.

Bucyk had notched some important points throughout his tenure with the Bruins, but they had all seemingly occurred on the road. But when he scored his 400th goal and his 1,000th point, he had the full weight of the crowd at Boston Garden cheering him on. Bucyk would get to reach a couple more milestones in Boston. Later that season he picked up his 1,000th point as a Bruin at home, and a few years after that, he potted his 500th career goal before the Bruins faithful.

NOVEMBER 10

TERRY O'REILLY GETS FIRST HAT TRICK, 1977

In his first appearance back after serving a suspension, Terry O'Reilly got one goal for every game he had been banished. On November 10, 1977, O'Reilly notched a hat trick, his first three-goal performance, in a 5–2 victory over Los Angeles, a performance that even earned him the admiration of Kings goaltender Rogie Vachon, who asked him where he got those moves. But a different set of moves landed Taz in hot water two weeks earlier, on October 26, when he got a little out of control in a game against the Minnesota North Stars.

Following a tripping penalty he didn't agree with, an incensed O'Reilly reportedly skated past referee Denis Morel and caught him with the blade of his stick, earning him a game misconduct. At that point, O'Reilly chucked one of his gloves at the official. Hey, the Tasmanian Devil didn't always have the brightest ideas. It could have been much worse for O'Reilly, but after spending more than two hours meeting with NHL vice-president Brian O'Neill, he got off pretty light with a three-game ban.

NOVEMBER 11

ART ROSS PULLS GOALIE AGAIN, 1943

With time winding down in the third period and the Bruins trailing by a goal to the Black Hawks, head coach Art Ross pulled his goaltender for an extra attacker. It was November 11, 1943, but it wasn't the first time Ross had done that. More than a decade earlier, he brought netminder Tiny Thompson to the bench for an extra player in a playoff game, but the Bruins were unable to capitalize and lost 1–0. A year later, in a regular-season matchup against the Rangers, Ross pulled Thompson in overtime, but Cecil Dillon shot the puck into Boston's yawning cage for his second tally in the extra frame (it's a long story).

Although Ross pioneered the tactic in the NHL, he may have borrowed the idea from *Toronto Star* columnist Lou Marsh, who in 1928 wrote that he had "been waiting patiently for some quick-witted coach or manager to … yank out his goalkeeper, and replace him with a forward." But the gambit failed yet again that night in Chicago. The Hawks' Clint Smith found nothing but net.

NOVEMBER 12

MILAN LUCIC BOWLS OVER RYAN MILLER, 2011

Milan Lucic broke the Buffalo Sabres. With just under seven minutes remaining in the first period on November 12, 2011, Lucic was charging for the puck all alone in the Buffalo zone when goaltender Ryan Miller made a play for the disc. Big mistake. Lucic didn't downshift whatsoever when he saw the goalie bolt from his crease and barrelled right into him. Miller landed on his backside and his helmet went flying. But the worst part was Buffalo's response. No one stood up for their netminder.

There are few things more sacred in hockey than the goaltender, and you protect them at all costs. If a Sabre had done that to Tim Thomas he would have been hanged, drawn, and quartered as a warning to the rest of the league. Maybe they wouldn't have gone that far, but Lucic said they "would've taken care of business." Miller stayed in the game but didn't return for the third period. Buffalo went on to lose 15 of their next 22 games and the franchise spiralled into an identity crisis, searching for what was clearly missing that night.

NOVEMBER 13

BRUINS ACQUIRE STANISLAV CHISTOV, 2006

When Stanislav Chistov was drafted fifth overall by the Mighty Ducks in 2001, the Russian army responded by dragging him out of his hotel room and bringing him to a garrison military base in Moscow. The powers that be weren't too keen on potentially losing one of the top players on Omsk Avangard in the Russian Superleague, so they claimed he was in the army, unbeknownst to both Anaheim and the young winger. After a protracted political battle that lasted more than a year, Chistov eventually received his discharge papers and made his way to Southern California.

He played two seasons in Anaheim before he was dealt to the Bruins on November 13, 2006, for a third-round draft pick. Just over a week later, Chistov notched his first goal in a Bruins uniform, his first NHL tally in nearly three years. He finished out the year in Boston, picking up 13 points in 60 games before returning to Russia to suit up in the newly formed Kontinental Hockey League. Chistov played more than a decade in the KHL before retiring.

NOVEMBER 14

DON SWEENEY HITS 1K, 2002

Ray Bourque had some simple words of encouragement for former teammate Don Sweeney: keep on trucking. On November 14, 2002, Sweeney appeared in his 1,000th game, becoming the 180th player in NHL history to reach the milestone but just the fourth Bruin to accomplish the feat. The only other Boston defenceman to pull it off was Bourque, of course.

Sweeney, who was drafted 166th overall by the Bruins, played four years at Harvard University before swapping crimson for black and gold after graduation. He made his Boston debut on October 6, 1988, and became a fixture on the club's blue line for the next 14 seasons. When his tenure with the Bruins came to an end, only Bourque and Johnny Bucyk had appeared in more games. Sweeney may have finished his playing career in Dallas, but he wasn't away from Boston for too long. In 2006, a couple of years after hanging up his skates, the team named him director of player development, and after working his way up the front office, he succeeded Peter Chiarelli, whom he played with at Harvard, as GM in 2015.

NOVEMBER 15

BRUINS ACQUIRE BILLY G, 2000

Bill Guerin was watching his daughter Kayla at her skating lessons when he learned he had been traded from the Oilers. It was November 15, 2000, and the clunky cellphone he had with him was in the car, so the news hadn't been delivered to him by his agent, Bob Murray. Rather, as he later recounted on the *Spittin' Chiclets* podcast, while he was at the rink, he noticed some guy appeared to be staring at him. Eventually, the gawker worked up the courage to tell Guerin that he was surprised to see him there. Perplexed, Guerin asked him what he was talking about.

That's when the stranger told him he just heard on the radio he had been traded. Now the guy had Guerin's attention. If it was true, Guerin figured he might as well ask him if he knew where he was going. The answer was Boston. Guerin, a native of Worcester, Massachusetts, initially worried he wouldn't be able to live up to the hometown expectations, but he quickly put those concerns aside, scoring 64 points in his first 63 games in black and gold.

NOVEMBER 16

BOBBY ORR GETS FOUR ASSISTS, 1969

It was the first four-assist night for No. 4, but it certainly wouldn't be the last. On November 16, 1969, Bobby Orr recorded four helpers in Boston's 7–4 victory over the Kings. It was an extraordinary performance for a defenceman, but something that Orr would make quite ordinary over his career in black and gold. Just over a month later, he proved that Christmas is truly the season of giving when he helped set up five goals in a game against the Penguins.

Orr accomplished the feat two times in each of the next two seasons, and then on January 1, 1973, in a matchup against Vancouver, he collected six assists, matching the NHL record originally set by Babe Pratt in 1944, and later matched by Pat Stapleton in 1969, for the most assists in a game by a defenceman, a benchmark that has since been matched but never beaten. Following that six-helper effort against the Canucks, Orr hit the four-assist mark six more times, bringing it up to a baker's dozen throughout his tenure in Boston.

NOVEMBER 17

RÉAL CHEVREFILS GETS FIRST HAT TRICK, 1956

Réal Chevrefils had a lot of potential. Early into his tenure with the Bruins, head coach Lynn Patrick believed the winger could be one of the best players in the NHL. Talented as he was, Chevrefils struggled with alcoholism and was eventually shipped out to Detroit. But he wasn't even in Motor City for a full season before he was traded back to the Bruins, along with Jerry Toppazzini, for Murray Costello and Lorne Ferguson.

The story goes that Wings GM Jack Adams tried to get Chevrefils help and even hired private investigators to keep tabs on him, but Adams couldn't get through to the young player and, exasperated, sent him back to Boston. In his first full campaign back in Beantown, things were looking up for Chevrefils, and with the way he was playing to start the year, it looked like he was going to prove Patrick right. He notched his first career hat trick on November 17, 1956, and finished the season with 31 goals and 48 points, career bests in both categories.

NOVEMBER 18

ANDY BRICKLEY SCORES HAT TRICK AGAINST FORMER TEAM, 1989

It was a revenge game for Andy Brickley. Although he was in his second season with the Bruins, Brickley, a native of Melrose, Massachusetts, always wanted to show New Jersey they had made a mistake. A year earlier, the Devils left him unprotected in the NHL's annual waiver draft and he was claimed by Boston. He was held pointless in the first pair of games he played against the Devils, but on November 18, 1989, he made them pay.

In the third period, Brickley notched a power-play goal that ignited a comeback. Cam Neely added another, and Brickley picked up two more to collect his second career hat trick and power Boston to a 6–4 victory. Brickley managed to stick it to his former team, but he wound up injuring himself in the game. It wasn't obvious in the moment, but the next day he couldn't even walk. He made it back in the lineup, but the injury lingered. It turned out Brickley was suffering from a rare condition called myositis ossificans in which a bruise, probably caused by a check, calcified and turned into bone.

NOVEMBER 19

KEITH CROWDER SCORES GOAL 12K FOR BOSTON, 1983

It didn't make any headlines, but Keith Crowder's first goal in a game against the Rangers on November 19, 1983, was a pretty significant milestone in the history of the Bruins. Forty-five seconds after Tom Fergus tied the game 3–3, Crowder fired a wrist shot from 20 feet out to take the lead. It was Boston's fourth straight goal that frame, but more importantly, it was the 12,000th regular-season goal scored by the black and gold.

None of the newspaper coverage I managed to pull from that matchup mentioned the significance of the goal. It would make for a better story if I told you I painstakingly added up every Bruins goal from 1924 until then, but the reality is that thanks to the digitization of game sheets and the accessibility of online data, it's much easier to pinpoint milestones that may have gone overlooked in the past. Bruins fans will be really happy to know that, despite joining the NHL seven years after the Maple Leafs, Boston still hit the benchmark before Toronto.

NOVEMBER 20

FIRST GAME AT THE GARDEN, 1928

It was the largest crowd to ever witness a hockey game. On November 20, 1928, the Bruins played their first game at Boston Garden. Some estimates had the crowd as big as 17,000, and those who couldn't get into the new arena actually crashed through the doors. The police had to be summoned to toss the interlopers out. But those who were out on the street didn't miss much. There was only one goal, and it was scored by the Canadiens with time winding down in the second period.

With intermission just a few seconds away, Bruins players were reportedly making their way off the ice when Sylvio Mantha snatched the puck in his own end and quickly proceeded the other way. By the time they clued into what was going on, Mantha was all alone and beat netminder Tiny Thompson with a shot that was no more than ankle high. Although it was an inauspicious start to their tenure in the Garden, the Bruins would finish the season in the new barn as Stanley Cup champions.

NOVEMBER 21

PATRICE BERGERON HITS 1K, 2022

As soon as Brad Marchand scored the goal, he gleefully pointed at Patrice Bergeron. The Bruins captain had assisted on many of Marchand's goals throughout the years, but this was different. That helper marked Bergeron's 1,000th career point. On November 21, 2022, he became just the fourth player in franchise history, joining Johnny Bucyk, Phil Esposito — who fittingly happened to be in the arena calling the game for the Lightning on the radio — and Ray Bourque in reaching the milestone.

I think longtime NESN play-by-play commentator Jack Edwards said it best on the broadcast when he exclaimed, "One thousand points for a one-in-a-million player." The significance certainly wasn't lost on Bergeron's teammates, who poured over the bench to mob him in celebration. A month later, on December 17, the Bruins officially honoured Bergeron with a ceremony at home. The Boston captain was showered with gifts and applause, but the coolest thing might have been that incoming NCAA president and then Massachusetts governor Charlie Baker proclaimed that the day would be known as "Patrice Bergeron Day."

NOVEMBER 22

THE JACKSONS BEAT TORONTO, 1942

It was the Bruins against the Leafs, but it was really the Jackson brothers taking on Toronto. On November 22, 1942, Boston hosted the Leafs in a high-scoring affair that was headlined by Art and older brother Busher. After Busher, who went by Harvey on his tax returns, picked up an assist in the first period, Art scored just 18 seconds into the middle frame. Before the halfway mark, Busher picked up another helper and Art found the back of the net again. In the final stanza, it was all the Jacksons.

Art bulged the twine to complete the hat trick, his second career three-goal performance, and Busher added a goal of his own to seal a 7–6 victory. Art, like his older sibling, started his NHL tenure in Toronto, but after a quick initial stop in Boston and then New York, he made his way back to Beantown. He was a key contributor for the next five seasons with the Bruins and helped the club win its third Stanley Cup in 1941.

NOVEMBER 23

ANDY MOOG GETS EIGHTH CAREER SHUTOUT, 1989

Andy Moog was one of my favourite players when I was a kid. I wasn't an Oilers fan or a Bruins fan, but I was definitely an Andy Moog fan. I don't know if it was because I liked saying his last name or how slick his black-and-gold set-up was, especially that bear mask, but for whatever reason, his hockey cards were some of my most cherished, and I probably have a few of them still lying around. After starting out his career in Edmonton, Moog was sent to Boston for Geoff Courtnall, Bill Ranford, and a second-round draft pick in 1988.

Moog initially shared the crease with Réjean Lemelin but eventually took over the starting duties by his third campaign. During the 1989–90 regular season, Moog picked up a few shutouts, including one on November 23, the eighth of his career, and, along with Lemelin, ended up taking home the William M. Jennings Trophy for the fewest goals allowed. Moog then backstopped the Bruins to the Stanley Cup Final, where they were once again halted by his former team, the Oilers.

NOVEMBER 24

JOHN ADAMS GETS FIRST SHUTOUT, 1972

You would figure a guy named John Adams wouldn't have to look too hard for work in Boston, but after he won a Stanley Cup with the Bruins, it took more than two years before he finally saw some NHL action. Yes, I know that's confusing. During the team's 1970 championship run, Adams, a goaltender, was called up as a backup reserve behind Gerry Cheevers and Eddie Johnston. Adams never played, but the team decided to add his name to Lord Stanley's silver mug. He spent the next two years in the minors in Oklahoma before he finally suited up for Boston. With Cheevers tending the twine in the rival World Hockey Association for the 1972–73 campaign, Adams was recalled when Ross Brooks went down with a broken collarbone.

The Stanley Cup champion goalie made his Bruins debut on November 18, earning a victory against the Islanders, and six days later, he stopped all 32 shots he faced from the Atlanta Flames to record his first, and what would prove to be his only, big-league shutout.

NOVEMBER 25

BUZZ BOLL SCORES FOUR, 1943

Buzz Boll's hockey career flashed before his eyes. During the 1943 off-season, while working on his farm back home in Saskatchewan, he accidentally got one of his hands caught in a threshing machine. He only ended up losing part of a thumb, but it could have been much worse. Back then it wasn't uncommon for NHL players to hold down summer jobs. Pentti Lund, who is believed to have been the league's first Finnish player when he suited up for the Bruins a few years later, worked as a setter on a sawmill carriage in a lumber mill, another dangerous gig. Chicago's Bill Mosienko, on the other hand, seemed to have it all figured out. He operated a bowling alley in his hometown of Winnipeg and got quite good at knocking down the pins.

Although Boll missed the start of the season while he recovered from his injury, it apparently hadn't set him back. On November 25, 1943, he scored four goals, his first hat trick in nearly eight years, in Boston's 6–2 victory over the New York Rangers.

NOVEMBER 26

JACK STUDNICKA MAKES DEBUT IN 8–1 WIN, 2019

Jack Studnicka had plenty of support in his first NHL game. On November 26, 2019, he made his Bruins debut against the Canadiens. Heading into the final frame, Boston was up 6–1. Charlie Coyle extended the lead and then, with just over two minutes remaining, Studnicka set up Danton Heinen to make it 8–1 and collect his first big-league point. Studnicka, who was taken 53rd overall in 2017, may have had some pre-game jitters, but when you're surrounded by players like David Pastrňák and Brad Marchand who can put on an offensive performance like that, it's much easier to get comfortable and not worry as much about making a mistake.

Studnicka played one more game for the Bruins that season before he was sent back down to the minors. Despite being a rookie, he led Providence in scoring with 49 points in 60 games. Studnicka played parts of two more seasons for Boston until, after mostly sitting in the press box to start the 2022–23 campaign, he was traded to Vancouver for goaltender Michael DiPietro and prospect Jonathan Myrenberg.

NOVEMBER 27

DIT CLAPPER TAKES THE ICE, 1946

Dit Clapper was pulling double duty. Heading into a game against the Rangers on November 27, 1946, the Bruins were down a defenceman with Johnny Crawford out with a leg injury, so coach Clapper laced up his skates. It wasn't unfamiliar territory for Dit, who once again I will reiterate had one of the best ever hockey names. The previous year, while still playing full-time for Boston, Clapper served as player-coach.

Clapper originally joined the Bruins in 1927 as a defenceman, but bench boss Art Ross moved him to right wing. He'd later score 41 goals in that position. He played up front for nearly a decade before he moved back to patrolling the blue line, forming a formidable pairing with Eddie Shore. He got his first taste of coaching during the 1944–45 campaign, during games when Ross was not able to travel with the team. Clapper's return to the ice in 1946 proved to be more than a cameo; he filled in five more times that season before hanging up his skates for good.

NOVEMBER 28

LEO LABINE RECORDS SIX POINTS, 1954

As I mentioned already, Leo Labine was known as "the Lion"— most Leos are. I would know, as I have a nephew named Leo. But it wasn't just alliteration that lent itself to the nickname; on November 28, 1954, Labine certainly played with the heart of a lion in a 6–2 triumph over the Red Wings. He factored into every Bruins goal and managed to earn a handful of club and league records along the way.

After picking up an assist in the opening period, during the second frame, Labine notched a hat trick in four minutes and 22 seconds, the fastest three goals from any point in a game by a Bruins player in nearly three decades. He also added two assists that session, matching an NHL record for the most points in a single period. While that mark was later surpassed by Bryan Trottier more than two decades later, it's still the gold standard for the Bruins. To top it all off, Labine finished the game with six points, matching the club record held by Bill Cowley, which went unchallenged until Bobby Orr made his way to Boston.

NOVEMBER 29

BOBBY ORR GOES UNDER THE KNIFE, 1975

Everyone expected that Bobby Orr would be back before the season was over. Just a few days after scoring a goal and an assist in a game against the Rangers, on November 29, 1975, Orr underwent a procedure on his left knee, the second of the campaign. A couple of months earlier, he had bone chips removed from the wonky joint. Despite this further setback, surgeon Dr. Carter Rowe figured the superstar defenceman would be skating again within six to seven weeks, and there was no doubt in his mind he would be playing again that year.

But as the weeks turned to months, Orr never made it back onto the ice. While the Bruins faithful eagerly anticipated his return, they did not realize he had already played his last game for the team. During the off-season, Orr, following misguided advice from his duplicitous agent, Alan Eagleson, turned down an offer from Boston and ended up signing with the Black Hawks. Orr just wanted to get back on the ice, but knee injuries once again curtailed his time, and ultimately his career, in Chicago.

NOVEMBER 30

BRUINS TRADE JUMBO JOE, 2005

As I am writing these words, the San Jose Sharks are raising Joe Thornton's No. 19 to the rafters of the SAP Center. There's no doubting what Thornton meant to the club. He has the most assists in franchise history and is behind only Patrick Marleau for the most points. Thornton's number was right where it belonged, but I couldn't help but wonder if it would be hanging high above the ice at TD Garden had the Bruins not traded him to San Jose on November 30, 2005, for Wayne Primeau, Marco Sturm, and Brad Stuart.

With a player of Thornton's calibre, it's certainly possible, but it was clear that he wasn't a fit with the management group at the time. And had Thornton stayed, the Bruins probably wouldn't have won the Stanley Cup in 2011. Sure, the pieces they received in return weren't necessarily instrumental, but creating space for players like Patrice Bergeron and David Krejčí to develop down the middle, and providing the club with the salary cap room to sign free agent Zdeno Chara in the off-season, certainly changed the fortunes in Boston.

DECEMBER

DECEMBER 1

FIRST BRUINS GAME, 1924

When the puck hit the ice at Boston Arena, history was made. On December 1, 1924, the Bruins kicked off their very first game, marking an important milestone not only in franchise history but for the league as well; it was the first NHL game played in the United States. Teams from the league had competed at U.S. sites before, but those games were against clubs from other circuits. Although the Bruins' first game should have been the hottest ticket in Beantown, there were reportedly quite a few empty seats.

After falling behind 1–0 to the Montreal Maroons, another expansion team, Boston rallied and took the game 2–1 for their first victory. While the team got off to a good start, it didn't last very long. The Bruins dropped their next 11 games, posting a goal differential of −41 over that run before finally picking up their second win on January 10, 1925, against the Canadiens. Owner Charles Adams hoped the team's name would inspire ferociousness on the ice, but that season they played more like teddy bears, finishing with just six triumphs.

DECEMBER 2

JOHNNY BUCYK PASSES MILT SCHMIDT, 1967

When I was going through old newspapers to do some of the research for this story, I happened to come across some advertisements for hockey equipment. The first was for the Johnny Bucyk model of Bauer skates, featuring a silver arrow blade, built-in tendon guard, hard box toe, and black leather boot. You'll never believe the price. If you play hockey or have kids in the sport, then you already know how expensive skates are these days.

I couldn't believe it when I saw they were going for $11.90. Eleven dollars and ninety cents! Even if you adjust for inflation, that's still one heck of a deal. But that's not all. A pair of Bucyk shin pads and gloves were listed for just a penny shy of five bucks. What a score! Bucyk was certainly getting his money's worth. On December 2, while presumably wearing those $12 Bauers and perhaps even those bargain-bin gloves, he scored his 230th goal as a Bruin, surpassing Milt Schmidt, who was then the Boston GM, for the most goals in franchise history.

DECEMBER 3

BRUINS RETIRE PHIL ESPOSITO'S NUMBER, 1987

After Ray Bourque slipped the jersey over his head and handed it to Phil Esposito, he turned his back to the Bruins legend to reveal that he was wearing another sweater underneath. Esposito's eyes widened as he realized what was going on. Bourque had worn No. 7 since breaking into the league in 1979, the same single digit worn by Esposito that Boston was now retiring on December 3, 1987, but now he was sporting a new look: a freshly stitched No. 77.

Esposito had been adamant that he did not expect Bourque to give up his number, but there was no way he could keep wearing it once it was hanging in the rafters of the Garden. Esposito was genuinely touched by the heartfelt gesture. He told the crowd, "What this young man did tonight is something that I'll never, ever, ever forget, no matter what happens in my life." Bourque wore his new number for the rest of his NHL career, and after he hung up his skates, No. 77 joined Esposito's No. 7 high above the ice in Boston. A class act, that Raymond Bourque.

DECEMBER 4

FRANK BRIMSEK GETS FIRST SHUTOUT, 1938

Maybe I'm just getting old, but they don't make hockey nicknames like they used to. One of my favourites has to be the moniker Frank Brimsek earned just a handful of games into his tenure in Boston: Mr. Zero. I love it because it sounds like the name of a comic book villain, but also for its simplicity. They dubbed him Mr. Zero because that's how many goals the opposing team got by him: zero. And the best part is it was hardly an exaggeration.

After recording his first shutout against the Black Hawks on December 4, 1938, Brimsek rattled off five more shutouts in the next six games, setting a Bruins record for the most consecutive scoreless minutes between the pipes. He finished the season with 10 shutouts, unquestionably taking home the Vezina and Calder trophies as the league's top goaltender and rookie, respectively, and making a pretty darn good case for the Hart. His strong play continued in the playoffs. Brimsek recorded a sterling 1.25 goals-against average, backstopping the Bruins to a Stanley Cup.

DECEMBER 5

ESPO VS. ESPO, 1968

When the Bruins hosted the Canadiens on December 5, 1968, Phil Esposito spotted a familiar face at the other end of the ice. Making his first NHL start was his younger brother, Tony. The elder Esposito was playing his second season in Boston, while Tony was just getting his first taste of big-league action — he was called up after Montreal suspended Gump Worsley for a month when he refused to fly to Oakland. The Gumper hated air travel.

Tony had been called in to relieve Rogie Vachon a few games earlier, but this was his first start. Phil didn't exactly hold back on his baby bro. Less than eight minutes into the game, he slipped a puck past Tony to open the scoring for the Bruins. After the Canadiens took a 2–1 lead, Tony was just 10 minutes away from recording his first career NHL victory when Phil, once again, got the better of him. With the clock winding down in the third period, Phil wired a shot from 45 feet out to tie the game.

DECEMBER 6

TYLER SEGUIN SCRATCHED, 2011

As the broadcast panned to the press box at the MTS Centre in Winnipeg, Tyler Seguin sat there with a scowl across his face. He wanted to be out on the ice with his teammates when they took on the Jets on December 6, 2011, but Seguin was scratched for missing the morning team breakfast and meeting. And it wasn't the first time it had happened. It was part of an apparent pattern of off-ice behaviour that was increasingly distressing the Bruins' brass.

When Seguin was asked about what happened, he initially offered a lame-duck excuse that he had mistakenly set his alarm clock to Boston time. The only problem with that "dog ate my homework" of a justification was that Winnipeg is on Central Time, which means Seguin would have actually been an hour early for the meeting. Clearly, he still had some growing up to do. Years later, in his second season in Dallas, Seguin was scratched for the final game of the campaign for being late to practice. Old habits die hard.

DECEMBER 7

JOHNNY BUCYK HIGHLIGHTS, 1963, 1967, 1968, 1975

I'll give you three Johnny Bucyk stories for the price of one for this page. A Chief-trick, if you will. Let's start with what Bucyk did on December 7, 1963. On that day he notched a goal and four assists in an 8–6 victory over the Rangers. It was his second career five-point performance, made all the more notable because it was just his third game back after being sidelined with a separated shoulder.

Exactly four years later, in another game against the Blueshirts, Bucyk potted two goals at the Garden to pick up his 576th point with the Bruins, surpassing then GM Milt Schmidt for the most in franchise history. And then, a year after that, Bucyk became the first member of the Bruins to notch 250 goals. So, that's three, but since we're coming to the end of the book and I'm feeling generous, here's another. On December 7, 1975, Bucyk, who was then in his 21st NHL season, collected his 507th career goal to tie him with Jean Béliveau for the sixth most in league history.

DECEMBER 8

MOE ROBERTS MAKES FIRST APPEARANCE, 1925

Nobody had better bookends to his NHL career than Moe Roberts. He made his big-league debut for Boston on December 8, 1925, when Bruins goaltender Charles "Doc" Stewart — this is where I absolutely need to mention that Stewart was known as Doc because he was a licensed dentist and practised dentistry in the off-season — left the game with an injury. Roberts, who was just five days shy of his 20th birthday, entered the crease and became one of the youngest goaltenders in NHL history.

He made one more appearance for the black and gold and then, after seven games for the New York Americans in the 1930s, didn't play for an NHL team for nearly two decades. But on November 25, 1951, Roberts, then an assistant trainer for the Black Hawks, was pressed into service when Harry Lumley, who was 20 years younger than him, got hurt. Now a few weeks away from his 46th birthday, Roberts stopped every shot he faced in the third period. And so, he managed to be both one of the youngest and oldest goaltenders to stand between the pipes.

DECEMBER 9

GORDIE ROBERTS HITS 1K, 1992

It was a big moment for Gordie Roberts, but it was just as big for U.S. hockey. On December 9, 1992, Roberts, a Detroit native, appeared in his 1,000th game, becoming the first American-born player to reach the milestone. Although it came in a 5–2 loss to the Sabres, it didn't diminish the accomplishment. A standout in junior, first for the Detroit Jr. Red Wings and then the Victoria Cougars, Roberts turned pro in the World Hockey Association for the New England Whalers, where he would later be teammates with another Gordie you might have heard of.

Roberts made it to the NHL when the two leagues merged and then made stops in Minnesota, Philadelphia, St. Louis, and Pittsburgh, where he picked up two Stanley Cups, before joining the Bruins for the 1992–93 campaign. He played two seasons in Boston before finishing his career in the International Hockey League. A couple of years after Roberts hung up his skates, his former teammate, the other Gordie, was in the IHL, for a couple of shifts anyway, to promote the Detroit Vipers' home opener.

DECEMBER 10

JOHNNY BUCYK HITS 1K, 1970

If I ever had the chance to meet Johnny Bucyk, the first thing I'd ask him, of course after asking him how he was doing, would be "Do you still have the $1,000 bill?" Let me explain. On December 10, 1970, in a pre-game ceremony at the Garden, Bruins president Weston Adams Jr. presented Bucyk with a $1,000 bill to commemorate his 1,000th NHL game. Bucyk certainly earned the bonus that night. He scored two goals and set up four others in an 8–2 victory over the Sabres.

Following the game, reporters asked him how he was going to spend his crisp banknote, but in between puffs on a cigar, which you were allowed to do in the dressing room back in those days, he told them he was going to keep it. Now I have no doubt that Bucyk was certainly a man of his word, but players weren't paid as much back then as they are now, so no judgment here if the Chief ever had to pull it out of his wallet. He'd certainly get a lot of change from breaking that bill.

DECEMBER 11

MARTY MCSORLEY SUITS UP FOR BRUINS, 1999

Marty McSorley should have gone to England. He would have done himself and everyone else in the league a huge favour. When the 1999–2000 campaign began, the veteran enforcer was still in need of a contract. When a couple of months went by and he still wasn't signed, he was thinking about heading across the pond to play in Britain's elite hockey league for the London Knights, where his brother, Chris, was the bench boss.

But instead of heading overseas, McSorley signed a contract with the Bruins on December 7, 1999, and made his Boston debut a few days later. But as the season unfolded it became clear that he really, really should've gone to England. Late in the game against the Canucks on February 21, 2000, McSorley viciously two-handed Donald Brashear across the head with his stick. McSorley was suspended indefinitely and charged with assault with a weapon. He was later found guilty and sentenced to a conditional discharge. McSorley's NHL suspension ended on February 21, 2001, but he, rightly, never played another game in the league.

DECEMBER 12

EDDIE SHORE LAYS OUT ACE BAILEY, 1933

Eddie Shore was seeing red. Halfway through the second period in a game against the Leafs on December 12, 1933, the Bruins defenceman was furious after he had been knocked down by a check. Thinking the perpetrator was Toronto's Ace Bailey, Shore went after him. He hit Bailey from behind, sending the Leafs winger to the ice, where he hit his head and was knocked unconscious. It looked grim for Bailey. After he was rushed to hospital, a priest was called to read him his last rites.

While Bailey fought for his life, his father, having heard the extent of the injuries over the radio, packed a suitcase for Boston. He wasn't going there to check in on his son. Rather, he was looking to kill Shore. The Leafs' brass, however, got wind of his plan and were able to defuse the situation. Bailey made a full recovery, but he never played hockey again. A few months later, an all-star benefit game was held at Maple Leaf Gardens. In a poignant moment, Bailey embraced Shore at centre ice.

DECEMBER 13

CRAIG JANNEY GETS FOUR ASSISTS, 1990

Everything was going Craig Janney's way. He had assisted on four of Boston's first five goals in a game against the Hartford Whalers on December 13, 1990, but then, with less than nine minutes remaining in the third period, he caught an elbow from Ed Kastelic. It was the kind of incident head coach Mike Milbury was hoping to avoid. After noticing Janney had been getting roughed up in some games, he put him on a line with Chris Nilan and Cam Neely.

Milbury referred to them as his bodyguards, going as far as saying Janney would be so well protected it would be like he was back in the womb. Well, not quite — Janney had to be helped off the ice and didn't return to the game. Some of the coverage would appear to have suggested Kastelic tried to give him a dental exam with his joint, but following the match, Janney said the hit had just flared up a nagging shoulder injury. In any case, he was back in the lineup two nights later when the Bruins hosted the Devils.

DECEMBER 14

ADAM OATES SCORES FOUR, 1995

Normally, Adam Oates was setting up the plays, but one snowy night in a game against Florida, he was finishing them. On December 14, 1995, Oates scored four goals, a career high, in a 6–4 victory over the Panthers. Oates, who was one of the league's smoothest passers, scored the only two goals in the second period and then completed the natural hat trick just over seven minutes into the final frame. He added a fourth with less than four minutes remaining, stemming a near comeback from the Panthers, who scored three unanswered goals after Oates notched his sixth career hat trick.

When asked about what prompted the goal-scoring output, Oates said that maybe it was because he didn't have too much time to think about the game. The Boston area had been hammered by a snowstorm, and Oates managed to arrive at the FleetCenter just 10 minutes before warm-ups began. While his silky mitts were better known for his dishes — he did manage to pick up one assist that night — it's worth remembering that all but one of his seven career hat tricks were scored during his time with the Bruins.

DECEMBER 15

BOB JOYCE SCORES TWO GOALS, 1988

You'd probably never guess who was leading the Bruins in goal-scoring heading into the 1988 Christmas break. Well, I suppose you already know it's Bob Joyce because his name is in the title, so let's just get on with it. After playing for the University of North Dakota, where he set a single-season record of 52 goals in 48 games, a mark that still stands as of this writing, Joyce spent most of the 1987–88 campaign with the Canadian national team. He went to the Winter Olympics and then finished the season with the Bruins.

The next year, his first full season in Boston, Joyce got off to a hot start. After scoring two goals in a game against Edmonton on December 15, he led the black and gold in goals with 11 in 31 games. But Joyce couldn't keep up that goal-scoring pace he had in college. He finished with 18 goals, tying him with Ray Bourque for the fifth most on the team. Any time you're tied with Bourque in anything, you're doing something right.

DECEMBER 16

DAVE REID NETS FIRST HATTY, 1995

If there was anybody the Bruins wanted out on the ice when they were short-handed, it was Dave Reid. Since Reid joined the team in 1983 after they drafted him 80th overall a year earlier, the only other players in black and gold who had more short-handed goals than him over the next decade were Rick Middleton and Steve Kasper. That stat is even more impressive when you remember that Reid did a three-year sabbatical with the Leafs before returning to the Bruins for the 1991–92 campaign.

So when Kyle McLaren earned a double minor late in the third period in a game against the Flames on December 16, 1995, Reider was going out there. His penalty-killing pedigree notwithstanding, it was also a prime opportunity for Reid, who had already scored twice, to complete the hat trick. He had been in the league for more than a decade but had yet to notch three goals in a game. With Calgary's net empty and just 9.9 seconds remaining, Reid fired the puck into the yawning cage from 75 feet out to finally bag some hats.

DECEMBER 17

COLBY CAVE SCORES FIRST GOAL, 2018

I am certainly not alone when I say I wish I had the power to write a different ending to this story. Growing up in Saskatchewan, Colby Cave dreamed of making it to the NHL. After playing junior for the Swift Current Broncos, Cave went undrafted, but like a good Canadian prairie boy, he was not deterred and continued to pursue the sport with a relentless drive. Following his final season with the Broncos, Cave signed with the Bruins organization in 2015 and spent the next three years plying his trade for Providence in the American Hockey League. He was called up for a few games in the 2017–18 campaign but was back in the minors to start the next year. A couple of months into the season, however, Cave made his way back to Boston. And then, on December 17, 2018, in his 16th game with the Bruins, he got the big-league moment he had spent his whole life dreaming of.

With 26 seconds remaining in the second period in a matchup against the Montreal Canadiens, Cave, who assisted on Joakim Nordström's opening tally, caught a beautiful dish from Charlie McAvoy and put the puck through Carey Price's pads to score his first NHL goal. As he celebrated with his teammates, he had a smile from ear to ear. Not many players get their first tally on a future Hall of Fame goaltender. And while it looked like it could be a glimpse of things to come in Boston, it proved to be his only tally in black and gold. A month later, Cave was placed on waivers and claimed by Edmonton.

He picked up two more goals with the Oilers down the stretch and another the following season. If life were fair, Cave would have had more goals and more celebrations ahead of him. But just a couple of years after that milestone with the Bruins, the hockey community was mourning when Cave passed away after undergoing surgery to remove a colloid cyst that was causing pressure on his brain. That may have been how Cave's story ended, but that's not how he will be remembered. The joy he found in life and in the game is what endures. Rest in peace, Caver.

DECEMBER 18

CHARLIE MCAVOY PUTS UP GORDIE HOWE HAT TRICK, 2017

If I were putting together a highlight reel for Charlie McAvoy's Calder Trophy consideration, this would probably be my opening clip. Less than a minute into the third period of a game against the Blue Jackets on December 18, 2017, McAvoy drilled Pierre-Luc Dubois behind the Boston net. Dubois took exception — evidently, the refs did as well as they later nailed the rookie blueliner with an illegal check to the head penalty — and gave him a shot to the side of the noggin.

McAvoy didn't hesitate. They dropped the gloves. McAvoy tossed uppercuts and over-the-shoulder punches, eventually bringing Dubois to the ice in a practically unanimous decision. After feeling some shame in the box, McAvoy, who already scored in the second period, picked up an assist to complete the Gordie Howe Trick, a rare hockey feat consisting of a goal, an assist, and a fight in the game. Made famous by none other than Mr. Hockey, you may be surprised to learn he only did it twice, which means McAvoy is halfway to matching him.

DECEMBER 19

PHIL ESPOSITO SCORES SEVEN POINTS, 1974

Phil Esposito didn't mince words. He said what he felt, and too bad if it hurt your feelings. Following an 11–3 rout of the Rangers on December 19, 1974, in which Esposito scored a hat trick and added four assists, matching Bobby Orr's franchise record for the most points in a game, he really stuck it to the Rangers when speaking to reporters in the dressing room following the lopsided match.

"I needed a program to know their team," he said. Ouch. With all respect to the Blueshirts, they were absolutely decimated by injuries. They reportedly had eight veterans on the shelf and nine rookies in the lineup that evening. Although New York took an early 2–0 lead, the Bruins scored nine unanswered goals to put the game out of reach. Rookie netminder Curt Ridley, who was making his very first NHL start, allowed six goals before he was pulled mercifully in favour of Ed Giacomin, who didn't fare much better. "Don't blame their goalies," Esposito said. "We poured it on them like there was no one in front of them."

DECEMBER 20

JOHN MCKENZIE NOTCHES HAT TRICK, 1970

Before John McKenzie was known as "Pie" for his resemblance to Pie Face, a cartoon spokesperson for a chocolate company, he answered to "Cowboy" and "Bronco" because he grew up in Alberta and was once a rodeo competitor. I'll tell you, if my nickname was once Bronco but I became forever known as Pie, I might have had something to say about it, but McKenzie took it in stride. The iconic sobriquet actually started out as Pie Face and was shortened to Pie, so I guess he still came out ahead. Besides, it could have been worse. Pie Face's sweet companion was Fat Emma.

McKenzie broke into the NHL with Chicago in 1958 and then made stops in Detroit and New York before joining the Bruins in 1966. During his time in Boston, McKenzie consistently flirted with the 30-goal mark. He was always just a tally or two away, but he finally made it officially in the 1970–71 campaign. He notched a hat trick on December 20, propelling him to finish the year with 31.

DECEMBER 21

LOU CRAWFORD SCORES FIRST NHL GOAL, 1991

Lou Crawford never gave up on his NHL dream. After seeing his older brothers Bob and Marc graduate to the big leagues, he kept at it. Following a Memorial Cup victory with the Kitchener Rangers, adding to his family's impressive hockey trophy collection, Crawford spent nearly a decade in the minors but managed to pick up two Calder Cups along the way. He finally got a cup of coffee with the Bruins in the 1989–90 season, but after a handful of games, he was sent back to the American Hockey League, where he stayed for a few more years.

Just when Crawford thought the NHL might have passed him by, he was called up again. On December 21, 1991, in his third game back with Boston, Crawford scored his very first goal and NHL point. He played 19 games for the Bruins before finishing his career in the minors. Like his older brothers, Crawford got into coaching after hanging up his skates, leading his hometown Belleville Bulls to their first and only Ontario Hockey League championship.

DECEMBER 22

MILT SCHMIDT NAMED BRUINS COACH, 1954

Marie Schmidt got an early Christmas present: her husband's skates. Milt was ready to hang them up. The news was a relief to Marie. Over the course of his 16 seasons with the Bruins, Schmidt had endured a laundry list of injuries that included a broken collarbone, a fractured ankle, torn rib cartilage, and a broken jaw. Each time Marie nursed him back to health so he could get back onto the ice, but she was always worried that another injury, potentially a major one, was just around the corner. So on December 22, 1954, Schmidt handed in his retirement papers.

But Schmidt wasn't exactly leaving the organization. Rather, he was transitioning into a safer role, head coach. Although being a bench boss in Boston carried its own list of occupational hazards, Marie didn't have to watch each game on pins and needles for those. The plan had always been for Schmidt to coach. The Bruins thought he might have finished out that season, but it was just as well for GM Lynn Patrick, who had been pulling double duty.

DECEMBER 23

BRUINS GO AFTER FANS AT MSG, 1979

Nothing screams "peace on Earth and goodwill to all men" quite like ascending into the stands in full hockey equipment and beating a fan with his own shoe. Following a feisty game against the Rangers on December 23, 1979, which ended with a scrum along the boards after New York goalie John Davidson had some choice words for the Bruins, fans at Madison Square Garden started throwing debris at the Boston players. Stan Jonathan got hit in the face with a rolled-up program, cutting him below the eye, while another patron tried to snatch Terry O'Reilly's stick out of his hands.

Before the fans even realized what imminent danger they were in, O'Reilly, along with Peter McNab, Al Secord, and Mike Milbury, climbed over the glass and into the stands. McNab grabbed someone who looked like he was trying to flee and started throttling him in the seats, but the most enduring image from the chaos was Milbury taking a fan's shoe off his foot and hitting him with it. That's just how the Big Bad Bruins say Merry Christmas.

DECEMBER 24

LEAFS BLANK ORR-LESS BRUINS, 1966

After Bobby Orr injured his knee in early December of his rookie season, the Bruins weren't sure when their young star would be back. When I was researching this story, I came across an article that mentioned Orr might have been ready to return Christmas Eve 1966. But get this — not as a defenceman, but as a centre. Apparently, Boston was looking to ease him back into the mix by moving him up front for a couple of games.

It wouldn't be long before Orr would revolutionize the role of the blueliner with his dizzying end-to-end rushes and offensive contributions, but could you imagine how lethal he would have been as a forward? He was winning Art Ross trophies from the back end, so who knows how many points he could have piled up as a smooth-skating pivot. It's a fun hockey history thought exercise, but it never came to pass. Orr missed the Christmas Eve matchup, a 3–0 loss to Toronto, but was back in the lineup the next day in his usual spot on the back end.

DECEMBER 25

BOSTON'S CHRISTMAS GAMES

The National Hockey League often gets compared with the other major North American leagues, usually for what it does wrong, but I think one thing the NHL does right is the true holiday break it gives its players. Other leagues may be able to capitalize on the eyeballs at home over the holidays, and I'd be lying to you if I said I wouldn't love to watch an NHL game on Christmas day in my pyjamas with a cold glass of eggnog, but I think it's special that the league gives players the opportunity to spend meaningful time with their families by not scheduling games on Christmas Eve or Christmas.

Now this wasn't always the case. The league stopped playing Christmas games after 1971. Boston played its first-ever Christmas game in Montreal in 1924, a 5–0 loss to the Canadiens, and over the next forty-seven years, went 17-18-2 in Christmas contests. And while they lost more than they won, the Bruins went out on a high note, beating the Flyers 5–1 in 1971. Merry Christmas!

DECEMBER 26

DON MARCOTTE SCORES LAST NHL HAT TRICK, 1981

Don Marcotte didn't score many hat tricks. He didn't need to. During his tenure with the Bruins, he was one of the top two-way forwards in the NHL. Marcotte was regularly tasked with shadowing the league's top players such as Guy Lafleur, who considered him one of the toughest checkers he encountered. Lafleur later told the *Vancouver Province* that the only room Marcotte left for him was in his pants, and even then, "if he could find room to jump in my pants, he would have jumped in my pants." Now that's commitment. And while Marcotte wasn't expected to score like the Flower, he was still a consistent 20-goal scorer for the Bruins and hit the 30-goal mark in the 1974–75 season.

Even as Marcotte entered the twilight of his career, he was still strong on both sides of the puck and could chip in offensively. Although he had scored only once through the first 24 games of the 1981–82 campaign, Marcotte notched his fourth career hat trick, his first in more than four years, in a 9–6 victory against Hartford on December 26.

DECEMBER 27

DEAN PRENTICE PENALTY SHOT, 1964

Something wasn't right with Dean Prentice. After crashing into the boards, he felt a terrible pain in his back. But the veteran winger pulled himself up off the ice, then learned he had been awarded a penalty shot. While he probably should have retired to the dressing room, Prentice was about as tough as they come and took the shot, beating Black Hawks goaltender Denis DeJordy to tie the score at two goals apiece in a game on December 27, 1964.

Following the game, Prentice went to the hospital for evaluation but returned home when initial tests showed he had no broken bones. Only after he returned to Boston did more X-rays reveal he had suffered hairline fractures to two of the vertebrae in his lower back. This meant that when Prentice took that penalty shot, he had a broken back! Prentice missed the rest of the season, spending months in a body cast, but by the summer he was working in a brewery warehouse hauling kegs and cases of beer. They don't make 'em like they used to.

DECEMBER 28

PETE PEETERS RECORDS SEVENTH CAREER SHUTOUT, 1982

Pete Peeters — a goalie so nice they named him twice. In just his first full season in the NHL with the Flyers during the 1979–80 campaign, Peeters put together a 27-game unbeaten streak before finally losing his first big-league game. Later that year, he backstopped Philadelphia to a Stanley Cup Final but faltered to a bourgeoning powerhouse Islanders team that would win its first of four straight titles. A couple of years later, Peeters was traded to the Bruins, and he picked up pretty much where he left off with that exceptional rookie campaign in the City of Brotherly Love.

On December 28, 1982, Peeters stopped every shot he faced to record his league-leading fourth shutout. It was also his seventh straight win. Dating back to November 13, Peeters hadn't lost a game; he had a dozen victories and three ties. But he was just getting started. He would push the streak even further in Boston than in Philly, going 31 games without a loss, becoming the only goaltender in NHL history to have two unbeaten streaks of 25 games or more.

DECEMBER 29

LEFTY WILSON SPRINGS INTO ACTION, 1957

If there were a patron saint of emergency backup goaltenders, it would be Ross "Lefty" Wilson. Long before they began stealing the show in the NHL, Wilson pioneered the EBUG. A career minor-league netminder, Wilson joined the Red Wings in 1950 as a trainer and practice goalie. A few years later, when Terry Sawchuk left a matchup against Montreal, Wilson tended the twine for most of the final frame. Two years after that, Wilson found himself at the other end of the ice when he took over for Toronto's Harry Lumley, who left the third period against Detroit with an injured thigh.

Those appearances gave Wilson more time in the big leagues than he ever imagined, but on December 29, 1957, he played nearly a full game for the Bruins. Just before the halfway mark of the first period in a game against the Wings, Boston's Don Simmons left with a dislocated shoulder. Wilson, once again, dutifully went between the pipes for the opposing team. He gave up one goal but made 23 saves, earning the tie.

DECEMBER 30

CHRIS ODDLEIFSON SEALS HAT TRICK AGAINST FORMER TEAM, 1973

Everyone loves scoring against their former team. It was certainly a driving force behind Chris Oddleifson's performance on December 30, 1973. Squaring off against the California Golden Seals, who drafted him 10th overall a few years earlier using the pick Montreal gave them in a swap that wound up netting the Canadiens Guy Lafleur, Oddleifson notched four goals, his first NHL hat trick, in an 8–1 rout. He relished lighting up his former teammates, but he never actually played a game for the Seals. Early in the 1971–72 campaign, he was traded to Boston, with Rich Leduc, for Ivan Boldirev.

Not exactly known for his goal-scoring prowess, Oddleifson nearly doubled his output with that feat. Through the first 32 games of the season, he had five goals, tied with Carol Vadnais and Fred O'Donnell for the eighth most on the Bruins, but after his revenge game, he moved up to sixth and was just one behind Johnny Bucyk. Following the game, he joked with reporters that Phil Esposito better watch his back — he only needed 26 more to catch him.

DECEMBER 31

BOB MILLER SCORES HAT TRICK, 1977

Bob Miller didn't listen when his coach, Don Cherry, told the young winger not to worry about scoring goals. On December 31, 1977, in a 7–0 trouncing of the Red Wings, Miller notched three, his first NHL hat trick. Probably one of the few times when disobeying Grapes wouldn't get you stapled to the bench. What Cherry was trying to tell Miller was that the team valued him for his skating and forechecking, so if the goals weren't coming or they dried up a bit, it wasn't a big deal — just focus on your game.

But Cherry and the Bruins certainly wouldn't say no to a three-goal performance. Late in the first period, Miller scored two goals in a span of 45 seconds to give Boston a 4–0 lead, making Detroit netminder Ron Low wish he could start the New Year early. Miller completed the hat trick just before the halfway mark of the final frame. Although scoring wasn't part of Miller's job description, he chipped in 20 goals that season, giving the Bruins eleven 20-goal scorers among their ranks, a record that still stands to this day.

ASSISTS (ACKNOWLEDGEMENTS)

As always, writing one of these books is truly a team effort.

Thanks to the crew at Dundurn Press, chiefly Meghan Macdonald, Elena Radic, and Kathryn Lane, for allowing me to bring the Hockey 365 universe to Boston.

If you picked up this book because you judged it by its cover, then I have Ron Beltrame to thank for that. I have no doubt that his fine design work has led to more sales than I deserve.

Big thanks to Patricia MacDonald for editing *Bruins 365*, her fourth book with me. To give you an idea of how important Patricia has been to this series, it was she who kept me from including "don't poke the Asselstine" in this one.

Thanks to my parents, Patti and Tony, as always for supporting my work and helping me square up some of the family details included in this book.

This is my fifth Hockey 365 book. I'd like to say that I've gotten it down to a science, but I couldn't do it without my wife, Chantal's, support. Whether it's letting me sneak in some writing over a coffee on a weekend morning or get in some extra editing at night, it's a big help and I have no doubt the books are better for it. I love you.

Zoe, you definitely have your papa's love of reading. It makes me so happy to see you with a book in your hand, and I have no doubt I will absolutely melt if I ever see you turning the pages of one of mine. Sophia, you're like the Big Bad Bruin in our house, only you're the littlest and the cutest. *Je vous aime, mes filles.*

Finally, to all the Bruins readers who didn't realize I was a Leafs fan, I'm sorry (no refunds), but thank you for picking up this book and entrusting me with your team's history.